BIODIVERSITY PROSPECTING:

Using Genetic

Resources for

Sustainable

Development

Walter V. Reid   Ana Sittenfeld
Sarah A. Laird   Daniel H. Janzen
Carrie A. Meyer   Michael A. Gollin
Rodrigo Gámez   Calestous Juma

World Resources Institute (WRI), USA
Instituto Nacional de Biodiversidad (INBio), Costa Rica
Rainforest Alliance, USA
African Centre for Technology Studies (ACTS), Kenya

A Contribution to the:
WRI/IUCN/UNEP *Global Biodiversity Strategy*
May 1993

Kathleen Courrier
Publications Director

Brooks Belford
Marketing Manager

Hyacinth Billings
Production Manager

Cover Photos
Merck & Co./Black Star, Steve Winter; INBio; Walter V. Reid

Pam Reznick
Cover Design

Each World Resources Institute Report represents a timely, scholarly treatment of a subject of public concern. WRI takes responsibility for choosing the study topics and guaranteeing its authors and researchers freedom of inquiry. It also solicits and responds to the guidance of advisory panels and expert reviewers. Unless otherwise stated, however, all the interpretation and findings set forth in WRI publications are those of the authors.

CONTENTS

FOREWORD

More than half the world's plant and animal species live in one tropical forest or another—and nowhere else on Earth. Coral reefs and other coastal ecosystems add hundreds of thousands, if not millions, more species to the thin and variegated film of life that covers the globe. As the search for wild species whose genes can yield new medicines and better crops gathers speed, these rich habitats also sport more and more specimens of a relatively new breed—the biodiversity prospector. Like the nineteenth-century California gold rush or its present-day counterpart in Brazil, this "gene rush" could wreak havoc on ecosystems and the people living in or near them. Done right, though, bioprospecting can bolster both economic and conservation goals while underpinning the medical and agricultural advances needed to combat disease and sustain growing human numbers.

What "doing right" means in this context is the central question of *Biodiversity Prospecting*, by WRI Vice President Walter V. Reid and seven of his colleagues, here at WRI and elsewhere. The need for answers is urgent since all the major pharmaceutical firms are already hard at work screening the genetic storehouses found in Brazil, Costa Rica, China, Micronesia, and other biologically diverse countries. Arguing that the very great potential benefits from such ventures may be overwhelmed by the actual harm they cause, the authors describe the kinds of organizations, contracts, and laws needed to ensure that both human communities and their natural surroundings benefit from the bioprospecting boom.

Although many institutions around the world are pioneering this new field, the report focuses on Costa Rica's National Biodiversity Institute (INBio) because its arrangement with Merck & Co., Ltd.—the world's largest pharmaceutical firm—represents new ways to promote conservation, as well as manage information and inventory. Indeed, INBio's stated aim is conserving biodiversity, not exploring its commercial potential, which it views as merely one way to finance conservation. The authors do not view the INBio-Merck arrangement as a model that other would-be contractors should follow, but as a promising pilot project that offers lessons vital to the success of bioprospecting ventures elsewhere.

At the Earth Summit last year, the United States refused to sign the biodiversity convention joined by more than 150 nations, claiming that agreements like that between Merck and INBio would obviate the need for an international treaty. The authors of *Biodiversity Prospecting* take the opposite view, asserting that contracts entered into by one or another gene-rich country will be feasible and effective only in the context of international agreements that settle such questions as who owns biodiversity, how access to it can be controlled, and how intellectual property rights and profits can be equitably divided between local communities and prospecting corporations. As this book goes to press, President Clinton has just reversed the U.S. position and promised to sign the biodiversity convention, so there is reason to hope that the United States will play a constructive role in resolving all these issues.

Since wealth and technology are as concentrated in the North as biodiversity and poverty are in the South, the question of equity is particularly hard to answer in ways that satisfy everyone with a stake in the outcome. The interests of bioprospecting corporations are not the same as those of people who live in a biodiversity "hot spot," many of them barely eking out a living. The authors describe ways that hard-pressed rural communities can benefit from bioprospecting in their vicinity—for instance, through the training and jobs provided by INBio's parataxonomist program. They also stress that people have a right to regulate and charge for access to the biodiversity that surrounds them and to be compensated for their intellectual contributions to the discovery and development of new products. Unfortunately, as the authors note, experience has taught that these rights mean little in practice unless they are clearly defined and strongly defended by local and national governments. Since such clarity and support are often absent, the authors recommend that corporations and governments in the industrial world assume more responsibility for ensuring that bioprospecting is done legally and with the informed consent of the communities involved.

The contract between Merck and INBio is a private contract and not open to public inspection. *Biodiversity Prospecting* includes a draft contract that can help pharmaceutical companies and collecting organizations negotiate agreements. The draft contract, as the authors note, is not a universally applicable model, however, and is not intended for wholesale adoption. Rather, it is an educational tool intended to enable collectors and institutions in developing countries to enter negotiations with large corporations and their representatives with some knowledge of the issues and potential solutions.

Altogether, the essays in *Biodiversity Prospecting* explore many different strands of thought and theory that come together in this relatively new industry, elaborating on issues only touched on in other publications. Its recommendations extend those laid out in the *Global Biodiversity Strategy* and in such WRI reports as *Conserving the World's Biological Diversity, Keeping Options Alive: The Scientific Basis for the Conservation of Biodiversity,* and *Trees of Life: Saving Tropical Forests and Their Biological Wealth.*

We would like to thank the Dutch Ministry of Foreign Affairs, the Norwegian Royal Ministry of Foreign Affairs, the Swedish International Development Authority, the United Nations Development Programme, the Canadian International Development Agency, The Surdna Foundation, the Sasakawa Peace Foundation, and the W. Alton Jones Foundation for their generous support of WRI's general research on biodiversity conservation issues. For their foresight and support, we are deeply grateful.

Jonathan Lash
President
World Resources Institute

ACKNOWLEDGMENTS

We would like to thank the many colleagues and friends who contributed ideas, experiences, and encouragement to this project. In particular, we are grateful to Michael Balick, Chip Barber, John Barton, Mario Boza, Lynn Caporale, Jason Clay, Gordon Cragg, John Duesing, David Downes, Elaine Elisabetsky, Cary Fowler, Geoffrey Hawtin, Elaine Hoagland, Jeff McNeely, Kenton Miller, Robert Repetto, Nigel Sizer, and Darrell Posey for their valuable comments on drafts of the manuscript, as well as comments from Stephen King, Jeff Kushan, Annie Petsonk, and Carmen Suro-Bredie on portions of the manuscript. Our thanks to Kathleen Courrier and Page Shepard Demello for skillfully editing the report, to Hyacinth Billings for her help in preparing the text, to Sue Terry for her help in obtaining numerous reports and references, to Helena Albuquerque for assistance with research and references, and to the co-authors of the individual chapters for their valuable contributions. Finally, a special thanks to Jodilee Nelson who cheerfully assumed the task of coordinating and making sense out of the seemingly infinite revisions, comments, queries, edits, conference calls, and meetings involved in the project.

W.R.
S.L.
C.M.
R.G.
A.S.
D.J.
M.G.
C.J.

I.
A NEW LEASE
ON LIFE

Walter V. Reid, Sarah A. Laird, Rodrigo Gámez, Ana Sittenfeld,
Daniel H. Janzen, Michael A. Gollin, and Calestous Juma

In September 1991, Costa Rica's National Biodiversity Institute
(INBio)—a private, non-profit organization—and the U.S.-based
pharmaceutical firm Merck & Co., Ltd., announced an agreement
under which INBio would provide Merck with chemical extracts
from wild plants, insects, and micro-organisms from Costa Rica's
conserved wildlands for Merck's drug-screening program in return for a two-year research and sampling budget of $1,135,000
and royalties on any resulting commercial products. INBio agreed
to contribute 10 percent of the budget and 50 percent of any royalties to the government's National Park Fund for the conservation
of national parks in Costa Rica, and Merck agreed to provide technical assistance and training to help establish drug research capacity in Costa Rica (Aldhous, 1991).

This agreement represents a watershed in the history of "biodiversity prospecting"—the exploration of biodiversity for commercially
valuable genetic and biochemical resources. (*See* Eisner 1989, 1992.) For
decades, ecologists and environmentalists have been arguing that
pharmaceutical and other commercial applications of biodiversity
should help justify its conservation. However, industry investment in
natural products research since the mid-1960s has been small, and it actually declined in the pharmaceutical industry during the 1960s and
1970s. Clearly, the INBio-Merck agreement demonstrates a shift in industry focus and the true economic potential of these resources.

1

This ground-breaking agreement also shows how companies can return a portion of the benefits of pharmaceutical development to the developing country where the chemical compounds originated. Further, it ensures that some of these proceeds will directly finance conservation while the remainder will indirectly finance conservation through biodiversity research and development in association with the national parks. Coming as it did during the final negotiations of the International Convention on Biological Diversity, the Merck-INBio agreement validated what was becoming—after heated debate—an underlying tenet of the convention: the fair and equitable distribution of the benefits of the use of genetic resources among *all* those who invest in their continued existence.

Although its close link to conservation efforts has earned it exceptional attention, the Merck-INBio agreement is just one of a rapidly growing number of biodiversity prospecting ventures. For example, Japan has launched a major biodiversity research program in Micronesia, the U.S. National Institutes of Health is screening wild species for compounds active against HIV and cancer, and both Indonesia and Kenya are establishing inventory programs similar to INBio's, and are exploring possible biodiversity prospecting activities.

This flurry of interest and enthusiasm in biodiversity prospecting is taking place in a policy vacuum. Virtually no precedent exists for national policies and legislation to govern and regulate wildland biodiversity prospecting. Yet, the more than 150 countries that signed the International Convention on Biological Diversity in 1992 now must pass implementing legislation that establishes just such a policy framework.

The stakes are high as countries begin to fill this policy vacuum. Done well, biodiversity prospecting can contribute greatly to environmentally sound development and return benefits to the custodians of genetic resources—the national public at large, the staff of conservation units, the farmers, the forest dwellers, and the indigenous people who maintain or tolerate the resources involved. But carried out in the mold of previous resource-exploitation ventures, biodiversity prospecting can have a negligible or

2

potentially harmful effect on biodiversity conservation and environmentally sound development.

This report offers suggestions to governments, non-governmental organizations, scientists, and industry on designing effective and equitable biodiversity prospecting programs, with a particular focus on the use of biodiversity in the pharmaceutical industry. The premise of *Biodiversity Prospecting* is that appropriate policies and institutions are needed to ensure that the commercial value obtained from genetic and biochemical resources is a positive force for development and conservation.

The value of biodiversity as a raw material for pharmaceutical and biotechnology industries is only a portion of its value to society. It makes good economic sense—and often meets ethical norms—for countries and communities to conserve biodiversity whether or not they become biodiversity prospectors. Indeed, it is entirely possible—and sometimes highly appropriate—for nations to invest in biodiversity conservation without ever seeking to commercialize genetic and biochemical resources. The normative question of whether or not countries should commercialize genetic and biochemical resources is not addressed here, but the urgent need to ensure that the commercialization already under way supports conservation and development is. In particular, three problems must be overcome if biodiversity prospecting is to contribute to national sustainable development and the long-term survival of wildland biodiversity.

First, growing commercial interest in biodiversity will not necessarily fuel increased investment in resource conservation. Genetic and biochemical resources are often described by economists as "non-rival public goods." In other words, their use by one individual does not reduce their value to others who use them. Because any user benefits from investments in their conservation, market forces will lead to less conservation of the resource than its value to society warrants.[1] In fact, unregulated biodiversity prospecting and drug development could speed the destruction of the resource. In one particularly egregious example, the entire adult population of *Maytenus buchananni*—source of the anticancer

3

compound maytansine—was harvested when a mission sponsored by the U.S. National Cancer Institute collected 27,215 kg in Kenya for testing in its drug development program (Oldfield, 1984).

Second, there is no guarantee that the institutions created to capture the benefits of biodiversity will contribute to economic growth in developing countries. Quite the opposite has been the case historically. The chief commercial beneficiaries of genetic and biochemical resources found in developing countries have been the developed countries able to explore for valuable resources, develop new technologies based on the resources, and commercialize the products. The Convention on Biological Diversity provides a framework that may boost developing countries' negotiating strength and foster needed investments in conservation, but it will be up to individual nations to pass the laws and establish the regulations needed to achieve these benefits. From a conservation standpoint, unless developing countries *do* realize benefits from these resources, summoning the political will to conserve them will be difficult.

Finally, biodiversity prospecting is just one of many forms of biodiversity development that could take place in the countryside to help raise living standards there. In most countries, the people living side by side with wildland biodiversity—farmers and villagers, indigenous peoples, forest dwellers, medicinal healers, and fisherfolk—hold the key to its survival. If local and national citizens do not get something out of maintaining wildland habitats, the habitats will be converted to timber plantations, farms, or other productive uses harmful to biodiversity. Yet, in many cases sustainably managed wildlands won't yield enough direct economic benefits to support large local populations, so governments will have to ensure that a share of the national benefits from activities such as biodiversity prospecting are used to meet rural development needs. How well biodiversity prospecting institutions contribute to sustainable development thus ultimately depends on how effective local and national government policies for conservation and development are.

Many institutions involved in biodiversity prospecting are described in this report, but most attention is given to INBio because

4

of the world-wide interest it has generated and the demand for detailed information on its structure, objectives, and operations. INBio is a product of Costa Rica's biological, political, and social environment. And Costa Rica, with its high percentage of conserved wildland, highly educated population, relatively small indigenous population, small size, and considerable scientific capacity is a friendly climate in which to attempt innovative structures for biodiversity management. The processes that are being fostered at INBio as a pilot project are, however, relevant throughout the tropics. No doubt, the biodiversity management needs in other countries will require unique solutions, but useful guidance can be obtained from the experiences of INBio and other institutions discussed here.

This report is aimed at two overlapping audiences—one interested primarily in the general policy issues related to biodiversity prospecting and another in specific guidance on the design of organizations, legislation, and contracts for biodiversity prospecting. This chapter—oriented to the first audience—introduces the issues related to biodiversity prospecting and broadly sketches the types of policies needed in "source countries" to ensure biodiversity's sustainable and equitable use. It addresses fundamental questions of ownership and access to biodiversity, the economic opportunities provided by biodiversity, the costs and benefits of public versus private control of the resource, and the rights of indigenous people and other local "custodians" of biodiversity.

The subsequent chapters provide detailed guidance on specific biodiversity prospecting activities. In Chapters II and III, Rodrigo Gámez, Ana Sittenfeld, Alfio Piva, Eugenia Leon, Jorge Jimenez, and Gerardo Mirabelli describe INBio's institutional structure and current biodiversity-prospecting program. Since INBio was designed to meet both conservation and development objectives, these chapters may help others trying to launch similar institutions or activities.

Biodiversity prospecting typically involves several types of written or implied contracts: between the collector and the company interested in the resource, between the collector and the state, between the collector and the communities providing ethnobotanical data, and sometimes between local collectors and larger collecting institutions. In Chapter IV (and Annex 2), Sarah Laird explores the nature of collector-company contracts and tells how they can be shaped to serve conservation, development, and equity. In Chapter V, Dan Janzen, Winnie Hallwachs, Rodrigo Gámez, Ana Sittenfeld, and Jorge Jimenez examine the "contract" or research agreement between the collector and the state from these same perspectives.

Chapter VI, by Michael Gollin, explores one of the more contentious issues of biodiversity prospecting—Intellectual Property Rights (IPR)—evaluating whether or not IPR regimes can be structured to support conservation. And, in Chapter VII, Calestous Juma tackles the question of how countries should structure their technology policies to ensure that the use of biodiversity leads to the development of a technical infrastructure that will yield long-lasting benefits.

In this rapidly evolving field, it is not surprising that this report leaves some questions unaddressed. But it should nonetheless help policy-makers at least become aware of the questions surrounding the potential for biodiversity prospecting. Historically, the exploitation of a "new" resource has led to its exhaustion and to the destruction of local communities and cultures. It will be no easy task to ensure that biodiversity prospecting harnesses these same forces in support of biodiversity conservation and rural development.

Growing Demand for Genetic and Biochemical Resources

The driving forces behind the evolution of new biodiversity-prospecting institutions has been the growing demand for new genes and chemicals and a growing awareness that an abundant and virtually untapped supply of these resources exists in wildland biodiversity. While genetic and biochemical resources have long been important raw materials in agriculture and medicine, biotechnology is opening a new frontier. Furthermore, democratization and economic development in many developing countries has fanned interest in the local development of in-country resources.

6

In the pharmaceutical industry, after a hiatus in natural products research in the 1970s, interest has intensified over the past decade. As a source of novel chemical compounds, natural products research is an important complement to "rational drug design"—the chemical synthesis of new drugs. Natural products research has been revived by the development of efficient automated receptor-based screening techniques that have increased a hundred-fold the speed with which chemicals can be tested. Although only one in about 10,000 chemicals yields a potentially valuable "lead" (McChesney, 1992; Principe, unpublished ms.), these new techniques have made large natural products screening programs affordable. Researchers are thus returning to such natural sources of biologically active chemicals as plants, insects, marine invertebrates, fungi, and bacteria.

Another and quite different stimulus to natural products research has come from decades-old ethnopharmacology—the study of medicines used by traditional communities. Leads based on the use of plants or animals in traditional medicine can greatly increase the probability of finding a commercially valuable drug. For small pharmaceutical companies, drug exploration based on this indigenous knowledge may be more cost-effective than attempting to compete in expensive random screening ventures. For example, Shaman Pharmaceuticals—a small company in California—bases all of its drug exploration on plants used in traditional medicine (King, 1992). One of its most promising products is an anti-fungal agent derived from a species commonly used as a folk remedy for wound-healing in Peru and parts of Mexico. Other examples of natural products research programs now under way include the U.S. National Cancer Institute's five-year $8-million program to screen 10,000 substances against 100 cancer cell lines and HIV, and new screening programs at SmithKline Beecham, Merck & Co., Inc., Monsanto, and Glaxo. *(See Table I.1.)*

In the United States, some 25 percent of prescriptions are filled with drugs whose active ingredients are extracted or derived from plants. Sales of these plant-based drugs amounted to some $4.5 billion in 1980 and an estimated $15.5 billion in 1990 (Principe, unpublished ms.). In Europe, Japan, Australia, Canada, and the U.S.,

7

Table I.1. A Sample of Companies Active in Plant and Other Natural Product Collection and Screening

Abbott Laboratories
Active since: 1950
Collectors: University of Illinois; independent collectors
Capacity: 20–50 primary screens
Natural Product Focus: Microbes, plants
Therapeutic Groups: Anti-infective, cardiovascular, neuro-science, immunoscience

Boehringer Ingelheim
Active since: 1986–89
Collectors: University of Illinois, New York Botanical Garden (pilot program in 1986); independent collectors
Capacity: 8–12 screens; 5,000 compounds per year
Natural Product Focus: Plants, microbes
Therapeutic Groups: Cardiovascular, respiratory, gastroenterology

Bristol-Myers Squibb
Active since: company established
Collectors: Scripps Institute of Oceanography; Oncogen (pokeweed protein); independent collectors
Capacity: not available
Natural Product Focus: Fungi, microbes, marine, plants
Therapeutic groups: Anti-infective, cancer, antiviral

CIBA-GEIGY
Active since: 1989 (marine); 1992 (tropical plants)
Collectors: Chinese Academy of Sciences; Harbor Branch Oceanographic Institute; independent collectors
Capacity: 4,000 samples tested (1991)
Natural Product Focus: Microbes, marine, plants
Therapeutic groups: Cancer, cardiovascular, anti-inflammatory, CNS, respiratory, anti-allergy

Eli Lilly
Active since: active in 1950s and 1960s
Collectors: now collaborates with NCI, Shaman Pharmaceuticals and independent researchers
Capacity: not available
Natural Product Focus: Plants, algae
Therapeutic groups: Anti-infective, diabetes, cardiovascular, cancer, CNS, pulmonary, anti-viral, skeletal diseases

Glaxo Group Research
Active since: 1988
Collectors: Royal Botanic Gardens Kew; Chelsea Physic Garden; Institute of Medicinal Plant Development (Beijing); Biotics, Ltd.; University of Illinois/NCI
Capacity: not available to the public
Natural Product Focus: Fungi, microbes, marine, plants
Therapeutic groups: Gastrointestinal, respiratory, anti-infective, cardiovascular, dermatology, metabolic diseases, cancer, anti-inflammatory, infectious diseases

Inverni della Beffa
Active since: late 1950s
Collectors: in-house and independent collectors in Asia, Africa and South America
Capacity: in-house screening of hundreds of samples per year
Natural Product Focus: Plants
Therapeutic groups: Cardiovascular, gastro-enterologic and anti-inflammatory

Merck & Co., Inc.
Active since: 1991
Collectors: INBio; New York Botanical Garden; MYCOsearch
Capacity: not available to the public
Natural Product Focus: Fungi, microbes, marine, plants
Therapeutic groups: Respiratory, anti-allergy, anti-inflammatory, cancer, cardiovascular, anti-infective, antiviral, gastrointestinal, prostate, bone disease

Table I.1. (Continued)

Miles, Inc.
Active since: 1991
Collectors: contract companies; independent collectors
Capacity: not available to the public
Natural Product Focus: Microbes, plants, marine, fungi
Therapeutic groups: CNS, anti-infectives, cardiovascular, anti-
diabetes, rheuma diseases

Monsanto
Active since: 1989
Collectors: Missouri Botanical Garden
Capacity: 9,000 samples per year, mainly from North America
and Puerto Rico; number of screens is not available to the
public
Natural Product Focus: Plants, microbes
Therapeutic groups: Anti-infectants, cardiovascular, anti-
inflammatory

National Cancer Institute
Active since: 1960–1980; 1986–present
Collectors: U.S. Department of Agriculture (1960–80); Mis-
souri Botanical Garden; New York Botanical Garden; University of Illinois; Kunming Institute of Botany, China;
Central Drug Research Institute, India; Brigham Young University; Harbor Branch Oceanographic Institute; Australian
Institute of Marine Sciences; Coral Reef Research Foundation; Smithsonian Oceanographic; University of Connecti-
cut; University of Hawaii at Manoa; University of Miami;
Michigan Biotechnology Institute; Tel Aviv University
Capacity: 1960–1980: received almost 35,000 species of plants,
16,000 marine extracts, and 180,000 microbe extracts; under
current program, receives almost 10,000 plant, marine, in-
vertebrate, fungi, and algae samples each year
Natural Product Focus: Plants, microbes, insects, marine, fungi
Therapeutic groups: Cancer, AIDS, antivirals

Pfizer
Active since: not available
Collectors: Natural Product Sciences (now lapsed); New York
  Botanical Garden
Capacity: not available to the public
Natural Product Focus: Plants, spider venom
Therapeutic groups: Cardiovascular, anti-inflammatory, anti-
  infective, psychotherapeutic, anti-diabetes, atherosclerosis,
  cancer, gastrointestinal, immunoscience

Pharmagenesis
Active since: 1990
Collectors: In-house experts in herbal medicine and over 15
  collaborating entities throughout China and Asia
Capacity: 2,000–3,000 samples per year; 50 screens
Natural Product Focus: natural products used in Traditional
  Asian Medicine
Therapeutic groups: Immune, endocrine, CNS, cardiovascular

Phytopharmaceuticals
Active since: 1992
Collectors: University of São Paulo, Brazil; Chinese Academy
  of Sciences; independent collectors
Capacity: not available
Natural Product Focus: Plants
Therapeutic groups: Cancer

Rhone-Poulenc Rorer
Active since: 1991
Collectors: University of Hawaii; Beijing Medical University;
  Shanghai Medical University; Tianjin Plant Institute, China;
  independent collectors
Capacity: hundreds of samples per year; 9–20 screens
Natural Product Focus: Plants, marine, microbes
Therapeutic groups: Cardiovascular, anti-infective, AIDS,
  CNS, respiratory, bone disease, cancer

11

Table I.1. (Continued)

Shaman Pharmaceuticals, Inc.
Active since: 1989
Collectors: In-house botanists and a network of collaborators in Africa, Asia, and South America
Capacity: 200 samples per year
Natural Product Focus: Plants
Therapeutic groups: Anti-viral, anti-fungal, analgesics, diabetes

SmithKline Beecham
Active since: 1987
Collectors: Biotics, Ltd.; Royal Botanic Gardens, Kew; University of Virginia; Scripps Institution of Oceanography; Morris Arboretum, University of Pennsylvania; MYCOsearch; in-house collectors
Capacity: 2–3,000 samples per year; in-house library of 17,800 natural product extracts; 10–15 screens
Natural Product Focus: Microbes, plants, marine
Therapeutic groups: Anti-infective, cardiopulmonary, CNS, gastrointestinal, anti-inflammatory

Sphinx Pharmaceuticals
Active since: 1990
Collectors: Biotics, Ltd.; independent collectors
Capacity: 15,000 samples per year; 3 screens

the market value for both prescription and over-the-counter drugs based on plants in 1985 was estimated to be $43 billion (Principe, 1989).

Biotechnology has also opened the door to greater use of biodiversity in agriculture. Genetic diversity has always been a key raw material in agricultural research, accounting for roughly one half of the gains in U.S. agricultural yields from 1930 to 1980 (OTA,

12

Natural Product Focus: Plants, marine, fungi, algae
Therapeutic groups: Psoriasis, anti-fungal, cancer

Sterling Winthrop
Active since: 1988
Collectors: Mississippi State University: Brigham Young University; New York Botanical Garden (one shipment); independent collectors
Capacity: few hundred samples per year
Natural Product Focus: Microbes, plants, marine
Therapeutic groups: Cancer, anti-inflammatory

Syntex Laboratories
Active since: 1986
Collectors: Chinese Academy of Sciences
Capacity: receive 10,000 plant extracts per year; 10 screens
Natural Product Focus: Plants, microbes
Therapeutic groups: Anti-inflammatory, bone diseases, immunology, cancer, gastroenterology, cardiovascular, antiviral, dermatology, oral contraceptives

Upjohn Co.
Active since: 1986–87
Collectors: Shanghai Institute of Materia Medica
Natural Product Focus: Microbes, plants
Therapeutic groups: CNS, cardiovascular, anti-infectives, AIDS

1987). But whereas previously only close relatives of crops could be used in breeding programs, now the genes from the entire world's biota are within reach.

Traditional crop and livestock breeding methods will still comprise most crop-breeding activity for years to come. But genetic engineering is an important new addition to breeders' toolboxes. For example, a gene responsible for a sulfur-rich protein found in the

13

Brazil nut has been isolated, cloned, and transferred into tomatoes, tobacco, and yeast (Molnar and Kinnucan, 1989). And pest-resistant genes from the bacterium *Bacillus thuringiensis* (Bt) have been transferred to tobacco, tomatoes, potatoes, and cotton (Gasser and Fraley, 1992). All told, more than 40 species of food and fiber crops have been "transformed" through genetic engineering and, as evidence of likely rapid growth in the commercial importance of genetic engineering, almost 600 field tests of genetically engineered crops have now been undertaken in more than 20 countries.

Most of the initial commercial applications of genetic engineering will involve genes from bacteria and viruses since these groups are easy to work with. But plants, animals, fungi, and invertebrates are increasingly important sources of genes as well. A trout growth hormone gene, for example, has been transferred into carp (Crawford, 1990). Genes that produce a natural antifreeze in the winter flounder have been transferred into tobacco, where they protect the plant from freezing temperatures (Gladwell, 1990). And efforts are now afoot to transfer an insect-resistance gene from the cowpea to the potato (Ward and Coghlan, 1991).

The products of agricultural biotechnology are just now entering the marketplace, but by the year 2000 farm-level sales are expected to reach at least $10 billion and possibly as much as $100 billion annually, nearly equal to the total world market for agrochemicals and seeds in 1987 (World Bank, 1991). Research expenditures are equally striking. In 1987, total R&D expenditure on agricultural biotechnology was estimated at $900 million (Giddings and Persley, 1990).

The demand for genetic resources in agriculture is thus likely to grow substantially as techniques for genetic manipulation are improved and investments in research begin to pay off. While much of this demand will be for genes from domesticated species, wild species too will increasingly be the focus of searches for novel genes. For example, the number of requests for samples of wild species of rice received by the International Rice Research Institute doubled between 1988 and 1990 (D. Sendahira, IRRI, pers. comm., Dec. 1990).

14

Apart from new chemical leads for pharmaceuticals and new genes for agriculture, other new uses of biodiversity abound. A Brazilian fungus discovered in 1986 has been patented by a University of Florida researcher as a natural fire ant control (IFAS, 1990). Chemicals extracted from the neem tree have been patented as natural insecticide (Stone, 1992). Scientists have now genetically engineered plants to produce biodegradable plastic (*WSJ*, 1992). Naturally occurring micro-organisms can be used in various environmental applications, including oil spill clean-up (OTA, 1991). And genetically modified organisms are proving valuable in such applications as mining, wastewater treatment, carbon-dioxide scrubbing, chemical detoxification, and bioremediation.

Growth in this "biotechnology industry" foretells increasing demands for novel genetic and biochemical resources. Between 1985 and 1990, the number of biotechnology patent applications filed in the United States grew by 15 percent annually—by 9,385 in 1990 alone (Raines, 1991). Total product sales for the U.S. biotechnology industry in 1991 totaled approximately $4 billion—a 38-percent increase over 1990—and by the year 2000 sales are expected to have grown more than 10-fold to some $50 billion (IBA, 1992).

What is at Stake?

All else being equal, the growing demand for genetic and biochemical resources should increase the potential market value of the raw material. But, given the high revenues generated from the final products developed in the agricultural and pharmaceutical industries, it is easy to misjudge how much money might actually be involved.

Many of the industries using genetic and biochemical resources produce high-value commodities and thus enjoy substantial gross earnings from the commercial product. Two drugs derived from the rosy periwinkle—vincristine and vinblastine—alone earned $100 million annually for Eli Lilly (Farnsworth, 1988)—a figure that is sometimes erroneously cited as the "value" of the rosy periwinkle. But sales of a product provide little indication of the potential market value of the unimproved genetic material in the source country.

Most of the industries using these resources are capital-intensive ventures that invest substantial time and money in the production of a commercial product, and most are far removed from the original source of the genetic or biochemical material.

In the U.S. pharmaceutical industry, a commercially marketable drug requires an estimated $231 million and 12 years on average to develop (DiMasi et al., 1991). These costs cover the process of screening candidate compounds, isolating active compounds, testing for possible toxicity, and undertaking clinical trials, as well as failed attempts to discover and produce a new drug. Developing agricultural products through genetic engineering also entails substantial costs. For example, the successful introduction of Bt genes into plants took several years and cost some $1.5 million to $3 million (Collinson and Wright, 1991).

In any given trial, the likelihood of discovering a valuable compound for the pharmaceutical industry is quite low. By most estimates, only about one in 10,000 chemicals yields a promising lead, and less than one fourth of the chemicals reaching clinical trials will ever be approved as a new drug (McChesney, 1992; DiMasi et al., 1991; Principe, unpublished ms.). For example, of 50,000 extracts put through an HIV screen in the natural products research program of the National Cancer Institute, only 3 are likely to wind up in clinical trials, and of 33,000 extracts screened for cancer only 5 are receiving further study (Sears, 1992).[2]

Given the high value added in both the pharmaceutical industry and agriculture, the abundance of unimproved genetic and biochemical resources, and the low probability that any specific sample will have commercial value, the holders of unimproved material are likely to receive a relatively low payment for access to the resource, current heightened demand notwithstanding. In agriculture, Barton (1991) estimates, the total revenue that might be gained if developing countries sought royalties for unimproved genetic material could amount to less than $100 million annually.[3]

Even in the pharmaceutical industry, possible earnings from the sale of raw materials are smaller than might be thought given the industry's worldwide sales of roughly $200 billion—more than 30 times that of the seed industry (Lisansky and Coombs, 1989). In this industry, typical royalties paid for samples of unknown clinical activity (e.g., new synthetic chemicals) amount to only 1 to 5 percent of net sales—a range of royalties likely to apply to natural products as well. Consider an institution that supplies 1,000 chemicals to a pharmaceutical company in return for a 3-percent royalty on the net sales of any commercial product. Given the need to screen roughly 10,000 chemicals to find a single lead, a 1 in 4 chance of a lead being developed into a commercial product, a 5-percent discount rate, a 10-year wait before a product is ready to be marketed, and 15 years of patent protection while it is being marketed, and assuming that a drug, if discovered, generates $10 million net annual revenues, the present value of the agreement to the supplier is only $52,500.[4] More sobering, there is a 97.5 percent chance that the 1,000 chemicals will not turn up any commercial product at all, and if they do, royalty payments won't begin until more than a decade after chemical screening commences.

However, the prospects for success are raised with natural products, since any extract from a species will contain hundreds or thousands of different chemicals that might result in a pharmaceutical "lead." Moreover, the probability of success can be increased through the use of multiple—and higher quality—screens. Thus, for natural products research using current technologies, the probability of success could easily be ten times that of the example above, and thus produce promising leads at a rate of about 1 per 1,000 samples.[5] The probability of developing at least one commercial product in the above example would then grow from 2.5 percent to 22 percent, and the present value of the agreement would grow accordingly, to $461,000. And, if a "blockbuster" drug—earning $1 billion in sales annually—happens to be discovered under this scenario, that value would swell to $46 million.

Biodiversity prospecting does involve financial risks. With the odds against striking it rich, it often makes economic sense for biodiversity prospectors to hedge their bets by seeking advance payments and relatively small royalties rather than forgoing collecting fees and holding out for higher royalties that may never materialize.

17

Moreover, a risk exists that the market for natural products could quickly become saturated. While a number of pharmaceutical firms have natural products research efforts under way (*see Table I.1*), most are small in scale, and the demand for chemical extracts from plants, animals, and microbes might be saturated by a handful of large-scale suppliers. As, say, Costa Rica, Indonesia, India, Brazil, and Mexico establish biodiversity prospecting institutes, the growing supply may well lead to steadily declining prices for raw materials.

Finally, there is no sure way of projecting future demand for biological samples on the part of the pharmaceutical industry. Within a decade or two, advances in synthetic chemistry, biotechnology, and medical sciences may curtail interest in natural products. On the other hand, wild species will continue to be a source of novel genes and proteins, as well as a source of insights into chemical and physiological processes. Nobody knows whether natural products will fall from favor in several decades or become even *more* valuable in medicine and in industrial applications.

In sum, while biodiversity prospecting can return profits to source countries, institutions, and communities, the amounts involved are likely to be small relative to the market value of the final products, a decade or more may pass before significant revenues materialize, a good chance exists that no commercial drugs will be produced, and late-comers may find a market already saturated with suppliers. On the other hand, given the scale of revenues generated in the pharmaceutical industry, even a relatively small share of net profits may amount to extremely large revenues for a developing country. And, if nations add value to genetic resources domestically and build technical capacity for improving the resource themselves, biodiversity prospecting could become an important component of a nation's economic development strategy.

The Evolution of Biodiversity Prospecting Institutions

The increasing value of wildland genetic resources to private industry—combined with many countries' growing sense of national identity and desire for greater control over their destiny—has created incentives for new kinds of institutional arrangements for capturing the return on investment in the use of biodiversity. In particular, genetic resource property rights, international agreements, and the use of intermediary organizations are three critical institutional arrangements whose evolution must be guided to ensure the sustainable and equitable use of biodiversity. (For wildland biodiversity, a "sustainable use" is one that does not diminish the diversity of wild species through time.)

Property Rights

For decades, the major trend in the evolution of intellectual property rights for improved genetic and biochemical resources has been a gradual expansion in the scope and strength of ownership. As a result, two different systems now govern ownership and access to genetic and biochemical resources. On the one hand, "unimproved genetic material"—wild species and traditional varieties of crops and livestock grown by farmers—is treated as an ownerless, open-access resource.[6] On the other, intellectual property rights (IPR) regimes—including patents, plant breeders rights, and trade secrets—establish ownership for new varieties of plants and animals developed by commercial breeders and chemicals isolated and developed by pharmaceutical firms.

The biodiversity prospecting "industry" falls squarely between these two systems inasmuch as it seeks to locate wild resources with commercial potential. Not surprisingly, considerable controversy surrounds the applicability of property rights to wild biodiversity and to information about its potential use.

"Intellectual" property rights are used to grant private ownership to genetic and biochemical products because of the ingenuity involved in finding, identifying, and developing them. Unlike personal property regimes, intellectual property law secures ownership in the particular form or expression embodied in things, not over the tangible properties of the thing itself. Like knowledge or information, the costs entailed in discovering and developing new genetic or biochemical products can be quite high, but once

19

developed the product can be replicated easily at low cost, thereby undermining the ability of a seed company or pharmaceutical firm to recoup its development costs. Without protection for intellectual property or, alternatively, public funding to support development costs, less investment in research and development would take place than is socially desirable.[7] For example, agricultural research investments yield extraordinarily high returns—often more than 50 percent—but capturing the economic returns from the research is so difficult that little private investment occurs (Evenson, 1990).

Historically, unimproved genetic and biochemical resources were regarded as the common heritage of humankind, freely accessible by anyone. Scattered efforts to control ownership amounted to what would today be considered "trade secret" protection. Brazil, for example, tried unsuccessfully to prevent the export of rubber tree seeds, and for good reason. Just 20 years after the first rubber trees were established in Malaysia, the Brazilian rubber industry that had once commanded 98 percent of the world supply was exporting virtually nothing, while Singapore became the rubber capital of the world (Brockway, 1988). Similarly, Andean nations' attempts to prevent the export of Cinchona—the source of an anti-malarial compound—were eventually overcome, again by British plant explorers (Juma, 1989).

As early as 1873, however, a new type of ownership was extended to certain genetic resources: the patent. In that year, Louis Pasteur was awarded a patent in the United States for a yeast culture, giving him a limited monopoly over the culture, enforced by the state, in recognition of his intellectual contribution to the creation of the product (Juma, 1989).

Beginning in 1930, IPR for genetic and biochemical resources began to expand rapidly in breadth and scope. In 1930, the United States passed the Plant Patent Act, which allowed patenting of asexually reproduced plants such as roses, other ornamentals, and fruit trees. In the 1940s, European countries established Plant Breeders Rights (PBR) protecting sexually reproduced plants and the United States followed suit in 1970 with its Plant Variety

20

Protection Act.[8] To address issues arising from international trade in species protected by Plant Breeders Rights, the International Convention for the Protection of New Varieties of Plants—commonly referred to as the UPOV Convention—was adopted in 1961.[9]

With the exception of early patents like that granted to Pasteur, intellectual property rights granted for plants and animals were not formal "utility" patents. Neither Plant Breeders Rights nor Plant Patent legislation requires the same standards of novelty, utility, and non-obviousness (that is, innovation that would not be obvious to the average person skilled in the art) required for a utility patent and, in turn, neither system provides as much protection for the innovation as utility patents.

The most significant step in the expansion of IPR coverage for genetic resources took place in 1980, when the U.S. Supreme Court ruled in the case of Diamond vs. Chakrabarty that a genetically altered bacterium could be granted a utility patent under standard patent law (U.S. Supreme Court, 1980, 447 U.S. 303). Then, in 1985, the U.S. Patent and Trademark office ruled that a corn plant containing an increased level of a particular amino acid could also receive a utility patent. In 1988, the first animal was patented—a mouse carrying a human cancer gene used in medical research. The extension of patents to human life took place over the same period. Human cells—cancerous cells taken from a leukemia patient—were first patented in 1984. In 1991, the U.S. National Institutes of Health filed patent applications for the structure of 337 human gene fragments identified with an automated sequencing machine and in 1992 applied for patents on a further 2,375 gene fragments (Roberts, 1992). (The first of these applications was rejected by the U.S. Patent and Trademark Office in 1992, but reportedly will be amended and re-submitted.)

Countries differ widely in the patent protection they offer for living material. At one end of the spectrum, the United States grants patents on novel DNA sequences, genes, plant parts, plant or animal varieties, and biotechnological processes. In contrast, while they do grant patents for plant and animal genes, European countries have only recently extended patent protection to plant

21

varieties. Recently, a patent was also granted for the Harvard mouse in the United Kingdom, though the court decision allowing the patent indicated that a criterion of clear human benefit must be used in determining the patentability of an animal. Many developing countries exempt biological processes and products entirely from their patent regimes.

Chemical compounds and processes have long been subject to patent protection in most industrialized countries, though drugs and other types of chemical products are sometimes excluded from patentability. For example, patent protection for pharmaceutical products was extended only in 1958 in France, 1968 in the Federal Republic of Germany, 1976 in Japan (when it ranked second in world drug production), and 1978 in Italy (Chudnovsky, 1983). As recently as 1990, Finland, Norway, and Spain did not patent pharmaceutical processes and products (Lesser, 1990).

The gradual expansion of IPR protection raises an important and fundamental question: How can anyone "own" genes or biochemicals that occur in nature? In most fields, patents are granted only for innovations, not for discoveries. Is it right for someone to possess an exclusive right to a naturally occurring gene or chemical?

No uniform standards exist for the treatment of discoveries by intellectual property regimes in different countries, particularly for discoveries relating to natural products like genes and chemicals. In many industrialized countries, patents are allowed if the discovery requires notable input of human effort and ingenuity (Lesser, 1990). For instance, in the case of agriculture, a gene will usually be patentable only if it is used in a species in which it did not evolve or which it could not have been transferred to through conventional breeding (Barton, 1991). Similarly, a longstanding U.S. legal doctrine holds that the purified form of a chemical can be patented if the chemical is found in nature only in an unpurified form (Barton, 1991). Thus, in the United States, Europe, and Japan, pharmaceutical companies can patent chemicals derived from natural sources and genes that have been transferred to unrelated organisms.[10] In contrast, a number of developing countries exclude drugs and/or biological materials from patent protection.

22

International Agreements

Even as the scope of property rights for improved genetic resources expanded over the past century, unimproved genetic resources retained their "common heritage" status until well into the 1980s. Beginning in the mid-1970s, however, questions surfaced in international forums over the nature of the institutions governing access to these resources.

In agriculture, a significant fraction of so-called "unimproved" genetic resources was actually the product of the hard work and ingenuity of farmers as they selected and bred crop varieties to fit local conditions and tastes (Mooney, 1983; Fowler and Mooney, 1990). Similarly, many pharmaceutical products developed from natural products were first "discovered" by traditional healers. Why, more people began to wonder, didn't these intellectual contributions receive the same IPR protection as the contributions of plant breeders and pharmaceutical companies? Or, alternatively, if these contributions were freely available to all, shouldn't the same apply to the products developed by pharmaceutical firms and seed companies?

A second concern revolves around ownership of the genes, seeds, and chemicals themselves. Developing countries began to question why individuals and companies based in the gene-poor developed countries were obtaining resources free-of-charge from the gene-rich developing countries, then patenting the genes and chemicals and selling the patented products back to the country where they originated. Since these were the raw materials used in agricultural breeding and pharmaceutical development, why shouldn't companies pay for them just as they would pay for, say, coal or oil?

In the agricultural arena, these debates quickly escalated in the early 1980s into a bitter "Seed War" between the North and the South. Since then, the resolution of this dispute through international mechanisms has moved at a glacial pace. In 1983, a Commission on Plant Genetic Resources was established through the Food and Agriculture Organization (FAO) of the United Nations and the "International Undertaking on Plant Genetic Resources" was signed by most developing countries and some industrialized

23

countries. This Undertaking initially held that *all* genetic resources (including the elite lines of private plant breeders) should be considered common heritage and thus freely accessible. Needless to say, few developed countries with established seed industries supported the Undertaking.

In 1987, the Commission on Plant Genetic Resources accepted the legitimacy of IPR protection for breeders in exchange for recognition of the concept of "farmers' rights." These were defined to be communal rights, vested in the international community through the International Undertaking on Plant Genetic Resources, recognizing the contributions of local communities and farmers in creating and maintaining genetic resources. In this same year, the Commission established a "Fund for Plant Genetic Resources" to fulfill the obligations inherent in the concept of farmers' rights by compensating developing countries for the use of their genetic resources, though donor countries never have provided more than token sums for this Fund.

The debate over ownership and access to genetic resources shifted venue in the late 1980s to the negotiations for a Convention on Biological Diversity. *(See Annexes 3 and 4.)* Here, countries quickly agreed to recognize that biodiversity was a sovereign national resource and a "common concern" of humankind—not a common heritage. But up until the very end of the negotiations, developed and developing countries couldn't agree on mechanisms for protecting intellectual property and for allocating the benefits of the use of biodiversity. The final convention, signed by more than 150 nations at the Earth Summit in June 1992, recognizes nations' obligations to ensure that both the countries supplying biodiversity and those using it receive economic benefits and even notes that countries should encourage the "equitable sharing of the benefits arising from the utilization of [the knowledge, innovations and practices of indigenous and local communities]."

Biodiversity Prospecting Intermediaries

The final element of the evolution of biodiversity prospecting institutions has been the recent emergence of new intermediary arrangements to facilitate access to genetic and biochemical resources and their transfer to the pharmaceutical, agriculture, or biotechnology industry. A wide range of such institutions already exists, and many more are being planned.

One outstanding example is Costa Rica's INBio. This private, non-profit organization was established to facilitate the conservation and sustainable use of biodiversity. It uses its income and donations to support a wide array of conservation actions—from carrying out the national biodiversity inventory in collaboration with the Ministry of Natural Resources, Energy, and Mines (MIRENEM) to conducting and facilitating biodiversity-prospecting activities to support its conservation mission. Many other private non-profit intermediaries are based in developed countries. For example, the New York Botanical Garden, the Missouri Botanical Garden, and the University of Chicago have all contracted with private pharmaceutical companies and with public research organizations to provide samples of biodiversity for pharmaceutical development. Increasingly, these intermediaries also enter into contractual relationships with the countries—or appropriate institutions within the country—where they pursue their collecting activities.

Private for-profit intermediaries also exist in both developed and developing countries. Biotics, Ltd., a private firm based in the United Kingdom, works as a broker, providing pharmaceutical companies with plant genetic resources. Biotics buys samples and, through a contract, agrees to share any royalties with the source country institution. Similar contracts are drawn up between Biotics and the pharmaceutical firms, which would ultimately hold the patent on any discovery. Numerous collectors in developing countries also make a business of supplying plant and animal samples to industry. While most large pharmaceutical companies rely on other organizations to collect natural products, smaller firms—such as Shaman Pharmaceuticals—may both collect biodiversity samples and develop drugs.

Public organizations have also begun to serve as intermediaries. Mexico's National Biodiversity Commission—established in February 1992—may seek to play much the same role for Mexico

25

that INBio does for Costa Rica. Similarly, Indonesia—and the Asian Development Bank—have considered establishing a Biodiversity Marketing and Commercialization Board. Elsewhere, the U.S.-Japan Environmental Partnership will be providing $20 million annually from 1994 to 1997 to establish several Natural Resource Conservation and Management Centers in Asia, some of which may undertake biodiversity prospecting. And three U.S. government agencies established a program in 1992 to fund "International Cooperative Biodiversity Groups" designed to "promote conservation of biological diversity through the discovery of bioactive agents from natural products, and to ensure that equitable economic benefits from these discoveries accrue to the country of origin" (NIH et al., 1992: 3).

Finally, some collaborative efforts between the public and private sectors have been established. For example, 24 Japanese corporations—including Suntory, Nippon Steel, and the Kyowa Hakko Pharmaceutical Company—and the Ministry of International Trade and Industry have established the Marine Biotechnology Institute in Micronesia. Researchers at this institute, with some 80 employees, two research laboratories, and a research vessel, are looking for new anti-bio-fouling agents, oil-eating bacteria, phytoplankton that fix atmospheric carbon dioxide, and new pharmaceutical compounds. (No arrangements have been made to share royalties with Micronesia or to pay an exploration fee.) (Sochaczewski, 1992)

Biodiversity prospecting intermediaries have been established for various purposes. Some are strictly money-making ventures. Others carry out basic research or spur conservation or economic development. But nearly all of the commercial collection programs of these institutions are young and thus by nature experimental.

Biodiversity Prospecting Guidelines

Although the mission of some organizations engaged in biodiversity prospecting is primarily one of conservation, most have evolved primarily in response to growing commercial demand for the resource, rent-seeking by commercial ventures, and public policies designed to foster innovation in the extension of IPR. None of these factors provides a sufficient incentive for resource conservation, the survey and description of biodiversity, local economic development, or the distribution of the benefits from biodiversity to those who pay the direct or opportunity costs for developing and maintaining it.

Biodiversity prospecting has attracted the interest of environmentalists and developing countries because it may provide significant incentives and funds for conservation and could contribute to economic development in regions rich in genetic and biochemical resources. But this dual potential will not be realized unless new policies are established to steer the evolution of the institutions toward these ends.

The remainder of this chapter summarizes general principles that can guide the development of such policies. These guidelines, derived from more detailed chapters that follow and based largely on the experiences of INBio in Costa Rica, should help governments, NGOs, and industry develop appropriate property rights regimes, intermediary institutions, collecting agreements, contracts, collecting regulations, and technology policies. In the absence of detailed empirical and theoretical studies, these conclusions are tentative and must be modified to fit specific circumstances. But taken as a whole, they approximate the "state-of-the-art" of biodiversity prospecting policies today.

Role of Intermediaries

Whether through one or more organizations, countries should establish the capability to identify and locate biodiversity, to save representative samples of wild biodiversity in protected wildlands, and to use it non-destructively for the public good.

Few generalizations about the diverse intermediary organizations involved in biodiversity prospecting hold. Intermediaries can support—or undermine—the conservation and sustainable use of biodiversity, whether they are public or private and whether they are located in the source country or in a foreign land.

27

Nevertheless, more than any other component of biodiversity prospecting programs, well-designed intermediaries have the potential to promote conservation, development, and equity. As a pioneering institution, INBio's activity as a biodiversity prospecting intermediary has received particular attention as a "model." However, in Chapter II, Gámez et al. reject the assertion that INBio is a model, but accept that it is an instructive "pilot project."

Perhaps the most important insight from INBio's experience is that biodiversity prospecting activities are only a means to an end. INBio was established to help identify and inventory Costa Rica's biodiversity and to integrate its non-destructive use into the intellectual and economic fabric of the society. Biodiversity prospecting helps fund conservation, but, more important, it demonstrates the economic value of biodiversity and thus helps convince policymakers that biodiversity conservation should figure centrally into all development planning.

Whatever intermediary organizations are established, the array of institutions involved in biodiversity activities should fill three basic needs: *saving* representative samples of wild biodiversity in protected wildlands, *knowing* what this biodiversity is and where it is to be found in those wildlands, and *using* biodiversity non-destructively for societal aims. If biodiversity is to survive, the society in whose custody it resides must perceive it as an asset. That will happen only through understanding what biodiversity is and seeking ways to use it to satisfy local and national social and economic needs.

Any effort to save, know, and use biodiversity requires the joint efforts of widely different sectors of society—including universities, museums, conservation ministries, commercial firms, and rural communities. But INBio's experience demonstrates that one organization can catalyze the integration of these sectors. INBio's inventory of Costa Rica's species provides employment for rural people as technicians—"parataxonomists"—in this venture. The institute is generating abundant information that is needed to wisely manage the country's biodiversity for a wide variety of users, developing the capacity to undertake chemical screening and pharmaceutical development, and working with Merck & Co., Inc., and other corporations to develop—and share the benefits from—new products based on that biodiversity. In essence, INBio closes the loop between studying, saving, and using biodiversity.

In other countries, biodiversity management institutions may or may not be involved in biodiversity prospecting. They may build on existing public-sector institutions like universities, environment ministries, and national museums or they may take the form of new public or private institutions. Multi-national management and prospecting organizations may make sense in some regions, while provincial or state-level organizations may be needed in others.

Clearly, institutions designed to gather information on biodiversity management and to develop new products of value to the biotechnology or pharmaceutical industry address only one portion of biodiversity conservation needs. For example, such institutions can create some employment in rural communities and may develop new products that local entrepreneurs can market, but it is unlikely that they could make rural development their mission. Yet, actions to reduce poverty in rural areas and to provide alternatives to habitat conversion that meet the needs of rural communities rank at the top of biodiversity-conservation priorities (WRI et al., 1992). By contributing to economic and technological development, and by contributing user fees or taxes directly to the public sector, biodiversity-prospecting initiatives can provide a share of the resources needed to meet this broader array of conservation and development needs, but the responsibility rests with national and local governments to ensure that these resources are used appropriately. When governments are unable to meet these responsibilities, the potential for success of biodiversity prospecting will be diminished.

One serious concern is that the revenues governments earn from biodiversity prospecting and the economic gains stimulated by commercialization of new products based on biodiversity may sometimes enrich the few rather than contribute to rural development. Certainly, biodiversity prospecting institutions often return

29

some benefits directly to the individuals, landowners, and communities involved in biodiversity collecting activities. But, more typically, as when biodiversity is collected from public lands or without the benefit of local information, there is no alternative to effective public sector mechanisms for returning benefits to local communities. For those countries that have shown a commitment to biodiversity conservation and the development needs of rural communities, biodiversity-prospecting intermediaries can be a valuable element of biodiversity-conservation policies. Without such a national commitment, biodiversity prospecting may be nothing more than the newest unsustainable resource-commercialization venture.

Company-Collector Contracts

Contracts between companies and collectors can help ensure that the exchange of biological materials generates both immediate and long-term benefits for the source countries and communities.

Contracts are an important means of distributing the costs, benefits, and risks between the collecting organization and the companies interested in developing products from genetic and biochemical resources. Through them, the portion of benefits that will return to the country that possesses the biodiversity can be determined. Contracts can be established even if countries lack intellectual property regimes or legislation governing the activities of collectors. They are an extremely flexible form of agreement that could, in theory, be used to ensure that the source country receives financial returns from biodiversity prospecting and that these funds are used to promote resource conservation.

However, as Laird explains in Chapter IV, contracts alone will not make a country's conservation and development objectives materialize. Such agreements can be expensive and difficult to draft, negotiate, and enforce, and any company negotiating such a contract is motivated by the desire to acquire useful samples for screening,[11] not to conserve resources. As a result, any provisions

30

for conservation, the return of benefits to local communities, technology transfer, and so forth are likely to be limited (even if they are the collecting organization's primary goals).

Company-collector contracts typically involve a fee for samples and, occasionally, advance payments to the collector. In such cases, the collector must determine how to disperse these in the country of collection. As countries begin regulating access to genetic resources, the collectors' obligations to in-country collaborators and to collecting regions are likely to become more stringently defined. Laird notes that while most collectors take responsibility for determining equitable relationships with their in-country collaborators, collecting regulations must be developed that will hold up regardless of whether personal relationships do.

One of the most striking aspects of the Merck-INBio contract was the size of the advance payment to INBio for services. Customarily, pharmaceutical plant collectors receive payments of $50 to $200 per sample. In sharp contrast, the $1.1 million paid by Merck in exchange for samples is nearly ten times the traditional service payment. Merck & Co. was asked to pay virtually all of the real costs of a sample, rather than be subsidized by the social and institutional backup that a pharmaceutical collector normally receives but does not charge to the company. From Merck and Co.'s standpoint, this sum is warranted by the greatly increased quality of the samples that it receives from INBio during the initial two-year agreement and in future years if the agreement is renewed. How often payments of this magnitude will be made depends on how often sourcing institutions can offer samples of such quality, whether all collectors choose to charge all of the real costs to the purchaser, and whether competition among collectors drives prices to below-cost levels. As in many other markets, product quality is likely to be strongly proportional to the price paid for the sample and its associated services.

In Chapter IV and Annex 2, Laird et al. describe a number of provisions that could be included in company-collector contracts to further conservation, development, and equity. For example, contracts could specify that future supplies of raw material would

31

be obtained from the country of origin, that royalties would be distributed to individuals (such as traditional healers) that provided information on the resource, or that a specified fraction of royalties would be dedicated to conservation. While such stipulations may currently be uncommon, the rules of biodiversity prospecting are changing rapidly. For example, all INBio-commercial contracts state explicitly what portion of the research and royalty budget goes directly to the National Park Fund at the Ministry of Natural Resources, Energy, and Mines and what portion is used for other kinds of wildland conservation activities. Similarly, all INBio samples must come from inside the conserved wildlands so that there is no contest over where the funds should be spent.

Property Rights

There is no more fundamental and divisive issue related to biodiversity prospecting than the question of who owns biodiversity. Developing countries have long been frustrated with a system that labels their resources as "open access" but then establishes private property rights for improved products based on those resources. Is it possible to modify IPR regimes to internalize the cost of biodiversity loss and management and ensure that the source countries and the custodians of biodiversity within them receive more of the economic returns from its development?

It is uncertain whether Intellectual Property Rights can be extended to wild genetic and biochemical resources and whether such rights would hurt or help the objectives of conservation and development.

On the surface, the idea of extending IPR protection to wild species would seem to resolve the apparent imbalance between the rights of ownership for improved and unimproved genetic resources, thereby providing an incentive for resource conservation. Just as the individual who purifies a naturally occurring chemical is able to patent it, the individual (or nation) first spending the time and money needed to identify a new species and bearing the cost of maintaining that species could be granted exclusive rights to its use or sale (Sedjo, 1988; Sedjo, 1992). By assigning such rights,

32

some would argue, the opportunity cost of the loss of the resource could be internalized and market forces and legislation might then lead to an "optimal" investment in conservation, at least with respect to biodiversity's genetic and biochemical value.

Michael Gollin explores this possibility in Chapter VI and concludes that the extension of IPR to wild species is unworkable at present. From a pragmatic standpoint, patent offices would be deluged with speculative claims on species whose utility was unknown. But, more important, such a step would place more of the "public domain" in private hands than would be justified to maximize social benefits, Gollin concludes.

More generally, Gollin reviews the various types of IPR that exist today and concludes that all are of limited use in promoting the conservation of wild species (but also do not necessarily hasten the loss of biodiversity). On the other hand, IPR can help stimulate domestic innovation and technology acquisition, thus providing an incentive for the sustainable development of the resource within the source country and generating economic benefits that may then be used to support conservation or to compensate the custodians of biodiversity.

The most promising immediate opportunities for capturing greater benefits from biodiversity involve access restrictions, contracts, and value-added industries.

If extending intellectual property rights to unimproved genetic resources fails to capture benefits from the use of the resource, what other mechanisms are possible? Three mechanisms are described in this report: contracts, access restrictions *(see below)*, and the promotion of value-added industries. Efforts to add value to biochemical and genetic resources—such as those described in Chapter II by Gámez et al. and in Chapter III by Sittenfeld and Gámez—may be particularly rewarding since they contribute directly to the development of the source country's technological capacity. Strengthened capacity, in turn, allows source-country institutions to enter into more profitable partnerships with technology-intensive industries.

The economic returns generated from biodiversity can be enhanced either by providing a service related to the unimproved resource or by improving the resource itself. For example, in its agreement with Merck, INBio is basically selling biodiversity prospecting services, not any intellectual property right that it holds. Among the services it offers are sample identification, ready access to further samples from the same species and of the same quality; and known and user-sensitive sample-processing methods. The Merck-INBio agreement is not exclusive. Merck is free to buy samples from others in Costa Rica, INBio can provide samples to other organizations, and other organizations can collect the same samples and sell them to Merck or any other user. Although INBio's agreements include stipulations that for six months to two years it will not send the same sample to a competing company, in no sense does INBio control access to—or "own"—the resource.

Institutions can also increase economic returns by developing information about the resource. A biodiversity-prospecting institution could undertake preliminary chemical screening of samples to identify those with promising biological activity, thereby raising their potential market value. Such work could be undertaken with no intent to seek a patent; indeed it could be undertaken in a country with no patent protection for biological materials. The increased commercial value would stem from the new information on the materials' potential use. In the pharmaceutical industry, for example, it is common to receive royalties of 1 to 6 percent of net sales for unscreened chemical samples, 5 to 10 percent for material backed by pre-clinical information on its medical activity, and 10 to 15 percent for fractionated and identified material with efficacy data.

INBio is already establishing chemical screening and bioassay facilities to explore Costa Rican species for potentially valuable compounds. Once active substances are discovered, INBio will be in a stronger position to negotiate royalty arrangements with foreign companies and can even isolate new products by itself.

Indigenous People, farmers, and traditional healers can and sometimes should seek IPR protection. As a supple-

ment to these property rights, formal and informal contracts will often be a more promising avenue for ensuring just compensation for their knowledge. National collecting regulations can help ensure that equitable contracts are negotiated.

Today, traditional knowledge is rarely involved in the development of new pharmaceutical products from biodiversity. Natural products chemistry today is based primarily on research by scientists, physicians, and pharmacologists. The screening programs used by large pharmaceutical companies are more likely to make use of phylogenetic information—screening organisms related to those that have proven their pharmaceutical worth—than indigenous knowledge, and new genes for agricultural breeding are increasingly found among wild species where farmers have played little role. But, in some cases, the discovery of new medicines or promising genes is due in part to the knowledge of traditional healers or the work of generations of farmers. In such cases, how can these people be equitably compensated?

Knowledge of the therapeutic properties of wild species is often held in confidence by traditional societies, both because considerable training is needed before the materials can be used safely and effectively and because widespread knowledge of the cures would undermine the healers' vocation. Historically, ethnopharmacologists have not seen the need to protect these secrets (though often researchers have attempted to negotiate compensation for the information provided.) For example, the author of *Medicinal Plants of East Africa* (which gives complete descriptions of the taxonomy, distribution, and uses of the medicinal plants) writes in the foreword:

"Many of the herbal medicine men will not like this book since it may deprive them of their profession once their secrets are revealed. The majority of them were reluctant to show me the drug plants as a whole for this reason. In most cases, I was given the leaves or root of the plant already crushed or picked. But after some persuasion, I was shown the plant on the condition that I would not reveal it to anyone else" (Kokwaro, 1976).

35

Though such practices were once commonplace, today this would be considered a misappropriation of trade secrets that could and should be prevented by legal means, including lawsuits.[12]

Issues of equity in the distribution of benefits from the use of traditional medicines and traditional crop varieties have underlain international debates over biodiversity for more than a decade (Mooney, 1983; Elisabetsky, 1991). And today, the issue of what represents "just compensation" for the holders of traditional knowledge is far from resolved. Some of the questions that arise include: How can the efforts of generations of farmers be equitably compensated through their descendants for developments in agriculture? Should a traditional healer be compensated for indigenous knowledge, or should the debt be paid to the community or to the state? Is a one-time payment to the deserving party or group enough, or do the bearers of traditional knowledge have a basic right to the fruits of their inspiration that goes beyond the labor effort involved?

The subjectivity of any definition of equitable compensation ensures that no mechanism for allocating benefits will appear "just" to all. And North-South questions of equity will be particularly troublesome. In a cohesive and well-integrated society where it can be shown that privatizing specific types of knowledge leads to greater public good, this "implicit" compensation ensures reasonable equity in the distribution of benefits (Brush, 1991). For example, when the United States grants a patent to a U.S. drug company that develops an anti-cancer compound made from a local plant, "implicit" social benefits accrue nationally in the form of a lessened incidence of cancer. But it is hardly surprising that equity issues come up when the actors are traditional healers living outside of market economies in Brazil on the one hand and genetic engineers in the United States on the other. What benefits return to a remote region of the Amazon from a new drug designed to fight diseases common only in the developed world, and too expensive for purchase by local people in any event?

One mechanism for meeting global obligations to the generations of farmers and healers who have developed and protected the genetic and biochemical resources now used in industry is through an international financial mechanism such as the Fund for Plant Genetic Resources or the Convention on Biological Diversity (Fowler and Mooney, 1990). But can other mechanisms complement such international agreements? Specifically, can IPR be used to protect the knowledge of indigenous people, traditional healers, and farmers?

The answer is "sometimes." As Gollin explains in Chapter VI, most current IPR regimes would, in principle, allow the extension of IPR to cover the innovations and knowledge of traditional healers and farmers. Traditional healers could be granted patents for novel uses of a compound under most systems of patent protection. As a corollary, if a traditional medicinal use of a compound is public knowledge, then patent laws should be applied to prevent others from patenting that compound for the same purpose. Similarly, there is no compelling reason why a farmer who breeds a new variety of plant could not receive protection under most systems of Plant Breeders Rights.

Any number of practical problems crop up, however, when intellectual property rights are extended to these "informal" innovations and promoting their use in this context is somewhat disingenuous. The scope of protection of IPR is generally as much a function of the political and economic power of those seeking protection as it is of wise or just economic policy. Moreover, the utility of IPR regimes is always a function of the enforceability of the rights. Society can establish the legal framework governing such disputes, but, ultimately, the rights-holder must be able to identify infringements and challenge the infringing party. Clearly, a traditional healer in Brazil or a farmer in Ethiopia can rarely do either. Farmers and traditional healers cannot effectively claim ownership to a resource if they can't control access to it, and they are in no financial position to challenge IPR claims made by others.

Finally, the costs of enforcing the right may often outweigh any benefits. A farmer might well be able to file for Plant Variety Protection on a new plant variety, but why bother if the new variety is locally adapted to just one small region of the country? The market for the variety simply won't be big enough to repay the effort.

37

Thus, while farmers and traditional healers are in a position to seek formal intellectual property protection (in countries that provide it), seeking compensation for their knowledge and inventions more directly through contracts and informal agreements usually makes more sense. For example, by refusing access to knowledge or traditional seed varieties, individuals can at least establish a framework for negotiating an equitable settlement (WRI et al., 1992). These two avenues for compensation are not mutually exclusive and indeed recognition of the legal right may encourage formal negotiations for compensation.

Increasingly, biodiversity collectors, anthropologists, and scientists are recognizing their responsibilities to local communities and negotiating formally or informally for access to information held by the communities. Both Laird (Chapter IV) and Janzen et al. (Chapter V) cite codes of conduct that professional organizations and U.N. agencies are now developing to promote greater equity in the relationship of researchers with local communities and source countries.

National legislation regulating biodiversity collecting activities provides another, more formal, mechanism for ensuring that the rights of local communities and source countries are respected. Collecting permits could, for example, require collectors to obtain prior informed consent from local communities before collecting begins and, in some cases, to negotiate the terms by which they would be given access to land or to local knowledge.

Legal Guarantees

Each of the policy tools discussed above—organizational design, company-collector contracts, and intellectual property rights—can help achieve the objectives of conservation, development, and equity. However, without effective national regulation, the attainment of these objectives may be the exception rather than the rule. Private intermediaries are more likely to be established with profit, rather than conservation, in mind. The parties to contracts will rarely agree on both the need for conservation and technology transfer. And it will be easy for commercial collectors and companies to slight the contributions of farmers and traditional healers to new medicines and crop varieties.

The best means available to ensure that biodiversity prospecting does meet these broader social objectives is national policy, specifically biodiversity collecting regulations. Such regulations should be part of legislation established by countries to implement the Convention on Biological Diversity. (Costa Rica, for example, adopted a Wild Life Protection law on October 12, 1992, which declares all wild plants and animals to be "national patrimony" and requires collectors to: submit an application for a license that details their collection plans; deposit voucher samples with the national collection; and, send copies of publications resulting from the work to the national library. Collection for non-scientific purposes requires a special license and must involve the use of public bids, concessions, or contracts.) Sittenfeld and Gámez (Chapter III), Laird (Chapter IV), and Janzen et al. (Chapter V) examine a number of issues that could be addressed through the national legal framework.

The agreement reached between a biodiversity collector and society is, in essence, a research *contract*. Where past collecting activity has been regulated informally, if at all, the state should now ensure that in return for access to genetic and biochemical resources the collector assumes certain obligations with regard to conduct, liability, and payments. The most critical elements of such regulation are: i) user fees for access to genetic or biochemical resources on public or private land, and ii) requirements that collectors negotiate equitable arrangements with the local communities, the wildland administrators, the private landowners, the farmers, and healers who were the custodians of the biodiversity collected or who contributed to the discovery or development of valuable genetic or biochemical resources.

To increase the benefits they receive from biodiversity, countries and local communities should regulate access to the resource and charge "user fees" where appropriate.

Critics have charged that private biodiversity prospecting intermediaries inappropriately exploit the public domain for private benefit (Kloppenburg and Rodriguez, 1992). This criticism is often valid: private commercial collectors often do obtain genetic resources freely from the public domain and sell them for private gain. Public policies should thus seek to ensure that private collectors pay local or national governments for access to biodiversity.

Nobody would expect a nation to allow a private timber company to use public timber resources free of charge or to mine on public land without reimbursing the state. A similar system of user fees—or biodiversity prospecting concessions—should be established for access to public lands for biodiversity prospecting ventures (Sedjo, 1990; Simpson, 1992). Ideally, such fees would be used to maintain the biodiversity, thereby internalizing part of the costs of conservation. INBio, by investing 10 percent of Merck's initial payment of $1 million in traditional conservation activities, agreeing to spend half of all royalties on conservation through MIRENEM, half on conservation through its own activities, and conducting all of its activities as development of the conservation areas, basically paid such a user fee, even though no national legislation required it at the time.

In Chapter V, Janzen et al. describe in detail a system of regulated access to biodiversity. They argue that the time has come for *all* research on biodiversity—whether commercial or scientific—to be strictly regulated by public institutions (or their designated representatives). This does not mean that all researchers must pay user fees. For example, scientists carrying out basic research on biodiversity—such as inventory and taxonomic work—return "in-kind" benefits to a nation instead of direct payments. Similarly, governments might set lower fees for local (as opposed to foreign) collectors, thus giving them an incentive to develop local industries based on these resources.[13]

Janzen et al. also discuss the types of compensation that might be received for access to biodiversity. They argue that the nature of the compensation must be based on what the researcher has to provide, which isn't necessarily money. Nonetheless, some user fees may be appropriate even for those engaged in "basic" rather than commercial research. Scientists readily accept the notion that they must contribute to the overhead of their home institutions; they should not object to the idea that they should also contribute to the "overhead" of their research sites. (Nor should their granting agencies discourage such expenses.)

An alternative to systems of user fees would be for the state to control all aspects of the commercialization of the resource. Genetic and biochemical resources do have unique attributes that set them apart from other elements of a nation's patrimony—among them, its timber, minerals, and fisheries. For example, the sale of rights to a gene or chemical to a foreign company exhausts the local rights and control over the resource. Whereas local communities or future generations may have an opportunity to challenge forest or mineral leases, for genetic resources the deal is final. And the real value of the resource lies in the information contained in the genes or chemicals, not in its physical properties. Though an intermediary may be selling only a service related to the resource, its actions may make it easier for individuals with technological expertise not available in the source country to establish private property rights for that information.

But whether stronger control by national governments would better serve national interests is far from clear. Such a system could run into tremendous practical problems. For example, INBio is paid for the service and information it provides, not for licenses to intellectual property rights. A system that retains national control over all such information and services—as well as the right to the resource itself—would be unwieldy at best and fraught with inefficiency and corruption at worst. In many countries, the balance between local and national control over resources has shifted too far toward the latter, undermining prospects for sustainable use and equitable distribution of the benefits from resource use. With too much national control, for example, indigenous groups would lose their right to contract with a pharmaceutical company for the use of their knowledge. In an ideal world, the national government might assume that right and make sure that the local community is compensated equitably, but in most countries the retention of local control is more likely to achieve the social objectives.

41

In any event, where private biodiversity prospecting is allowed, governments should protect the public interest by regulating access to the resource, charging appropriate fees for that access, and using the revenue so generated to support conservation and rural communities near protected wildlands.

Biodiversity prospecting on private lands should be subject to regulation and "user fees."

The need for user fees is relatively clear on public lands, but somewhat problematic when applied to biodiversity collected on private lands. Almost all countries, for example, consider plants growing on private land to belong to the land owner, though wild animals are the property of the state. Individuals can cut a tree on land they own without the state's permission but—because wild animals move across property lines—must follow state regulations governing the harvest of wildlife.

The issue of ownership and access to genetic and biochemical resources is closer to that of the right to harvest wild animals on private lands than to that of plant ownership. When an individual cuts and sells a tree, nothing prevents another individual from cutting another tree of the same species on adjacent land and selling it. But only the first individual who sells a chemical extract that is later developed into a drug will receive the economic benefit associated with the discovery and associated property right.

Thus, following the same policy that governs the harvest of wild animals, nations should not allow all rights to these resources to be "bundled" with private property rights in land. While local land owners may regulate access to the resource and charge collecting fees, local and national governments should also regulate the exploitation of these resources and charge user fees where appropriate.

Technology Policy

Developing countries should establish technology policies that better enable them to benefit directly from their genetic and biochemical resources.

The long-term contribution to economic development, conservation, and the equitable sharing of benefits from genetic resources may be greatest if biodiversity-prospecting policies foster the development of national capacity in biotechnology. Efforts that don't will fall victim to the historical mistakes of other export industries based on raw materials in developing countries.

In Chapter VII, Juma argues that a narrow focus on the sharing of returns on the sale of products derived from biological material is misguided. This approach can give developing countries financial incentives to conserve biological diversity, but even longer-term benefits will stem from technological cooperation and capacity building in science and technology. For this reason, biodiversity prospecting should be considered part of the larger issue of national biotechnology policy and should be treated as a capacity-building activity.

Juma downplays the obstacles intellectual property rights pose to access to new technologies. Most of the technologies needed by developing countries to build capacity in these fields are already in the public domain. The obstacle is *not* proprietary rights, despite the attention they receive in international debates.

Both Gollin (Chapter VI) and Juma (Chapter VII) argue that intellectual property rights should be viewed as a tool for enlarging technological capacity in developing countries. IPR regimes established without due consideration to the need for effective legal, political, and economic systems conducive to private business activity and the protection of private property rarely serve their stated ends (Evenson, 1990). IPR protection—tailored to a nation's development needs—can foster advances in technological innovation, but that protection must be coupled with other institutional changes to increase knowledge of public domain technologies, upgrade technical training, and provide access to the credit needed to develop new technologies and markets.

Juma notes that even small countries with limited industrial capacity can move to the frontiers of biotechnology in specific fields by enhancing their human resource capacity. By investing in training,

43

establishing systems that provide ready access to information about both biodiversity and new technologies, and seeking ways to add value to genetic resources through screening and characterization, developing countries can turn short-term economic benefits into a long-term development strategy.

International Agreements

The Convention on Biological Diversity and other multilateral agreements are important foundations for sustainable and equitable biodiversity prospecting programs.

A central theme of this report is that a variety of national and sub-national actions and policies can help biodiversity prospecting contribute to sustainable development. Rather than relying strictly on multilateral agreements, therefore, countries, institutions, and individuals can use contracts, institutional design, national legislation, and common sense to steer the evolution of biodiversity prospecting institutions. Some have even argued that national policies and bilateral agreements like that between Merck and INBio are sufficient and that no multilateral action is necessary. In 1992, the United States used this argument as one justification for its refusal to sign the Convention on Biological Diversity.

In fact, multilateral agreements are necessary for several reasons. First, by themselves, bilateral biodiversity-prospecting agreements are likely to result in conservation and development benefits for only a limited number of countries. Countries that are quick to enter the market as suppliers of biodiversity and that have the necessary technical capacity to compete may reap substantial gains. But for most developing countries—and the bulk of the world's biodiversity—multilateral mechanisms are needed to provide financial and technical support for biodiversity conservation and technological development.

Second, the value of many of the economic benefits provided by biodiversity—clean water, healthy ecosystems, aesthetic pleasure—is not fully reflected in the market, so market-based strategies like biodiversity prospecting can only complement public sector financial support for conservation. While some of these benefits are strictly local or national, others—like the maintenance of healthy forest and marine ecosystems—are global and justify multilateral action.

Third, multilateral agreements will help increase the benefits that source countries can derive from their genetic resources. As suppliers of biodiversity saturate the market, the price for genetic and·biochemical resources will fall. The interests of source countries could be better served if uniform conditions were developed through multilateral agreements to govern access to biodiversity.

On the other hand, the ability of source countries to form effective genetic and biochemical resource cartels is probably limited. The demand for biochemical resources for the pharmaceutical industry, for example, is likely to be very elastic in response to price changes. Today's resurgence in natural products research is due in part to the decline in costs resulting from new screening technologies. If the price for access to natural products rises, pharmaceutical firms could respond with increased investment in synthetic chemistry and reduced investment in natural products research. In principle, the establishment of cartels is more likely in the case of genetic resources used in agriculture, but the relatively low value of the seed industry (compared to the pharmaceutical industry) could mean that the costs of creating a cartel, restricting the flow of crop genetic resources, and pursuing royalties and payments for these resources might easily exceed the economic benefits. Short of a cartel, though, countries could agree to establish minimum obligations for companies engaging in biodiversity prospecting.

Fourth, multilateral agreements can help level the playing field so that bilateral agreements can be negotiated fairly. Clearly, institutions in developing countries may have less negotiating experience than multinational corporations. Under a multilateral agreement, mechanisms could be established to provide information, legal advice, or the services of an ombudsman to help ensure equitable negotiations.

Many developing countries also lack the ability to effectively regulate access to genetic resources within the country. Without such capacity, laws requiring collecting permits or user fees could easily be circumvented by international collectors. By requiring prior informed consent of the source country for access to biodiversity, the Convention on Biological Diversity will help shift some responsibility for enforcement to the developed countries. Parties to the Convention, for example, could pass laws requiring that gene or biochemical patent applications within their country include evidence that the material in question was collected with the prior informed consent of the source country and of local landowners or land claimants.

Finally, as Gollin argues, an international agreement such as the Convention on Biological Diversity sets the stage for a "Grand Bargain" whereby developing countries would seek strengthened IPR so as to profit from their biological resources while the developed world would concede the possibility that each nation may tailor its intellectual property laws to meet its own conservation, development, and equity needs. Rather than weakening intellectual property laws—a fear that the United States cited when it refused to sign the convention—this new bargain is likely to strengthen them.

Notes

1. That is, the private returns of conserving the resource are less than social returns.
2. These five include Taxol, the most promising drug of the decade for treating breast, ovarian, and lung cancer. Since the success rate for cancer screening is based on technologies used in the 1960s, current technologies are likely to yield higher rates of "hits."
3. This estimate is based on his 1979 calculation (Barton and Christensen, 1988) of the U.S. markup of seed sales derived from proprietary protection, extrapolated to the 1990s and to the global market (totalling $1.5 to $2 billion). With a 5-percent royalty returning to the suppliers of the genetic material, this would amount to $75 million to $100 million.
4. If p is the probability of a single chemical yielding a useful lead, q is the probability that a lead will result in a commercial product,

and n is the number of chemicals screened, then the probability of producing one commercial product (C) is $C = 1 - (1 - (p \times q))^n$. In this example, $p = .0001$, $q = .25$, $n = 1000$, and $C = .0247$. If $R =$ the present value of the royalties from a single commercial product, then the present value of the agreement is calculated as $C \times R$.

5. Even this figure may be conservative. At a January 1986 workshop involving representatives of American and Swiss pharmaceutical companies involved in plant-based drug development, a consensus was reached that the probability of any plant yielding a *marketable* pharmaceutical (not simply a "lead") ranged from 1 in 1000 to 1 in 10,000 (Principe, pers. comm., 1993).

6. Clearly, a local crop variety bred by farmers is an "improved" variety even though it has not been commercialized. Similarly, the investment that a nation makes in conserving wild species or in inventorying and identifying its species arguably results in an "improvement" in that species analogous to that made by commercial breeders.

7. The costs and benefits of intellectual property regimes have been debated at length. By using the creation of a monopoly right to correct for a market failure, governments create new economic inefficiencies in the hopes of removing more serious ones. In one notable case of abuse of this right, a British subsidiary of Hoffman-La Roche was found to be claiming costs of $925 and $2,305 per kilo for materials available in Italy (where no patent protection was available for pharmaceuticals) at $22.50 and $50 per kilo, respectively, to justify artificially high drug prices (Boone and Mathieson, 1990). Since the costs and benefits of IPR protection differ among countries and among industries within countries, most analysts agree that intellectual property rights regimes must be tailored to countries' specific development needs. (Siebeck, 1990; WRI et al., 1992; Khalil et al., 1992) One generalization can be made about the forces influencing the evolution of IPR systems: industry will always seek to strengthen IPR protection, even if the strength of the protection exceeds socially optimal levels. From industry's standpoint, stronger IPR protection allocates ever more of the economic rent produced by a new innovation to the industry and less to the consumer. No market mechanism determines the optimal balance of this rent

capture—by establishing IPR regimes, governments assume the responsibility of making this determination.

8. Plant Breeders Rights grant an individual exclusive right to sell a specific variety but traditionally do not prevent farmers from saving and replanting the seed of the variety (farmer plant-back), or breeders from using that variety in a breeding program (breeders' exemption). Many in the plant breeding industry have argued that this level of protection provides an insufficient incentive for research investment and have advocated closing "loopholes" related to both farmer plantback and the breeder exemption. (In response, the March 1991 revision of UPOV allowed countries to restrict farmer plantback and alters the breeders' exemption so that "essentially derived" varieties—that is, new varieties based largely on the genetic makeup of a protected variety—must obtain a license from the owner of the protected variety.)

9. All UPOV members were West European until 1978. Since that time, other countries including Australia, Czechoslovakia, Canada, Hungary, Israel, Poland, South Africa, and the U.S. have joined and some developing countries are considering joining.

10. Typically, drugs developed from natural products are altered from their natural forms during the drug development process and these derivatives are also patentable. The trail of patents filed during drug development can help in determining whether wholly or partially synthesized drugs originated from natural precursors.

11. A number of companies now recognize the need for conservation in their policies, but generally support for conservation is contributed through philanthropic foundations associated with the company. However, these foundations cannot legally donate money to institutions involved in a commercial arrangement with the parent company. (See Chapter IV.)

12. Several professional societies are developing ethical guidelines seeking to ensure that the rights of holders of traditional knowledge are respected and that just compensation is provided to local communities for access to such information.

13. This difference in treatment might raise red flags under international trade agreements. On the other hand, many countries already have two-tiered user fees for access to national parks, with foreign nationals paying higher fees than local residents.

Bibliography

Aldous, Peter. 1991. 'Hunting licence' for drugs. *Nature* 353:290.

Barton, John H. 1991. Relating Scientific and the Commercial Worlds in Genetic Resource Negotiation. Paper presented at the Symposium on Property Rights, Biotechnology, and Genetic Resource, African Centre for Technology Studies and World Resources Institute, Nairobi, Kenya. June 10–14.

Barton, John H., and Eric Christensen. 1988. Diversity compensation systems: Ways to compensate developing nations for providing genetic materials. Pp. 339–355 *in:* J.R. Kloppenburg, Jr. (ed.) *Seeds and Sovereignty*, Duke Univ. Press, Durham, N.C.

Boone, Peter S., and John A. Mathieson. 1990. Intellectual property rights: Assessment of current policies and practices, and options for A.I.D. initiatives. *The Economics of Technology.* Working Paper No. 1, Bureau for Program and Policy Coordination, U.S. Agency for International Development, Washington, D.C.

Brockway, Lucile H. 1988. Plant science and colonial expansion: The botanical chess game. Pp. 49–66 *in:* J.R. Kloppenburg, Jr. (ed) *Seeds and Sovereignty*. Duke University Press, Durham N.C.

Brush, Stephen B. 1991. Intellectual property and traditional agriculture in the third world. Paper presented at the Roundtable on Intellectual Property Rights and Indigenous Peoples. Society for Applied Anthropology. Charleston, South Carolina.

Chudnovsky, Daniel. 1983. Patents and Trademarks in Pharmaceuticals. *World Development.* 2:3 pp 187–193.

Collinson, M.P. and K.L. Wright. 1991. *Biotechnology and the International Agriculture Research Centers of the CGIAR.* 21st Conference of the International Association of Agricultural Economists. Tokyo, Japan, August 22–29, 1991.

Crawford, Mark H. (ed). 1990. Transgenic Carp: Pond Ready? *Science.* 247:1298.

DiMasi, Joseph A., Ronald W. Hansen, Henry G. Grabowski, and Louis Lasagna. 1991. Cost of innovation in the pharmaceutical industry. *Journal of Health Economics* 10:107–142.

Eisner, Thomas. 1989. Prospecting for nature's chemical riches. *Issues in Science and Technology* 6(2):31–34.

Eisner, Thomas. 1992. Chemical prospecting: A proposal for action. Pp. 196–202 *in:* F.H. Bormann and S.R. Kellert (eds.) *Ecology,*

49

Economics, and Ethics: The Broken Circle. Yale University Press, New Haven, CT.

Elisabetsky, E. 1991. Sociopolitical, economic and ethical issues in medicinal plant research. *Journal of Ethnopharmacology* 32:235–239.

Evenson, R.E. 1990. Survey of empirical results. Pp. 33–46 *in*: W.E. Siebeck (ed.) *Strengthening Protection of Intellectual Property in Developing Countries.* World Bank Discussion Paper 112. World Bank, Washington, D.C.

Farnsworth, Norman R. 1988. Screening plants for new medicines. Pp. 83–97 *in*: E.O. Wilson and Francis M. Peters (eds.) *Biodiversity.* National Academy Press, Washington, D.C.

Findeisen, Christina and Sarah Laird. 1991. Natural Products Research and the Potential Role of the Pharmaceutical Industry in Tropical Forest Conservation. A report prepared by The Periwinkle Project of the Rainforest Alliance.

Fowler C., and P. Mooney. 1990. *Shattering: Food, Politics, and the Loss of Genetic Diversity.* University of Arizona Press, Tucson, AZ.

Gasser, Charles S., and Robert T. Fraley. 1992. Transgenic Crops. *Scientific American.* June, pp 62–69.

Giddings, Luthar Val, and Gabrielle Persley. 1990. Biotechnology and biodiversity. Unpublished manuscript prepared for the UNEP Negotiations on the Convention on Biological Diversity. U.S. Department of Agriculture, Hyattsville, MD, and International Service for National Agricultural Research, The Hague, Netherlands.

Gladwell, Malcolm. 1990. Genetics: Taking Natural Antifreeze from Flounder. *Washington Post.* 23 July p. A2.

IBA [Industrial Biotechnology Association]. 1992. U.S. biotechnology industry fact sheet. IBA, Washington, D.C.

IFAS [Institute for Food and Agricultural Sciences]. 1990. Press release. Gainesville, FL.

Juma, Calestous. 1989. *The Gene Hunters: Biotechnology and the Scramble for Seeds.* Princeton, NJ: Princeton University Press.

Khalil, Mohamed H., Walter V. Reid, Calestous Juma. 1992. Property rights, biotechnology and genetic resources. *Biopolicy International Series* No. 7, African Centre for Technology Studies, Nairobi, Kenya.

King, Stephen R. 1992. Conservation and Tropical Medicinal Plant Research, mimeo, Shaman Pharmaceuticals, Inc.

Kloppenburg, Jack, and Silva Rodriguez. 1992. Conservationists or corsairs? *Seedling* 9(2-3):12–17.

Kokwaro, J.O. 1976. *Medicinal Plants of East Africa*. East African Literature Bureau, Kampala, Nairobi, Dar es Salaam.

Lesser, William. 1990. An overview of intellectual property systems. Pp. 5–15 *in*: W.E. Siebeck (ed.) *Strengthening Protection of Intellectual Property in Developing Countries*. World Bank Discussion Paper 112. World Bank, Washington, D.C.

Lisansky, S.G., and J. Coombs. 1989. *Funding Mechanisms for the Fund for Biological Diversity*. CPL Scientific Limited, Newbury, U.K.

McChesney, James. 1992. Biological Diversity, Chemical Diversity and the Search for New Pharmaceuticals. Paper presented at the Symposium on Tropical Forest Medical Resources and the Conservation of Biodiversity, Rainforest Alliance, New York, January 1992.

Molnar, Joseph J., and Henry Kinnucan. 1989. Introduction: The Biotechnology Revolution. *In* J. J. Molnar and H. Kinnucan (eds.) *Biotechnology and the New Agricultural Revolution*. pp 1–18. Westview Press, Boulder, CO.

Mooney, Pat Roy. 1983. The law of the seed. *Development Dialogue* 1983(1-2):1–172.

NIH [National Institutes of Health], National Institute of Mental Health, National Science Foundation, and U.S. Agency for International Development. 1992. International Cooperative Biodiversity Groups: Request for Applications. June 12, Washington, D.C.

Office of Technology Assessment (OTA). 1987. *Technologies to Maintain Biological Diversity*. Washington D.C.: U.S. Congress, U.S. Government Printing Office.

Office of Technology Assessment (OTA). 1991. *Biotechnology in a Global Economy*. Washington D.C.: U.S. Congress, U.S. Government Printing Office.

Oldfield, Margery L. 1984. *The Value of Conserving Genetic Resources*. U.S. Department of Interior, National Park Service, Washington, D.C.

Principe, Peter P. 1989. The economic significance of plants and their constituents as drugs. Pp. 1–17 *in*: H. Wagner, H. Hikino, and N.R. Farnsworth (eds.) *Economic and Medicinal Plant Research, Volume 3*. Academic Press, London, U.K.

51

Principe, Peter P. Unpublished manuscript. Monetizing the pharmacological benefits of plants.

Raines, Lisa J. 1991. Protecting Biotechnology's Pioneers. *Issues in Science and Technology*. Winter 1991–92, pp. 33–39.

Roberts, Leslie. 1992. NIH gene patents, round two. *Science* 255: 912–913.

Sears, Cathy. 1992. Jungle potions. *American Health*. October 1992.

Sedjo, Roger A. 1988. Property rights and the protection of plant genetic resources. Pp. 293–314 *in:* J.R. Kloppenburg, Jr. (ed) *Seeds and Sovereignty*. Duke University Press, Durham N.C.

Sedjo, Roger A. 1990. Property rights, genetic resources, and the protection of biotechnological development. Unpublished manuscript, Resources for the Future, Washington, D.C. January 3.

Sedjo, Roger A. 1992. Property rights, genetic resources, and biotechnological change. *Journal of Law and Economics* 35:199–213.

Siebeck, W.E. (ed.). 1990. *Strengthening Protection of Intellectual Property in Developing Countries*. World Bank Discussion Paper 112. World Bank, Washington, D.C.

Simpson, R. David. 1992. Transactional arrangements and the commercialization of tropical biodiversity. Resources for the Future Discussion Paper, Washington, D.C.

Sochaczewski, Paul Spencer. 1992. Marine biodiversity: who benefits, who pays? Unpublished manuscript. World Wide Fund for Nature, Gland, Switzerland.

Stone, Richard. 1992. A biopesticidal tree begins to blossom. *Science* 255:1070.

U.S. Supreme Court. 1980. United States Supreme Court Cases 447:303. U.S. Government Printing Office, Washington, D.C.

Wall Street Journal. 1992. April 24, 1992.

Ward, Mike, and Andy Coghlan. 1991. Free genes for sweet potatoes. *New Scientist*. 16 February:28.

World Bank. 1991. *Agricultural Biotechnology: The Next Green Revolution?* World Bank Technical Paper No. 133. Washington, D.C.

World Resources Institute et. al. 1992. *Global Biodiversity Strategy*. WRI, IUCN, UNEP, Washington, D.C.

II.
Costa Rica's Conservation Program and National Biodiversity Institute (INBio)

Rodrigo Gámez, Alfio Piva, Ana Sittenfeld, Eugenia Leon,
Jorge Jimenez, and Gerardo Mirabelli

A growing consensus holds that tropical biodiversity will survive only to the extent that societies use it for intellectual and economic development. Doing so requires creative new structures and collaboration among groups that have traditionally been separate, if not opposed—biologists and businessmen, for example. In Costa Rica, a serious attempt to forge such new socioeconomic and "socioecological" collaborations is building those bridges.

Background

Costa Rica lies on the narrow land bridge of Central America—a biological crossroads between South and North America, and a mountainous barrier separating the Pacific Ocean from the Caribbean Sea. Emerging from the collision of tectonic plates, this geologically dynamic region boasts active volcanoes, rugged once-glaciated mountain peaks, and both Caribbean and Pacific coastlines. Moisture-laden trade winds alternate with seasonal droughts to produce diverse rainfall and temperature patterns. Such dramatic topographic and climatic variations have made this small area one of the world's biologically richest places. In just 51,000 km^2, Costa Rica contains at least a half million species arrayed in habitats from near desert to exceedingly wet rain forests and cloud forests, and from sea level to over 3500 m. Fully 4 percent of all terrestrial living species on Earth are found in Costa Rica—an enormous natural heritage and natural resource.

Over the last two decades, Costa Ricans have come to recognize the importance of preserving their biodiversity. Since around 1970, 25 percent of the country has been designated as national parks, national forests, and equivalent reserves, today consolidated as seven mainland Conservation Areas. While international encouragement and support have been crucial, Costa Rica's astonishingly rapid advancements in conservation stem mainly from sustained self-initiative. The persistence of enthusiastic conservation leaders from both major political parties and from the private sector has allowed first the national park system and now the conservation areas to prosper through six government administrations.

Other facets of the country's socio-political climate have also been favorable. Costa Rica has enjoyed stable democratic rule for more than a century, a large middle class, and widespread relative prosperity, even though per capita GNP ($1,500 in 1990) is only about 10 percent that of developed nations. The standards and indices of health, education, and literacy compare with those of industrial nations—largely because the national army was abolished in 1948, freeing additional funds for social programs. These funds, plus socio-political stability, have allowed the country to develop a broad-based education system that underlies scientific and conservation efforts: more than 2 percent of the population is seeking university degrees in any given year. Recognition of the country's long-term commitment to peace came in 1987, when President Oscar Arias received the Nobel Peace Prize for his efforts to get his Central American neighbors to stop fighting. In this healthy social climate, a national biodiversity institute is a realistic possibility.

Institutional Groundwork

The idea for a national biodiversity institute—Instituto Nacional de Biodiversidad, or INBio—evolved along with other dynamic changes in conservation thinking and policy in the last half of the Arias administration. The creation of the Ministry of Natural Resources, Energy, and Mines (MIRENEM) in 1986 raised environmental concerns to the cabinet level. Equally important, the national parks, forestry, and wildlife services were taken out of the Ministry of Agriculture and allowed to restructure and coordinate their programs within a new ministry. Under the vigorous leadership of its first minister, Alvaro Umaña, MIRENEM transformed and integrated Costa Rica's conservation programs, developing creative new administrative, financial, and institutional structures and policies. Besides creating INBio, MIRENEM consolidated, integrated, and decentralized the administration of protected wildlands in the new National System of Conserved Areas (SINAC), implemented a Forestry Action Plan, developed the National Conservation Strategy for Sustainable Development of Costa Rica, and came up with innovative financing for conservation activities through debt-for-nature swaps.

Support for these changes has come from all levels in Costa Rica. MIRENEM's first well-defined projects have attracted enthusiastic international approval and financing from a variety of sources, and the subsequent Rafael A. Calderón government's commitment to caring for the environment of Latin America, as well as Costa Rica, has helped sustain it.

INBio has its roots in the October 1987 establishment of MIRENEM's Biodiversity Office, under the responsibility of Rodrigo Gámez, former Director of the University of Costa Rica's Center for Cellular and Molecular Biology. Supported by a three-year MacArthur Foundation grant, the new office was created to direct and coordinate the highly participatory analysis and development of a "new strategy and conservation program for Costa Rica's wildlands." Participants included representatives of the National Park Service, Forestry Service, and Wildlife Service (all parts of MIRENEM), Fundación Neotrópica, Fundación de Parques Nacionales, and many other institutions and individuals involved with conservation in Costa Rica. The Biodiversity Office advised and assisted the then new Minister of Natural Resources and the National Park Service; it also facilitated the program's diverse conservation initiatives.

As a first step toward reorganizing Costa Rica's wildlands and capitalizing on two decades of conservation experience, a new conceptual framework for conservation was established. Three somewhat overlapping tasks were considered essential:

55

(1) Establishing large conserved wildlands, the Conservation Areas;
(2) Determining what biodiversity lies in these protected areas and where it is located; and
(3) Integrating the non-destructive use of this biodiversity into the intellectual and economic fabric of national and international society.

The first step was achieved mostly through the establishment of the National System of Conservation Areas (Sistema Nacional de Areas de Conservación). Among other benefits, the creation of the Conservation Areas helped Costa Rica recognize that it has two major types of non-urban productive land use: conventional agro-forest-pastoral landscape (about 70 percent of the country) with its well-known products, and wildlands conserved for their biodiversity products (about 25 percent of the country). The country cannot afford to neglect either.

INBio was created to carry out the second and third steps.

INBio's Emergence

The search for an effective means to support conservation through the environmentally responsible use of conserved wildland biodiversity by all sectors of society was the Biodiversity Office's second major task. Fresh from an international meeting in September 1988 in Bogotá, Colombia on the "Global Biodiversity Strategy" and the October 1988 Congress on the Costa Rican National Conservation Strategy for Sustainable Development, Director Gámez called a meeting attended by more than 50 individuals, including representatives of many national institutions working with Costa Rica's biodiversity. Participants agreed that Costa Rica should launch a major unified biodiversity program to replace the fragmented efforts of universities, museums, government agencies, and private organizations. Coincidentally, American biologist Daniel Janzen returned to Costa Rica after a fund-raising trip for Guanacaste National Park with the news that the international community was ready to consider financing a national commitment to understand, manage, and sustainably use biodiversity.

In the enthusiastic discussions and planning that followed, the idea of an independent biodiversity institute emerged. At a second national meeting, called by the Biodiversity Office in San José in February 1989, the conclusion was that even though national and international biodiversity research on Costa Rican organisms had been going on for more than a century, the information and specimens resulting from that research were so widely scattered that no existing institution could afford to organize and assimilate the current collections, much less manage the future products of a national inventory. Participants also concluded that a National Biodiversity Institute should be formed to:

- Develop a national-level strategy and carry out an inventory of Costa Rica's biodiversity;
- Begin integrating all national collections into one physical and administrative entity;
- Centralize all information on Costa Rica's biodiversity; and
- Put this information into an easily accessible format and distribute it to the public.

A Planning Commission chaired by the Director of the MIRENEM Biodiversity Office was proposed at the February 1989 meeting. The Minister of Natural Resources and the President embraced the idea enthusiastically, and the commission was officially established by Presidential decree on June 5, 1989. The nine members included representatives from three government ministries (MIRENEM, Science and Technology, and Culture), the National Museum, two major universities, the National Scientific Research Council, and two non-governmental organizations (Fundación Neotrópica and the Organization for Tropical Studies).

The outcome of the Commission's work was the creation of a private, non-profit, public-interest association—"La Asociación Instituto Nacional de Biodiversidad" (or INBio). The new institute was legally established and formally incorporated on October 24, 1989.

INBio's Legal, Physical, and Administrative Structure

INBio is governed by a 15-member Assembly and a six-member Board of Directors. As an autonomous non-profit private institution,

57

it can receive grants, enjoy tax-free status, and receive tax-free donations of specimens and materials from other Costa Rican institutions or international sources, but still manage its own funds and hire personnel. INBio is tightly linked to the national and private institutions that created it and use it—members of the Assembly and the Board of Directors are prominent members and directors of these organizations—but is not legally obligated to any of them. It is fully empowered to enter into contracts and agreements with national and international institutions and individuals.

INBio will eventually occupy a 15-hectare "campus" in the outskirts of San José (Santo Domingo de Heredia) within walking, bus, commuter train, and taxi range of more than half of Costa Rica's pop-

---

Box II.1. INBio's Basic Characteristics

In the press and in some international reports, INBio has been called a "model." More accurately, it is a "pilot project" with these characteristics:
- Bylaws that emphasize the conservation of national wildland biodiversity through non-damaging use;
- A commitment to generating income from wildland biodiversity to meet wildland biodiversity management costs and to boost the country's GNP;
- A strong national orientation;
- A policy of hiring nationals for positions at all levels;
- Cultural awareness and involvement in national policy;
- Multiple goals and multiple products;
- A budget determined by goals and products;
- A commitment to rigorous science;
- Dependence on taxonomy and natural history as primary technological tools;
- Responsiveness to challenges and recommendations related to biodiversity management and use;
- A commitment to serving as an information source on biodiversity management and use; and
- A policy of sharing data and information with other parallel users, but charging commercial users.

ulation. Not only highly accessible, the area also has an excellent year-round climate for office work, computer systems, and the storage and management of biological specimens. (Frequent minor earthquakes are the only drawbacks: all INBio's buildings will have to be earthquake-proof.) At present, INBio's main administration building houses the Division of Biodiversity Prospecting and the Division of Biodiversity Information Distribution. At the same location, it also has a new modern inventory building that contains the Division of the National Biodiversity Inventory and the Division of Biodiversity Information Management, as well as a small pension/dormitory for around-the-clock use by staff and visiting scientists.

INBio currently has a full-time administrative and scientific-technical staff of 66 at its headquarters, including the Director General and President of the Board, four division directors, and 8 other personnel. In addition, 41 full-time parataxonomists work out of 29 Biodiversity Offices within or on the margins of the seven Conservation Areas. INBio also benefits from part-time or short-term consultants and volunteers from Costa Rica, as well as foreign volunteer taxonomists and other professionals.

The Director of the INBio Division of the National Biodiversity Inventory has the primary responsibility for facilitating, prioritizing, and administering the work and collaboration of parataxonomists, inventory managers, and taxonomists. While the director must have a Ph.D.-level understanding of both taxonomy and ecology, equally important is a keen interest in facilitating the work of people of highly diverse backgrounds and levels of education, both in INBio's urban environment and in the Conservation Areas themselves.

The Financial Challenge

INBio must eventually become self-supporting. Similarly, Conservation Areas must eventually generate enough intellectual and financial income to cover both their management costs and the opportunity costs of conserving wildlands.

Three waves of financing are needed to launch INBio fully. The start-up stage, from April 1989 through late 1990, required around

59

$500,000 to cover the costs of land, buildings, training, and general operations. During the second stage, 1991–1992, about $2.5 million was used for intensive planning, infrastructure, and development. Most of the planning, like that leading to the establishment of parataxonomist and inventory manager positions, is "planning by doing." This amount is very small in comparison with developed-world budgets for the start up of an institute with such a mandate. Support for the first and second stages has come from private foundations (MacArthur, Pew, Alton Jones, Noyes, Wege, Claiborne and Ortenberg, and Moriah), the National Fish and Wildlife Foundation, the Conservation, Food and Health Foundation, the World Wildlife Fund-U.S., The Nature Conservancy, the World Resources Institute, the Natural History Museum (London), the Smithsonian Institution, Fundación Neotrópica, Fundación de Parques Nacionales, private donors, the government of Costa Rica (Ministry of Natural Resources, Energy, and Mines, Ministry of Science and Technology, and the Central Bank), the United States (Agency for International Development, National Science Foundation, and U.S. Department of Agriculture-ARS), Sweden (Swedish International Development Agency, and SAREC), and Norway (NORAD).

For the third stage, scheduled to begin during 1993 if all goes well, major funding is needed. It will cost roughly $30 million over ten years to conduct the National Biodiversity Inventory. An additional twenty million is needed for a permanent endowment to maintain the research and reference collections, the data bases, and public services. This long-term financing—basically start-up capital for a national-level investment in biodiversity development—will probably have to come from international sources, which INBio's Board of Directors are currently seeking.

Finding funds is still one of INBio's principal challenges, but INBio is hopeful that its financial goals can be realized. Indeed, prospects continue to improve as INBio grows and demonstrates its capacity to carry out its objectives, as well as its importance to Costa Rica and the international community concerned with the conservation and sustainable management and use of biodiversity.

INBio's immediate objectives are to:

- Undertake a total inventory of the biodiversity of Costa Rica between 1993 and 2003;
- Place that information in a computerized and physical format that Costa Ricans and others will find easy to use;
- Insure the preservation into perpetuity of the National Biodiversity Inventory Collections resulting from this activity;
- Facilitate access by national and international users to information related to Costa Rica's wildland biodiversity; and
- Greatly increase local "biological literacy" by providing information and fostering its use.

The National Biodiversity Inventory and Allied INBio Efforts

Unofficially, the inventory of Costa Rica's rich biodiversity has been progressing irregularly for more than a century in the hands of a wide variety of national and international conservationists and biologists (mostly taxonomists) working inside and outside of Costa Rica. Nearly all the taxonomic efforts have reflected the interests of an individual or an institution in one taxon or another and have supported centuries-old academic traditions rather than the practical management and use of Costa Rica's biodiversity. The results from these initial efforts form the irreplaceable and essential base from which the national inventory begins, and without them, Costa Rica would not have the skills and knowledge needed to inventory its biodiversity. The knowledge and specimens accumulated in past efforts are lodged largely in scientific publications and in foreign collections of specimens. It will be a major task to find this information, organize it, and integrate it with the mountains of new information and specimens generated by the new national inventory effort.

Also adding to the difficulty is the sheer size of the task. As much as 80 percent of the country's species have yet to be described and named. Costa Rica may contain some 13,000 species of plants, 10,000 fungi, 1,500 vertebrates, 290,000 species of insects, 75,000 species of aquatic organisms from fresh to brackish waters, 15,000 marine invertebrates, up to 50,000 spiders, mites, and other terrestrial invertebrates, as many as 10,000 species of nematodes,

61

and an indeterminate number of bacteria and viruses not exceeding 50,000, for a grand total of about 500,000 species. The percentage of species already known and the percentage already named vary greatly by group of organisms.

At its simplest level, INBio's inventory goal is to develop a taxonomically "clean" and organized database of the species that occur in the country, and to identify one or more localities where each occurs. At this level of resolution, the vertebrates, butterflies (diurnal Lepidoptera), some moths, dragonflies (Odonata) and non-epiphytic plants are nearly inventoried for Costa Rica. However, other major groups are only just initiated. As any taxon becomes well understood at the first level of resolution, INBio begins the yet larger task of understanding a species' distribution, natural history, ecology, morphology, behavior, phenology, genetic variation, etc. During the decade-long inventory—time enough to complete the task and still get the results out before much of Costa Rica's biodiversity disappears—INBio expects to attain at least the first level of understanding with all groups of organisms. How much it can do after that is largely a matter of funding. Some species of conspicuous use to society (e.g., poisonous snakes, relatives of crop plants, crop pests, endangered vertebrates, organisms that are sources of commercial research chemicals) have already been studied extensively in Costa Rica and will receive special attention by INBio. As more users and uses appear, more organisms will join the list for special emphasis. Likewise, select sites of special social or ecological value may be thoroughly inventoried well before the national inventory is complete. (To meet the decadal deadline, INBio plans to increase the funds and workforce for the inventory, rather than pile an impossible burden on current staff and resources.)

The goal of the inventory is *not* to list every organism in every hectare. In general, sections of Costa Rica designated for explicit conservation will receive highest priority attention, but agricultural zones will also be thoroughly inventoried. As many as 50 sites (29 to date) representing all of Costa Rica's terrestrial and freshwater conservation areas and habitats will be inventoried in depth. (When applied to insects, birds, plants, and mammals in various local biodiversity efforts in the past, this strategy has

62

worked very well.) The marine inventory will be undertaken later, once funds and institutional structure are in place. Additionally, some salvage inventory will be conducted in the 75 percent of the country fated for commercial exploitation (primarily agriculture) or otherwise unprotected, to insure that pockets of species have not been overlooked and to locate remnants of endangered species. The extensive preliminary survey work already done in Costa Rica, coupled with two decades of national and international conservation effort aimed at covering all the major habitats, insures that an inventory focused primarily on the Conservation Areas will capture at least 95 percent of Costa Rica's species.

Within this framework, all of the information—ecological, chemical, behavioral, genetic, etc.—to be gathered on Costa Rica's biodiversity can be organized, cross-referenced, manipulated, and offered to the country, region, and world through the public domain and commercial sales.

While seeking funding, INBio is conducting various parts of the inventory as small-scale trial runs and pilot projects. One such pilot project is the parataxonomist program. (*See Annex 1.*) A major component of the national inventory is collecting and preparing millions of specimens in the field and getting them to INBio, where INBio inventory managers, visiting and resident taxonomists, biodiversity information managers, and others can further process them. Rural Costa Ricans trained to work within INBio's "Parataxonomist Program" do most of this preliminary work. This program has captured the attention of tropical wildland managers and advisors confronted by problems similar to those faced in Costa Rica and has thus become a pilot project for other countries too.

The INBio-Merck and Co. biodiversity prospecting project is another pilot project that has unexpectedly attracted international interest. (*See Chapter III.*) And, the newly initiated INBio-Intergraph project to develop an easily accessible computerized system of biodiversity information in the public domain is another new addition to the growing number of taxonomic- and GIS-based institutions providing the information needed for biodiversity data management. (*See Box II.2.*)

63

Box II.2. The INBio–Intergraph Collaboration

Intergraph Corporation of Huntsville, Alabama, USA, and INBio have agreed to collaboratively develop a computerized Biodiversity Information Management System (BIMS) for INBio. Intergraph comes to the relationship as a world leader in interactive computer graphics and strategic mapping information systems, and as a supplier of integrated technical information-management systems to Fortune 500 companies. INBio is a pilot project in conserving tropical wildlands and the vast information contained in them. Should commercially marketable software be developed as a result of this relationship, INBio and Intergraph will share the income from sales of the software.

Intergraph is contributing approximately U.S. $750,000 in hardware, software, and services. These include customization and installation of the system by experienced Systems Integration teams from Intergraph, the training of two INBio staff members, and software upgrades and hardware maintenance over 18 months. Intergraph can quickly generate maps from aerial photographs and analyze physical, geographic, and biological variables on computer. Intergraph is also providing a large amount of storage memory to support INBio applications, which rely heavily on interactive graphics.

INBio personnel will maintain the system day to day and modify it as the needs of INBio users change. INBio is contributing experience and vision in industrial-scale techniques of collection, management, and use of information related to approximately 500,000 Costa Rican species—from viruses to vertebrates.

The INBio-Intergraph system will be part of INBio's core. Advanced computerized management of information is critical to INBio's mission of conserving Costa Rica's biodiversity by rapidly making it broadly useful, interesting, and even exciting—thus increasing its value to a broad cross-section of Costa Ricans and its survival prospects. This means collecting and manipulating information about Costa Rica's species purposefully for various intellectual and commercial users—the only way, INBio believes, to secure tropical biodiversity amid a world crisis.

Through this system, INBio will be able to manage and manipulate a suite of large databases holding traditional text and numeric information about Costa Rican organisms. (The structure of these databases and their data from the inventory will be in the public domain.) INBio's public databases will include published literature, information on species' geographical distribution, ongoing studies within Costa Rica, and other high-priority information. This information will be linked to graphic files, including drawings, photographs, and maps of organism distributions and conservation areas.

Potentially, a system like the one being developed at INBio will find many kinds of uses and users. In practice, however, its value depends primarily on how willing disparate goal-oriented users are to use it. To make it as attractive as possible, the system will be painstakingly designed by a joint INBio-Intergraph team for ease of use by INBio personnel, including many who do not have prior technical training. The difficulty of projects will be graduated so that users will grow into the power of the system.

The system's users are expected to include a broad range of INBio personnel in the Divisions of Biodiversity Inventory (Botany, Entomology, and others), Biodiversity Prospecting, and Biodiversity Information Dissemination, as well as collaborating national and foreign scientists and personnel from Costa Rican Conservation Areas. The Division of Information Dissemination will, in turn, use the system's output to meet the needs of diverse Costa Ricans, including school children, governmental planners, and businesses.

These pilot projects and INBio itself benefit from Costa Rica's commitment to establishing an effective system of protected wildlands. This act of great foresight has afforded Costa Rica the raw materials needed to build a biodiversity industry. The GIS and conservation information already in hand for the Conservation Areas—accumulated for more than two decades—provides an enormously valuable support base for the biodiversity inventory, and part of INBio's task is to integrate these two bodies of information.

INBio's chief collaborators are MIRENEM, the Ministry of Science and Technology, the Conservation Area administrations, and Costa Rica's two major universities. INBio also relies heavily on input from the far-flung network of taxonomists currently working in the world's museums, universities, and private collections.

The International Dimension

Since the entire Central American isthmus has much biodiversity in common, the process begun at INBio could well spread. Certainly, INBio's activities are stimulating the development of other INBio-like projects and institutions elsewhere in the tropics. For example, INBio has now developed collaboration agreements with Indonesia, Mexico, and Kenya that will facilitate the flow of ideas among these countries and others. And investing in these new south-south linkages will pay rich dividends for world society as a whole—among them, a wealth of basic biodiversity information in the public domain and the benefits of INBio's experiments in "on-the-job training for institutions."

For Latin America, the taxonomic dimension of INBio's inventory is even more direct. More than 80 percent of the species found in Costa Rica occur elsewhere on the continent, and more than half of them range into South America. Indeed, many Costa Rican organisms have a range that extends from somewhere in central Brazil or Bolivia up through Costa Rica to Guatemala or lowland tropical Mexico. "Cleaning up" the taxonomy of Costa Rican organisms thus gives scientists a substantial start toward precisely identifying and locating the large complexes of species found elsewhere in the neotropics. Similarly, unscrambling taxonomic snarls in a block of species in a genus or higher group of organisms from one centrally-located neotropical country usually makes it much easier to organize the remaining collected but undescribed species in that taxon. For all these reasons, INBio may find itself expanding its focus to cover all of Central America *if* funds and political circumstances permit and if invited by Costa Rica's neighbors.

On balance, Costa Rica's conservation program and the experiences being gathered at the National Biodiversity Institute represent one kind of indigenous answer to the complex problems of preserving tropical biodiversity and promoting sustainable development. It is hoped that this example will be useful to other tropical nations eager to preserve and benefit from their own biotic heritage.

III.

BIODIVERSITY PROSPECTING BY INBIO

Ana Sittenfeld and Rodrigo Gámez

Biodiversity prospecting—the search for wild species, genes and their products with actual or potential use to humans—is in its broadest sense, a process dating from the roots of humanity and before. It has long been practiced informally throughout the Costa Rican countryside. Here we examine biodiversity prospecting in Costa Rica's conservation areas, as currently conducted by INBio and as one of the first directly practical outcomes of Costa Rica's national biodiversity inventory. *(See Chapter II.)* Biodiversity prospecting at INBio has the express goal of generating income from Costa Rica's conservation areas so as to contribute to wildland management costs and to Costa Rica's intellectual capital and financial GNP. Ecotourism, watershed management, education, recreation, research, gene banking, and other wildland income-generators can also contribute to the survival of the wildlands.

INBio's biodiversity prospecting is focused on Costa Rica's conservation areas and the wild species in them because INBio is committed to insuring the survival of these areas—which make up about 25 percent of the country—by finding non-destructive uses of wildland biodiversity. Another reason for the emphasis is that the conservation areas are enormous and almost totally unexplored storehouses of biodiverse chemicals and genes. (As for the comparatively few species of wild organisms that do not occur

69

within the conservation areas, INBio's national inventory will include them, and they may even be considered for biodiversity prospecting, circumstances permitting.)

At INBio, biodiversity prospecting has many components:

- Supporting the taxonomic and inventory process *(see Chapter II)*;
- Finding sample species and specimens in the conservation areas;
- Collecting and processing replicable samples that are thoroughly documented;
- Screening samples for chemicals, micro-organisms, and genes;
- Relocating and resupplying samples for research purposes;
- Conducting research on leads from screens, the chemicals themselves, the producing organisms, and sample treatment;
- Developing with the national and international pharmaceutical, biotech, and agribusiness industries and other users contractual agreements that insure direct compensation for the costs of research, conservation, and development of wildland biodiversity;
- Facilitating contractual relations among the government, conservation areas, universities, other non-governmental organizations (NGOs), commercial users, and researchers; and
- Training and otherwise helping Costa Ricans to take charge of all these activities.

Historically, the extraction of tropical natural products for pharmaceutical or biotech screening has been largely a one-way process. For two major reasons, the movement of samples and information is from local and international suppliers—both academic and commercial—to industry; little of the product's value is returned to the source country, except to the collector's pocket. First, tropical countries have until recently been passive players in biodiversity transactions. Second, it's hard for industries in developed countries to accept as full partners tropical countries that appear to invest little or nothing in their biodiversity and its development.

But in the case of Costa Rica, these reasons no longer hold. A government planning commission and a large number of concerned biologists created INBio explicitly to facilitate the organized and non-damaging use of the biodiversity in the conservation areas. Moreover, Costa Rica has invested heavily in the support of its biodiversity, especially in the highly structured Costa Rican National System of Conservation Areas (SINAC).

Essential Types of Collaboration

INBio's activities represent first steps toward demonstrating that biodiversity resources can be made available to the commercial community without destroying the living capital in a conservation area. Yet, biodiversity prospecting to support conservation and further domestic economic and technological development won't succeed without close collaboration between the INBio-like institution, the national government, and the multiple owners, custodians, and caretakers of the wildland biodiversity resource.

Four types of collaboration are particularly vital. First, a national regulatory framework for biodiversity prospecting is needed to insure that conservation areas can and do become full economic and intellectual partners in the commercial development of wildland biodiversity. Such a regulatory framework is beginning to take form in Costa Rica: a new law permits government to allocate biodiversity prospecting concessions in the conservation areas. INBio and others have worked closely with the Ministry of Natural Resources, Energy and Mines (MIRENEM), the national assembly, and the conservation areas to facilitate the passage of this legislation. It has also fostered other contractual interactions and served as a pilot project by voluntarily conforming to the strictures required by the new law *before* it passed.

Second, infrastructure and technology must be developed. As an intermediary between the conservation areas and society, INBio integrates classical conservation, science, technology, and social goals. In a way, this entire process qualifies as technology transfer—whether putting the right name on a rainforest tree or writing a contract that fairly values conservation area maintenance as a contribu-

71

tion to a patented invention. Additionally, INBio works to get users to explicitly recognize all of the costs of biodiversity prospecting and to pay them. Currently, the bulk of the costs are hidden (and often, uncompensated) in the budgets that maintain taxonomists, ecologists, conservation areas, and development projects.

Third, formal contractual relationships among biodiversity's sources, intermediaries, and final users should govern the entire bioprospecting process—from sampling and processing to the arrival of final products on the marketplace. These contracts should guarantee compensation to the national system of conservation areas, to the regional conservation areas themselves, and to facilitators of the process. They should also provide for support for in-country research and development.

Fourth, biodiversity prospecting should attempt to move more R&D into the source country so as to contribute to the GNP. It is INBio's hope that many major users of natural product research samples from the conservation areas will eventually be located in Costa Rica, so the institute works hard to establish mutually beneficial relationships and convince the target industries to become more than simple consumers of samples. Many elements of the contract with Merck and Co., and other anticipated similar contracts, are designed to keep samples from disappearing from a Costa Rican social context.

At INBio, biodiversity prospecting has also required supportive behavior on the part of the developed countries and industries. This support has been expressed not so much in monetary contributions as in technical assistance—help in designing contracts, for example, and technology transfer that benefits both the commercial recipient and the source.

The Search for Wildland Chemicals

Biodiversity prospecting includes both the search for interesting chemicals made by wild organisms and the biotechnologists' search for genes (traditionally, the latter has been the domain of the breeder of plants and animals). (See Box III.1.) Only the first is dis-

Box III.1. A Matter of Definition

The chemicals in living organisms can be classified roughly as primary and secondary compounds. Primary compounds, which participate in the basic metabolic processes of growth and development, are widely distributed in nature and occur in one form or another in a large number of species of organisms. For example, low molecular weight carboxylic acids, the protein amino acids, many proteins, fats, lipids, sugars, and sugar derivatives fall into this group. Most secondary compounds are biosynthetically derived from primary compounds. They function mainly in the chemical mediation of the interactions among individuals and species—defense, attack, attraction, competition, etc. Many secondary compounds are already familiar as drugs, vitamins, colorants, etc.: caffeine, nicotine, L-dopa, digitalin, tannin, morphine, strychnine, aspirin, carotene, vitamin C, skunk oil, turpentine, rubber, cinnamon, quinine, aflatoxin, penicillin, gum arabic, snake venom, etc. Except for some widespread defensive compounds, such as cellulose, lignin, and starch, most kinds of secondary compounds have species-specific functions, so their distribution in nature is generally limited, often restricted to a particular taxonomic group.

Considering that each species synthesizes tens to hundreds of secondary compounds, a conservation area with several hundred thousand species houses several million secondary compounds. Tropical organisms are exceptionally rich in secondary compounds, partly because tropical organisms evolved and survive primarily through interactions with other organisms.

Secondary compounds have traditionally been the basis of the great majority of drugs derived from natural products. But the increasing sophistication of the search for drugs and the increasing number of non-drug uses for novel chemicals are also creating commercial and research-related demands for primary compounds—among them, the enzymes of normal cell operations, storage oils, and structural molecules.

cussed here since INBio will not begin an extensive search for genes until the biotech industry is ready to undertake research with INBio with genes from wildland organisms unrelated to local domesticates. Also not discussed here in detail is the fact that the wild organisms themselves are of great use in natural products research as bioassays, health hazard test organisms, living cultures, biosynthetic factories, etc. As these uses expand, the number of users of the storehouse that the conservation area represents increases.

New Demands and New Capabilities

As indicated in the introduction, Costa Rica has long been a source of wild natural products. For decades, samples were collected freely from the countryside and the national parks with no attempt to link extraction to conservation or to national economic development.

In the 1970s and 1980s, the pharmaceutical industry's interest in tropical wild samples declined sharply. Most companies believed they could cheaply and rapidly synthesize in laboratories all the novel "lead compounds" they needed, but this approach turned out to be incomplete. Now new diseases, new screening technologies, and new uses for naturally derived chemicals have combined with a deeper understanding of biochemical processes to renew industry's interest in natural products for drugs, agrochemicals, and industrial novelties.

On the supply side, INBio-like institutions and professionally managed conservation areas can now meet this renewed demand, providing greater access and more sophisticated means of resupplying chemical samples. In biodiversity prospecting, new developments in bioassay, chemical screening, and isolation techniques to guide the process of locating chemical activity and identifying active compounds are key to success. Microcomputers and robotics have allowed mass screening by automating several of the time-consuming steps in the drug discovery laboratory. Institutions like INBio can now provide large numbers of replicable samples from large numbers of identified wildland species. Rather than focusing on only a few species with known medicinal properties, the drug industry now also screens thousands of comparatively unknown species simultaneously for many kinds of chemical reactions. Mass screening makes field taxonomy, inventories, and a solid taxonomic base even more important than they have been and gives the administrators of conservation areas more incentive to become knowledgeable about the species the areas contain and effective custodians of those species.

The stakes in drug development are high and the payoff is uncertain. The process of finding a valuable compound has a high cost per useful molecule found since the probability with screens (or ecologically driven searches) of locating a molecule with a desired kind of reaction is low. For example, it might be necessary to test as many as 10,000 substances to find one that will reach the drug market. Given that a sample of a given plant species may easily contain 100 chemicals that occur only in it or a very few closely related species, developing one successful drug might require screening in the order of 1,000 plant species. On the other hand, the larger the number of kinds of screens used, the greater the chances of finding something of interest in a given sample.

The number of positive screening results can also be increased by getting clues from human ethnobiology, ecology (natural history), and phylogeny. Phylogenetic knowledge is particularly useful for inferring what is in an unknown species from what has been found in a close relative. However, ethnobiological and ecology-driven searches have inherent limits. There is no way to predict, for example, which insect in nature will be the source of a secondary or primary compound that will react with the surface of the AIDS virus.

The research and development cost of a new drug is generally extremely high—on average, $231 million per successful drug in the United States—and new drugs take nearly ten years to progress from source to market. This snail's pace should dash any hopes for immediate income from new drug discoveries. On the other hand, in a small country like Costa Rica, an eventual royalty payment of 1 to 5 percent for one highly successful drug could produce as much national net income during the life of the patent as does a major crop.

75

INBio does not expect major royalty returns in the immediate future from its biodiversity prospecting, but its contract with Merck and Co. has demonstrated that commercial partners will pay the real costs of obtaining biodiversity prospecting samples at the time of collection. *(See Chapter IV.)* (These costs include sample location, sample identification, preserving voucher specimens for future reference, and preservation and management of the target populations, in addition to such visible costs as those for collecting and preparing samples.) With this mindset, royalty possibilities become part of a long-term income portfolio.

INBio facilitates blind screening, ecology-driven searches, and taxonomically-driven searches. If the user wants large numbers of samples at a low cost per sample for blind (or relatively blind) screening, INBio's charges cover mainly the processing costs and the costs of the taxonomic and multiple-sampling efforts needed to produce them. Since most of the organisms screened under this approach are unknown ecologically and taxonomically, the costs of identifying the species, establishing a reference collection of voucher specimens, and doing the basic taxonomy of the flora and fauna become part of the budget. If the user wants to invest in a small number of in-depth ecology-, or taxonomy-driven searches, INBio tries to recoup the costs of maintaining the necessary knowledge and the personnel who can "read" nature and taxonomy. Here, the emphasis will be on previously described or otherwise well-known organisms, unless there is time to develop the necessary taxonomic and ecological background information on the spot.

Managing Biodiversity Information for Biodiversity Prospecting

A user must be able to thoroughly and accurately trace any INBio sample or extract. Thus, INBio's biodiversity prospecting program creates complex demands for specimen labeling and tracking, vouchers, samples, extracts, and related information. Furthermore, since the many chemicals in a species change throughout its life cycle, as well as in response to how the sample of that species is treated, every process to which a sample or extract is subjected must be documented. Killing, stressing, drying, heating, freezing, resting, extracting with different solvents at different temperatures and levels of pressure—all can alter the sample by destroying or producing desired chemicals. Obviously, a primary challenge for INBio is insuring that a resupplied sample contains the desired chemical found in the first sample.

The information from field sampling, screening procedures, sample or chemical purification, and chemical isolation are fully computerized and filed. INBio expects that this information will be permanent. Disparate and voluminous information on commercial opportunities, industrial initiatives, industrial processes, market strategies, and government legislation and regulations must also be organized and kept readily available. Moreover, INBio keeps this evolving body of complex information and processes alive and up to date even when key people leave.

The need to keep much of the institute's biodiversity prospecting information confidential to one degree or another adds to INBio's data-management burden. Precisely which samples are collected and how they are processed are generally trade secrets from the standpoint of the commercial user. On the other hand, general information about sample collection and many aspects of their processing are deliberately made public, and any number of employees, managers, and associated biologists are involved. If conservation area managers, for instance, are kept in the dark about the collection process, they will not understand what measures are needed to insure that the samples are removed without damaging a conservation area's biodiversity. Finally, since Costa Ricans have traditionally placed no premium on confidentiality, especially vis-a-vis information derived from public works, INBio has to take pains to allow the maximum public access to information—thereby gaining trust and understanding among all segments of the public—without violating commercial users' confidentiality.

Biodiversity inventory collections and databases. Like similar collecting institutions throughout the world, INBio puts its national inventory collections and all related specimen data on the date of collection, the collector, the location, and the collection methods, etc., in the public domain electronically and on hard copy. As the inventory progresses, these collections will gradually become more complete and more valuable to a broader array of users. (These inventory collections provide background for all kinds of users, and are not to be confused with the much smaller samples taken for biodiversity prospecting.)

The Division of Biodiversity Prospecting is free to use the inventory collections as reference for specimen identification and for locating species within Costa Rica. When biodiversity prospectors encounter unknown species, INBio curators and taxonomists make identifying that species a high priority and the curators seek immediate help from the broader taxonomic community to identify it.

Without the inventory and access to knowledgeable curators and taxonomists, biodiversity prospecting would be severely limited. *(See Box III.2.)* Accurate identification allows the biodiversity prospector to search closely related species for natural products identical or similar to those found in a sampled organism. If blind screening turns up an interesting alkaloid in one species of seed, an obvious next step is to screen the seeds of closely related species. Or, to use another example, if researchers suspect that a certain seed contains a mammalian toxin, they may find it easier to search for that toxin in closely related species that are easier to obtain, more abundant, and more tractable in the extraction process than the original.

INBio charges non-commercial users nothing to identify species. But in any INBio-commercial partnership, a significant contribution to the Division of the National Biodiversity Inventory to help meet the costs of maintaining the parataxonomists, inventory managers, and inventory operations is expected. It is hoped that some day biodiversity prospecting can even generate enough income so that Costa Rica can make a fair contribution to the world-level process of taxonomic and ecological research that underpins the entire biodiversity industry.

INBio also believes that all commercial operations based on Costa Rican wildland biodiversity should do more than just help meet the costs of conducting the national inventory and cover the

Box III.2. The Taxonomist's Role in Biodiversity Prospecting

To carry out biodiversity prospecting, it is necessary to be able to identify plants, animals, and micro-organisms, and to know something about their variation and geographic distribution. It is also necessary to be able to characterize the organism and give it an unique name. As a body of biochemical data is built up, the data must be linked to the name of each species through a voucher specimen, so that identities can be checked as additional data from other specimens are added to the database. Without voucher specimens and accurate taxonomic information, the data will become very confused. Many a sorry biochemist has come to a taxonomist after completing years of experiments, asking for identification of the species on which the experiments were conducted, only to learn that he actually used several species, each with unique chemical properties. When this happens, it is impossible to interpret the experimental results. The implications for biodiversity prospecting are obvious, as they are likewise for other users of biodiversity information.

By no means are all organisms known to science; the vast majority lack both names and phylogenetic affinities. In biodiverse tropical countries, as much as 90 percent of the biota may be unknown. The unknown organisms tend to be those with the most biomedical and agricultural potential—especially soil invertebrates and microbes, fungi, and marine algae and colonial organisms. These species live within tight competitive relationships, and many have evolved specific chemical defenses, such as the antibacterial properties found in penicillin.

The last step in taxonomic research is to place the species within a taxonomic hierarchy, or phylogeny. The phylogeny expresses genetic (historical) relationships among taxa and allows scientists to identify close relatives, as well as to understand such evolutionary processes as the evolution of disease resistance. Phylogenetic knowledge enables researchers to make predictions about the biology of a species, including its chemical properties. Knowledge that one plant species produces a

Box III.2. (Continued)

useful compound, such as quinine or rubber, permits a search for close relatives that may be even better producers. It also allows scientists to search for useful genes for biotechnological manipulation, such as the production of perennial corn using a gene from a wild relative of domesticated corn. In fact, the three legs of the biodiversity prospecting "stool" are ecological knowledge (which includes ethnobiological information), phylogenetic knowledge, and use of modern screening techniques.

Phylogenetic knowledge is constantly updated, even for already-named species. New biochemical techniques have allowed researchers to recognize many "cryptic" species, which must then be split into several species. Newly discovered species change prevailing concepts of genera and families. Information vital to conservation strategies, including reproduction, life history, and symbiotic relationships, is also gained by taxonomists and other scientists, using both museum specimens and field data.

Specimen Collectors

Plant and animal collectors are not necessarily taxonomists, and taxonomists are not necessarily (in fact, usually not) involved in biodiversity prospecting. While taxonomists do collect organisms, they usually do so in the context of taxonomic research: comparison, naming, biogeography, and phylogenetic studies. Only rarely are they contracted by a commercial firm or a governmental entity to serve as commercial collectors; and only rarely are commercial efforts based on the specimens collected by taxonomists (though with genetic research the potential for this collaboration is obvious).

Taxonomic research results are necessarily internationally available: the International Commission of Zoological Nomenclature and the International Association for Plant Taxonomy establish the rules for describing species. Because taxonomic research is comparative, information must be shared among international colleagues through networks and apprentices must be trained, much as medical doctors traditionally are.

Commercial plant collectors do not have the time and often do not have the knowledge to describe species, learn their key biological properties, and place them in a phylogenetic context. They require taxonomists to resolve species identifications, with the aid of museum resources (collections and libraries). They also require repositories for their own voucher specimens.

The purpose of a voucher specimen is to provide material for comparison with other related organisms or samples purporting to be the same species. (These specimens thus cannot be kept secret unless they are the vouchers for a trade secret.) Voucher specimens can also be treated as documentation for a patent or intellectual property claims, however. For safety, vouchers should be deposited in more than one repository. Traditionally, zoological taxonomists deposit the type specimen (holotype) of a new species in a developed world museum and sometimes deposit a series of "paratypes" (specimens believed by the taxonomist to be the same species) in a repository in the country of origin. Other paratypes are sent to one or two large internationally accessible museums. Vouchers for biodiversity prospecting need be deposited in only one repository if it is professionally maintained to protect against degradation of the specimens and violations of confidentiality.

The work of taxonomists is basic science, though it has many applications in biotechnology for agriculture, medicine, and natural products. Taxonomy is so fundamental to the rest of biology that it has been considered in the category of a "public good," and enters the public domain immediately as species descriptions and phylogenies are published. For this reason, the work of taxonomists is often taken for granted. Creating and maintaining databases developed in the course of taxonomic work, including those devolving from museum collections data, are also in the public interest, but to survive institutions must develop ways to recover development and maintenance costs. INBio has already realized this fact, and fees for some

Box III.2. (Continued)

categories of nonreciprocal users, including use contracts and subscriptions for database products, are probably inevitable.

Successful biodiversity prospecting tied to conservation of national resources requires the kinds of in-country incentives and safeguards spelled out in this book. But the safeguards will be counter-productive if they inhibit taxonomic research. Each country needs to develop mechanisms to encourage taxonomic research, infrastructure, and dissemination of basic knowledge (species names, descriptions, and relationships). A view of biodiversity resources that is so nationalistic that it prohibits access for taxonomic study threatens to thwart the international cooperation that is the basis for species identification and the use of a nation's biodiversity.

It is imperative that scientists affiliated with educational institutions not be compelled to be the enforcers of contracts between third parties over which they have no control or legal responsibility, such as corporations and conservation managers. Taxonomic collectors cannot guarantee the payment of royalties, future purchases of raw materials, and the like.

Researchers cannot anticipate the ways in which specimens that reach museum collections will be used. However, visitors to collections must present credentials and state their purpose.

costs of identification services. To date, with the notable exception of Merck and Co., businesses that harvest Costa Rican wildland samples for sale have had no interest in directly contributing to Costa Rican biodiversity conservation. But this is likely to change in response to the new Costa Rican legislation, which requires a concession from the government to prospect for biodiversity in conservation areas, and as a result of the pilot project agreements that INBio is promoting among many kinds of users.

Literature on biodiversity prospecting. An enormous literature exists on the natural products that can be derived from wild tropical

They work under supervision of museum staff, and cannot remove or alter material without permission. Herbarium sheets are not used for biochemical assay. In order for drug screening to be done using museum resources, a museum could require that the commercial interest present evidence of a pre-existing agreement with the country of origin. When botanists send duplicate specimens for exchange with other museums, they could also stipulate that the material not be used for screening without permission.

Museum scientists and particularly museum administrators have become more aware of third party (non-academic) interest and use of collections for profit-making ventures. They, like developing countries themselves, are looking to ways to recover costs so that their institutions can survive tough economic times and continue to serve society at large. The interests of developing countries and museums, whether in developing or developed countries, are coincident on this point, allowing for a natural alliance on control of use of museum specimens.

Source: K. Elaine Hoagland. 1993. "The Taxonomist's Role in Biodiversity Prospecting and International Institution-Building," Position Paper #1, The Association of Systematics Collections, Washington, D.C.

plants, insects, and micro-organisms, as well as on the physiological or ecological role and human uses of these natural products. While this information is of little use in the initial stages of blind screening (which tends to stress taxonomic diversity), it may guide progress once an interesting lead appears. In an ecology-driven search, this literature can provide invaluable clues on where to look and what class of compounds to look for. For example, if it is noted that no insect eats the leaves of some species of plant, a literature search on the natural products chemistry of that plant and its relatives may help the chemist begin searching for the defensive chemicals responsible for its leaf toxicity.

Of course, trying to absorb all the literature in natural products chemistry and stay up to date is expensive. Although INBio is working hard to stay fully plugged into the global network of electronic data bases and abstracting services, older literature pertinent to ecology-driven searches in the tropics has yet to be abstracted. Resources permitting, INBio would like to help capture these old journals and books electronically, both as a general service to all users of tropical biodiversity and as a specific aid in biodiversity prospecting.

Besides printed literature, traditional electronic data bases, and abstracting services, INBio will accumulate specimen-based and species-based databases from a wide variety of field studies in ecology, physiology, behavior, etc. This information should be helpful in both blind and ecology-driven searches. A database on caterpillar host-plants, for example, might well indicate the presence of a caterpillar that can digest a particularly noxious chemical found in the leaves of a particular plant species. Like the inventory specimen databases, these ecology databases should also belong in the public domain. Again, however, the commercial user should plan to contribute to the Division of Biodiversity Inventory for access to this information. Lest paying for what can be had for free appear strange, the reader is reminded that in, say, the United States, biodiversity users pay taxes that are then in part used to gather taxonomic and ecological information that is subsequently placed in the public domain through publication in scientific journals.

Collaborations with Universities, Government Agencies, and NGOs

As a non-profit non-governmental organization dedicated to the public service—helping a major natural resource survive—INBio works alongside universities, museums, government agencies, and conservation-oriented NGOs. These relationships can be either formal or informal. In either case, the collaborative process is the same.

The national biodiversity inventory is a formal collaboration with MIRENEM. *(See Box III.3.)* Any given biodiversity sampling

84

project is carried out according to an explicit written agreement between MIRENEM, the local conservation area administration, and the specific sampling project. As specified in all INBio contracts with commercial enterprises, a 10-percent payment to the National Park Fund at MIRENEM is included in the project budget and half of all royalties that INBio receives go into the same fund.

INBio also subcontracts as much as possible of the sample processing, extracting, chemical analysis, etc., to Costa Rican university laboratories, and it aggressively seeks out university and hospital laboratories for in-country projects in blind screening and ecology-driven search. The reasons are many: spreading the new income around in Costa Rica, broadening participation in bioprospecting, increasing national research capacity, and minimizing the psychological distance and economic differences between the conservation area and the final biodiversity user. Still, INBio would be foolish not to take advantage of the chemical processing hardware and technical capacity available in developed country universities and industrial complexes. Indeed, INBio biodiversity prospecting staff collaborate closely with foreign researchers, sometimes travelling to and using developed-country facilities.

INBio also aggressively seeks collaboration with museums and other sources of taxonomic expertise. The two-fold goal is to be able to tap into the world-wide network of taxonomic knowledge and services and to contribute specimens, data, and user demand to it. Indeed, INBio's basic inventory will be on the Internet by late 1993, and all information gathered in the national inventory will then be placed in the electronic public domain.

Fostering Drug Discovery and Local Expertise

The process of drug discovery—field sampling, laboratory processing and screening, and chemical isolation and so on—has long been managed and staffed largely by experts from developed countries. INBio assumes that Costa Rica's biodiversity won't be highly valued and appropriately managed in the long run unless the Costa Rican populace on whose lives it will have the largest positive or negative impact are involved. To this end, INBio

85

Box III.3. Cooperative Agreement Between the Ministry of Natural Resources, Energy and Mines (Costa Rica) and the Association, National Biodiversity Institute (INBio)

We, Hernan Bravo Trejos, adult married once, resident of San Ramon de Tres Rios, chemical engineer, cedula 1-376-823, as Minister of Natural Resources, Energy and Mines, as stated in Executive Decree No. 19709 of 8 May of 1990, referred to below as MIRENEM, and Rodrigo Gámez Lobo, adult, married, Doctor of Virology, resident of Heredia, cedula 6-046-360, as President of the Association The National Institute of Biodiversity, domiciled in Santo Domingo de Heredia, cedula juridica 3-002-103261-12, inscribed in the Public Registry, Section of Associations, in file #336, referred to below as INBio, sign the present agreement that is governed by the antecedents and clauses that are listed below:

Antecedents

1. MIRENEM administrates, through the National Park Service, the national parks and biological reserves, whose objective is the preservation of the natural resources of our country.

2. One of the fundamental reasons to preserve and protect the wild areas is scientific investigation that leads to the improvement of the knowledge and the conservation of the biodiversity existing in these areas.

3. INBio is a non-profit Association that has among its objectives to contribute to the preservation into perpetuity of Costa Rican biodiversity, promoting its integration with the intellectual and economic values of the society, through the generation and dissemination of knowledge about the identity, geographical distribution, and uses of the species of plants, animals, and microorganisms of the country.

4. In conformity with articles 5, 14, and 17 of the Regulations of the Scientific and Technological Registry and Article 67 and others of the Law No. 7169 (Law of Promotion of Scientific

and Technological Development), INBio is legally included in this Registry as a national scientific entity.

5. By accord #22 of the Board of Directors, of the 4th of May 1992, INBio authorized its President to sign the present agreement, that is governed by the following clauses:

Clauses

First:

a) MIRENEM and INBio agree to jointly carry out the inventory of biodiversity in the system of protected wild areas, through activities or research projects that will be carried out in the shortest time possible and conducted according to the regulations established in the Research Regulations of the National Park Service.

b) In accord with their resources, MIRENEM and INBio will supply the personnel, installations, and the equipment necessary to carry out that which was stipulated above. In addition, INBio shall donate to MIRENEM equipment and materials for the described objectives.

c) In order to carry out the inventory, MIRENEM grants to the technical and scientific functionaries of INBio an official and specific recognition status. INBio can contract personnel to work in the activities that are associated with the inventory in the Protected Areas under the norms established in Law 7111 or other related legislation.

Second: Based on the Regulation of Research of the National Park Service, MIRENEM shall grant to INBio permission to collect samples of various species of plants, animals, and other organisms, in order that these can be used in scientific research. INBio should communicate its annual program of research to the central offices of the National Park Service and to the respective Conservation Areas where the research will be carried out.

Third: The activities of specimen collection by INBio will be done in such a manner that it will not cause damage or alteration that would constitute a threat to the biodiversity of the wildland area, complying with the existing legislation and regulations.

Box III.3. (Continued)

Fourth: In all research projects, INBio will attempt to include an amount equivalent to 10 percent of the total annual budget of the respective project, for donation to the National Parks Fund for the ends indicated above. In the case that the project is financed by a commercial entity, INBio is committed to making a donation of no less than 10 percent of the budget to the National Parks Fund for the ends indicated above.

Fifth: When INBio receives as outcome of the scientific research benefits of an economic character, it agrees to donate to the National Parks Fund 50 percent of the financial benefits accrued to INBio, to be used for the management and conservation of the wild areas.

Sixth: INBio agrees, within its capacity, to provide to MIRENEM technical advice that MIRENEM requires for the study and evaluation of projects or other activities related to the conservation of biological diversity.

Seventh: Within its capacity, INBio shall put at the disposition of MIRENEM, by the mechanisms established for the case, the pertinent information contained in its Data Bases for Conservation to be used for decision making on the management and conservation of biodiversity and other matters related to its jurisdiction.

employs only local talent or nationals trained on-the-job in Costa Rica or abroad. All of INBio's directorate and staff are Costa Rican. Still, foreign researchers will continue to play a highly significant role in technology transfer at INBio for sometime and will probably always be involved as research collaborators.

At INBio, each facet of the drug discovery process is handled by two research leaders—one specializing in biology, the other in chemistry. The Director of the Division of Biodiversity Prospecting coordinates these traditionally different areas of science and develops

Eighth: All the matters pertaining to the execution of this agreement will be resolved by a commission composed of the Director of the National Park Service and the Director of INBio. When the matters pertain to other divisions of MIRENEM, the Director of National Parks will be substituted in the Commission by the respective Director.

Ninth: This agreement takes effect from the time of signing, having validity for five years, renewing itself automatically for periods of equal duration. In the case that any of the parties wishes to rescind it, this shall be communicated in writing to the other party six months in advance. Those projects in existence and those that will be in progress shall continue until conclusion.

Giving faith in the above, we sign in the City of San José, on the 11th of May of year one thousand nine hundred and ninety two.

Hernan Bravo Trejos, Minister
Ministry of Natural Resources, Energy and Mines

Rodrigo Gámez Lobo, President
National Biodiversity Institute

(Note: Original in Spanish)

the formal contractual relationships between the conservation area and the commercial product user.

Field sampling teams. Biodiversity sampling in the field will soon be handled primarily by Costa Ricans, with only marginal cheerleading and technical guidance from foreign researchers. Except in cases of dire necessity, INBio has avoided the temptation to use foreign consultants and international volunteers—who can unwittingly block opportunities for on-the-job training. It has aggressively hired Costa Ricans, from both the rural community and the university community, training them to view science and conservation in a new way. Tolerance of the high error rate generated by combining the human learning process with the intrinsically error-rich process of fieldwork has been essential.

INBio is now training its first national paraecologists and biodiversity ecologists—colleagues of the parataxonomists and inventory managers described in Annex 1. These field personnel carry out the most straightforward sampling but are still learning from experience and from international associates how to tackle more complex tasks. The parataxonomists do *not* collect biodiversity prospecting samples (in contrast to what has been reported in newspapers), but they do collect for the inventory and offer to biodiversity prospectors information on where organisms occur.

Laboratory processing and screening teams. Chemical extracts are produced in Costa Rica in a combination of first-step facilities at INBio, other chemistry laboratories at universities, and other research laboratories. Productivity is limited not so much by training needs as by the lack of processing machinery and physical space for operations, and by biodiversity consumers' unwillingness to collaborate fully in a process aimed at Costa Rican development and the generation of financial returns to the conservation areas.

Training in how to run, repair, manage, and evaluate screens (bioassay or chemical) in-country is a major benefit to INBio and Costa Rica from INBio-commercial contracts. To the degree possible, contracts specify that the screens needed for bioassays or chemical assays must be either developed or acquired in Costa Rica. As screens move to Costa Rica, the country gains both from direct involvement and from the increase in within-country expenditures on pharmaceutical R&D. In addition, screening at INBio for diseases and other problems commonplace in developing countries directly benefits Costa Rica. (Some INBio-university collaborations are already based on screens developed in Costa Rica, and INBio helps acquire the knowledge needed to develop new screens in-country.)

Chemical isolation. Through in-country screening, the field samples are linked to the process of isolating and purifying active chemicals. Once an extract is found to contain an active compound, further search of the hundreds of compounds in the sample requires repeated trials with the same and sometimes additional screens. Since the results from these screens guide the chemist, it is difficult to do screening in-house and the chemical refinement simultaneously in a distant developed-world laboratory. Until the chemist has the budget to purchase and maintain more equipment in Costa Rica, full use can be made of only certain kinds of screens. On the other hand, assurance of known chemical activity is often enough to prompt the commercial world to purchase extracts; the active molecule does not necessarily have to be isolated.

Creating a major industrial chemistry complex for compound identification and modification in Costa Rica is simply not a possibility at the moment, so INBio must specialize in highly reliable sourcing, resupply, and only certain kinds of screening results. But many R&D processes can be carried out in-country once a particular compound has become the focal point of drug development.

Agreements and Contracts with the Industrial and Commercial Sector

From INBio's perspective, the contractual challenge in biodiversity prospecting is not so much in information management. After all, biodiversity information resembles other kinds of information in the marketplace. Rather, it is making sure that the intellectual and financial net income get returned to the conservation areas. Likewise, as much as possible of the gross income should support the quality and survival of the conservation areas and Costa Rica's GNP. As the biodiversity prospecting industry grows, it may—like ecotourism and scientific research in the conservation areas—contribute even more to domestic production than to budgets for conservation area management. The size and nature of an industry based on the raw materials and information from the conservation areas will determine its economic contribution. INBio's goal is not to replace other wildland industries with biodiversity prospecting but rather to help develop the information base that supports them.

When INBio proposes business relationships with industry, its contractual arrangements include eight items:

1. *Direct payments in cash and barter (equipment, training, technological know-how) to enable INBio to develop and conduct the sampling, screening, and partial characterization processes and to train and finance local scientists and parascientists.* These payments—determined through negotiation—are made in exchange for the provision of samples and extracts to the user industry. They depend on the real costs of biodiversity prospecting and of maintaining and managing the conservation areas. The entire cost of a biodiversity sample is certainly not adequately represented by the hourly wages of going into the field, bagging up a bag of leaves, and drying them in an oven—even though this is what the pharmaceutical companies have traditionally directly paid for a sample. Direct compensation to a tropical country for the real costs of a sample can help finance conservation programs long before chemical prospecting can begin to pay returns through royalties or in-country industry.

2. *Payment of a significant percentage of INBio's initial project budget (10 percent) and of royalties (50 percent) as a direct contribution to the cost of maintaining the National System of Conservation Areas (SINAC).* These percentage-based payments contribute *directly* to meeting the management costs of maintaining the wild organisms sampled. Of course, all other funds that go to INBio also contribute to SINAC, since INBio is philosophically and administratively a non-governmental branch of SINAC.

INBio's current thinking is that the biodiversity prospecting contribution is best channeled through the government (the National Parks Fund) rather than through a non-governmental organization, though it is easy to imagine cases in which the reverse might be true, especially if government bureaucracies become too complex. An unresolved question in Costa Rica is how much of the earmarked income to channel to the central SINAC system and how much to the conservation area where the sample was collected.

3. *A significant fair royalty paid on net sales to industry from the commercialization of the biodiversity materials.* The willingness of commercial firms to pay fair royalties depends on the recognition that biodiversity

samples are not merely a few leaves snatched off of a "wild west frontier" but, rather, are products that the supplier—the conservation area and INBio—has systematically maintained and characterized at considerable cost. As the sampling and analysis system becomes more diverse and supplier-user feedback more complex, it may make sense to renegotiate the distribution of royalties among competing subcomponents of the supplier system.

4. *Help in gradually moving drug research and development to the source country, thus creating new kinds of jobs and novel avenues of industrial development.* Biodiversity prospecting is just one of many industrial activities in which developing countries have a chance to compete seriously, especially because they are sitting on a rich resource and because the industry may be able to function more efficiently in the tropics even if employment and environmental standards comparable to those in developed countries are adopted.

5. *Minimal exclusivity.* Often, one or another commercial user wants to be the sole recipient of certain samples or to deny its competitors the opportunity to collaborate in biodiversity prospecting. Such exclusivity may pose problems for Costa Rica and INBio, but without guarantee of some exclusivity, pharmaceutical companies naturally aren't very interested in purchasing samples. As a compromise, INBio has negotiated deals whereby the same sample sold to one commercial user is not sold to another for 6 to 24 months after the initial purchase. (Of course, nothing prevents any other enterprise from sending the same species to anyone else, and private for-profit companies have been doing this silently for years!) At INBio, the voucher specimens for samples in biodiversity prospecting are maintained as confidential collections separate from the primary national inventory. The electronic data associated with these specimens are confidential; only certain members of the Division of Biodiversity Prospecting have access to this information.

6. *Agreement on sample ownership and patent ownership.* Ownership of samples and extracts must be clearly defined, and the extract must either be destroyed after use or remain subject to the INBio royalty—no matter when the chemical discovery is made or how long the commercial user keeps the sample or something

extracted from it. Patents represent such an administrative headache and entail such high legal costs that INBio would much rather have a solid commercial contract guaranteeing a royalty than own the patent outright. Also, in Costa Rica patenting a product produced by a living organism is illegal—though this anachronistic law is likely to change as Costa Rica fully enters international trade.

7.   *The use of chemical synthesis, semisynthesis, and domestication of living sources, etc., to avoid continuous extraction of biotic material from conserved wildlands and to keep commercial "sourcing" in-country.* Researchers can normally make do with amounts of material that are small enough to be obtained without significantly altering the conservation area's populations or ecology—especially if ecologists guide collecting activities. However, few conservation areas will be able to provide commercial quantities of novel chemicals found through biodiversity prospecting. What these areas can provide are the plant and animal stock and natural history knowledge private farmers or ranchers need to produce larger volumes of the commercially valuable organisms found in the conservation areas. INBio encourages commercial users to consider Costa Rica as their first choice for such agricultural production or, alternatively, to start up chemical synthesizing industries there.

8.   *Protective legal mechanisms.* INBio's legal contracts with the commercial sector are generated in-house with *pro bono* legal counsel from the Costa Rican environmental law community and U.S. law firms specializing in patent rights and intellectual property. These contracts are also formally or informally approved by MIRENEM even though INBio (as a non-governmental organization) is not legally required to do so. Since all INBio biodiversity sampling takes place in conservation areas that MIRENEM controls, all sampling is done under concession from MIRENEM through a formal collaboration agreement. *(See Box III.3.)*

National Policy

National biodiversity legislation will come about through normal political processes. But an INBio-like institution can be sensitive to the evolution of this legislation and encourage it to increasingly support the non-destructive use of the conservation areas and their financial self-sufficiency. Solidarity among the biodiversity-rich countries, and encouragement from the developed countries to care for biodiversity resources, can help provide the opportunity for countries to manage their biodiversity resources as a whole through regulated concessions to INBio-like entities or as government industries. The alternative—allowing private individuals to "mine" and sell biodiversity in an unregulated manner without contributing to its maintenance—could destroy the resource and its productive potential for the country. Indeed, countries without a national biodiversity policy run the risk of irrevocable exploitation by unscrupulous businesspeople.

Under Costa Rica's new law, any entity that wants to collect or manage biodiversity samples from a conservation area (government land) for commercial or other uses must sign a concession agreement with MIRENEM. (For scientific research, such a research agreement or "permit" has been required for many years.) This legislation declares all wild animals (including invertebrates) to be "national patrimony" or "public domain," regardless of whose property they inhabit. Non-timber plants are viewed as private property of public interest but outside the public domain. Thus, even the private landowner needs a concessionary agreement from MIRENEM to collect or otherwise alter or manipulate non-timber wild biodiversity. The law also states firmly that "the terms and conditions of the concessions must favor national interests."

How this legislation will avoid running afoul of the Costa Rican constitution, which allows landowners to do what they wish to their own land, is an important legal question. Another is the still-unclear relation between Costa Rican indigenous peoples (a tiny fraction of the population), their lands, and the Costa Rican government. At present, INBio forgoes biodiversity prospecting in any region or area that could possibly be contested by indigenous peoples and encourages the government to clarify the rights of indigenous peoples so they can freely prospect for biodiversity on their own (with help from INBio, if they wish). Two indigenous parataxonomists work out of their own Biodiversity Offices within indigenous

95

zones as part of INBio's national biodiversity inventory, but all the specimens and data they collect or process are in the public domain.

Business Development

Biodiversity prospecting is both an ordinary and an extraordinary business. Like many businesses, it draws partners from very different sectors of society and responds to supply and demand. But the suppliers' bottom line is not maximizing income, but making sure that the conservation area survives. Also, the value of biological samples changes continually as more pharmaceutical uses are discovered for them. Finally, fidelity to the supplier of biodiversity samples depends on whether the user honors a contractual promise that at present only the patent office can police. There is simply no way for the supplier itself to directly verify that the purchaser does not use the sample at a later date without paying royalties. The only safeguards for now are a company's good reputation and the patent office's requirement that the commercial developer identify the source of a patentable molecule.

In the early stages of biodiversity commercialization, INBio has supplied samples only to well-established biodiversity users since they have been the most generous, the most eager to protect their reputations, and the most painstaking with contract development. These users also reward INBio for having its samples in a high-quality format (vis-a-vis processing accuracy, the possibilities for resupply and feedback, politically acceptable use of funds, etc.).

To commercialize biodiversity successfully, Costa Rica must stay on the cutting edge of new commercial developments, as it has in the development of its conservation areas, of INBio itself, and of the INBio-Merck and Co. contract, etc. Indeed, INBio must aggressively seek new users and point out new potential uses to current users, as well as help foster a political and legislative climate in Costa Rica that is hospitable to innovation.

Because wildland biodiversity products are not yet highly visible in Costa Rica—everyday fixtures of life such as coffee and penicillin notwithstanding—INBio can broaden its user base by generating

96

new product ideas. Bringing together under one roof various kinds of information managers and processors certainly helps, and INBio is already a highly heterogeneous "zoo" of parataxonomists, paraecologists, inventory managers, biodiversity ecologists, Ph.D. academics, amateur biologists, chemists, truck drivers, accountants, computer enthusiasts, conservationists, international consultants, lawyers, conservation area managers, bank presidents, virologists, and many more. While workplace harmony is sometimes elusive, diverse perspectives inevitably lead to new ways of thinking about wildland biodiversity and its socially productive uses.

Of course, the commercialization of wildland biodiversity is a two-edged sword. While it is a good way of getting tropical wildlands to pay for themselves and to get the general public on their side, it also antagonizes free-wheeling bioprospecting competitors who naturally want to continue to reap personal profits unfettered, as well as those who disapprove of the marriage of commerce and conservation on principle. This unavoidable antagonism must be handled at the negotiating table every time INBio makes a contract with the business world.

IV.

CONTRACTS FOR BIODIVERSITY PROSPECTING[1]

Sarah A. Laird

"No negotiation, no matter how artful, can result in a preagreed solution to every possible eventuality. No contract, no matter how carefully drafted, is entirely clear on everything that was intended by the principals, when they are no longer around to interpret its clauses. Thus, negotiations and contracts are, at best, agreements at a point in time, and good relationships predictably outgrow their original contracts. For the relationship to grow and mature well over the years requires careful management of expectations" (Sherblom, 1991:223).

As industry interest in genetic and biochemical resources increases and more research and conservation institutions realize that they must use or face losing their countries' biodiversity, contractual agreements between collectors and suppliers of biological samples, and pharmaceutical and biotech companies, will become more important. Through the relationships they represent, these contracts can ensure that a portion of the value generated from developing genetically or biologically derived products is captured by the country and people who have been biodiversity's custodians.

Contracts function within the strictures of international and national policy and law, and as such are limited by existing business practices and concepts of property. Revolutionary solutions to difficult problems like the equitable distribution of benefits will not come out of contracts; nor will contracts usher in a new era of conservation. But they can yield significant financial and non-monetary benefits for governments and communities within biodiversity-rich countries, strengthen scientific research and infrastructure, spur technology transfer, and create incentives for conserving biodiversity.

To understand these potential benefits, we must look at the experiences, current collection and business practices, policies, and relationships of companies and collectors. In particular, both industry's and collectors' attitudes and policies toward collaboration, the supply of samples, advance payments and royalties, technology transfer, non-monetary compensation, future supplies of raw materials, and indigenous peoples' intellectual property rights influence company-collector relationships and, eventually, the effectiveness of contractual agreements.

The Strengths and Limitations of Contracts

A contract is a set of lawful promises that make up a legal obligation resulting from the parties' agreement or understanding, where there is a duty of performance and a remedy at law in the event of a breach or a non-performance (Williston, 1990). Any contract reflects rather than determines a relationship, and a contract is only as good as the parties' ability to negotiate and agree to mutually satisfying terms.

In the case of contracts for the supply of biological samples, collectors generally agree to collect, taxonomically identify, and ship to soliciting companies a supply of samples for screening. Companies, in turn, provide collectors with advance funds, per-sample fees, their best efforts to screen samples, and, in some cases, royalties on any compounds commercialized from the collected samples. *(See Box IV.1.)*

Generally, both collectors and companies can achieve their immediate objectives through contracts. For instance, contracts can:

- Offer collectors and source countries advance payments, royalties, rights to supply future raw materials, research ex-

changes and funding, access to markets and technology, and direct payments to conservation "overhead."
- Channel benefits to conservation and local peoples that contribute to research efforts without requiring new definitions of property rights or special legislation.
- Ensure economic returns for the work involved in collecting samples as well as for the collected material itself, thus possibly avoiding the compensation problems associated with non-endemic species that exist in a number of countries and providing alternatives to the "spot" (one time) sale of samples that return no lasting benefits to the country of origin.

Other aspects of contracts as applied to the collection of biological samples and the resulting commercialization of natural products show up their limitations. Contracts may, for example:

- Prove expensive and difficult to draft, negotiate, and enforce. Legal language is difficult to enforce without a relationship of mutual benefit, and most companies have far more legal might than do collectors. This disparity in legal and financial resources can place a developing country party in a poor position to enforce the contract.
- Involve too many interests, parties, and issues. Such contracts are difficult to agree on and enforce. Restricting the number of specific objectives in a contract is likely to improve the odds that a deal will be struck and increase the agreement's longevity.
- Stifle creativity, flexibility, and expectations. For this reason, both industry and collecting institution representatives warn against over-reliance on prescribed models (Harder, Missouri Botanical Garden, pers. comm., 1992; Thomas, Biotics Ltd., pers. comm., 1992; Caporale, Merck Pharmaceuticals, pers. comm., 1992; Balick, NYBG, pers. comm., 1992).
- Raise questions about the control of a country's genetic and biochemical resources (or their "national patrimony"). As compared with the broadly applicable legal protection of national and international law and policy, contracts are too narrow to effectively control the activities of those who are not parties to the contract.

Box IV.1. Coming to Terms

Companies enter into contractual agreements with collectors to obtain regular and reliable supplies of samples. If the terms for obtaining samples from a particular biodiversity-rich country don't allow a company what it considers a reasonable projected return on its investment, it will simply look elsewhere. Collectors and countries of origin should insist upon significant returns from the development of products based on their genetic and biological resources, but they cannot expect a company to buck standard business practices, write off the $231 million it now reportedly costs on average (if failures are figured in) to develop a drug, or alter the profit-seeking motivations of corporate management.[1]

Many in industry will resist paying any "prospector's fees" and royalties:

"The typical developing country thinks that patents on pharmaceutical compounds are absurd and wicked, and does not respect them. So why should developed countries and the companies based in them respect a much more tenuous and newly asserted property right which is used to justify demanding *geographical fees* [royalties from biological samples]? The owner of a patent, after all, had to find a useful drug to get the patent. At most a developing country claiming a geographical

Parties to Contractual Agreements for the Supply of Biological Samples

What is the most effective and equitable way to draft a collector-company contract? What is the nature of collector-company relationships? And what motives and obligations underlie the agreements? Existing agreements provide insights into the answers for all of these questions. (*See also* Annex 2, a Draft Contract.)

fee can claim only to have been the country of origin of a plant or animal from which foreigners extracted a drug" (SCRIP, 1992).

To resolve such differences of perspective, each party must know its potential collaborator and recognize the need for mutual agreement and shared objectives. As James Sherblom (1991) puts it, this is a large part of the negotiating process:

"The first stage is usually a general discussion among businesspeople. The goal here is to establish whether there are consistent corporate cultures, complementary strategic goals, and a potential commonality of interest...You go forward only if a sense of goodwill has been established...The second stage usually involves scientific discussions including several scientists from each side. The goal here is to decide if the two groups could actually work well together, and to decide whether the proposed project has scientific merit. The third and final stage includes lawyers, contracts, work plans, and tremendous patience, and persistence from the champions on each side" (Sherblom, 1991).

Contracts represent relationships based in "good will" and, as described, a series of negotiating stages that move forward only as long as that goodwill is maintained. Contracts are the product of the negotiating process and, as such, do not dictate the terms of these relationships. Rather, they reflect them.

[1] For a breakdown of the costs involved in developing a marketable pharmaceutical, *see* DiMasi et al., 1991.

Industry

The interest of the pharmaceutical and biotech industries in wildlands' genetic and biochemical resources has intensified in recent years.[2] Many companies have made significant commitments to plant, insect, and micro-organism collection programs, and the numbers of new collectors are increasing. *(See Table I.1, Chapter I.)* Many of these companies now acknowledge the rights of biodiversity-rich countries to benefit from the development of products from their genetic and biochemical resources. Although most contractual agreements only partially address questions of equity and conservation, both collectors and companies increasingly recognize the need to go farther. Rosemary Hennings, spokeswoman for Wellcome PLC in the United Kingdom illustrated this shift in attitude in June 1992 in her response to a question about the International Biodiversity Convention: Wellcome was founded on the fortunes of a pharmacist who developed the muscle relaxant d-tubocurarine from Amazonian curare at a time when contracts or other mechanisms for returning benefits to countries of collection were not yet contemplated. Wellcome is not currently researching plants but, "were we to do so, we would of course pay royalties. We would never expect to get something for nothing" (Vromen, 1992).

Pharmaceutical companies are also increasingly aware of the public-relations and charitable potential of agreements with collectors of natural products. Lynn Caporale, Senior Advisor of Scientific Liaison at Merck Research Laboratories, notes of Merck's agreement with INBio:

"On our side it was undertaken as a way to obtain diverse samples for screening to help us in our work of discovering new treatments for serious diseases. Costa Rica has created in INBio a mechanism by which our need for diverse identified samples can be used to support local needs for conservation and sustainable development" (Caporale, 1992).

As another example, in October 1992, Eli Lilly and Company and Shaman Pharmaceuticals, Inc., agreed to "jointly develop certain antifungal drugs drawn from the knowledge of native healers." In return for an option to obtain exclusive worldwide marketing rights to products identified, isolated, and initially screened by Shaman, Lilly will make a $4-million equity investment in Shaman; in turn, Shaman's nonprofit arm, the Healing Forest Conservancy, will return a portion of its receipts to people and governments in the countries where Shaman works (Lilly, 1992; WSJ, 1992).

104

Glaxo Group Research (GGR) of Middlesex, U.K., has also addressed the conservation and development implications of its research. Its official policy is that it "understands the impact unauthorized and/or unrestrained removal of plant materials from their indigenous habitats can have on the environment and economy of a country and that third world sources may be particularly vulnerable" (Glaxo, 1992). But Glaxo does distinguish "between the supply of plant material for drug discovery and the broader philanthropic support of efforts to conserve resources of which this plant material is a part," and turns over the latter to its Charitable and Community Contributions department[3] (Glaxo, 1992).

Few profit-seeking companies pursuing biological samples will take a direct interest in how benefits are distributed within countries of collection or in how the collecting programs funded by royalty payments affect conservation and local communities in source countries. Doing so is seen as extrinsic to their areas of expertise and control. But most companies will select their collectors with these issues in mind, if only to avoid litigation and negative publicity.[4]

Collectors

The collectors that meet industry demand for biological samples range from individuals who collect samples for "spot" payments to university-based plant-collection programs, to botanical gardens supplementing their field-research budgets, to private for-profit "brokers," to private and public research institutes based in developing countries (see Box IV.2). Renewed interest in the financial—and, in some cases, conservation—potential of supplying biological samples to the pharmaceutical industry has begun to expand the range of possible collectors even farther, encompassing indigenous groups, conservation organizations, and eco-tourism operators. The exigencies of establishing the scientific and administrative infrastructure needed to reliably supply samples to industry have kept most of these new contenders in the background, however, and until very recently most plant collection for industry has been concentrated in a handful of institutions.

Box IV.2. What Industry Looks for in a Collector

From industry's perspective, what are the qualities of the ideal collector?

- supervision by qualified scientists and access to taxonomic expertise to properly identify samples;[1]
- sound management and administration;
- stable political and economic conditions in the collector's country;
- a literate and skilled local population; and
- assurance that the collector institution will continue to function at least for the term of the contract.

What this list suggests is that most companies would rather work with institutions than individuals. Why? As Glaxo's *Policy for the Acquisition of Plant Materials* states, "national and/or international organizations...possess the expertise and authority to obtain such materials from whatever source" (Glaxo, 1992).

[1]Proper identification is critical for industry research programs. Natural products chemists have identified promising compounds only to lack access to raw materials because of inaccurate identification of the species from which it came.

Many collectors are non-profit research institutions that enter into agreements with industry to cover the costs of botanical or pharmacological research. As Peter Lowry of the Missouri Botanical Garden put it, collecting is "a logical, appropriate way to supplement our resource base" (Lowry, Missouri Botanical Garden, pers. comm., 1992). The appeal of such collaboration is obvious. Plant-related sciences (such as taxonomy, ethnobotany, and pharmacognosy) and the compilation of national biodiversity inventories are under-funded, and collectors working in habitats facing impending destruction and practicing what Michael Balick of the New York Botanical Garden calls "salvage" botany and ethnobotany, supplement field-research budgets with collection contracts with industry and with the U.S. National Cancer Institute (NCI).

In-country Collaborators

In addition to the legal relationship a contracted collector has with a company, a more informal one usually exists between the collector and in-country collaborators. Most of these in-country collaborators are affiliated with scientific (usually botanical) institutions, though some are private individuals or businesses.

Many botanical gardens in developed countries have wide webs of institutional collaborators in developing countries. Some of The New York Botanical Garden's collaborators, for example, include the Botanical Garden and Caribe Council in Dominica, the Forestry Department, the Ix Chel Tropical Research Center, and the Belize Association of Traditional Healers. The Missouri Botanical Garden works with, among many others, the Centre Regional d'Etudes Nucleaires de Kinshasa (CREN-K) in Zaire and the Parc Botanique et Zoologique de Tsimbazaza and the National Botanical Garden in Madagascar. The Royal Botanic Gardens Kew has equally extensive and longstanding relationships with collaborators in developing countries (Balick, NYBG, 1992; Daly, NYBG, pers. comm., 1992; Harder, Missouri Botanical Garden, pers. comm., 1992; Lowry, Missouri Botanical Garden, pers. comm., 1992; Fellows, Royal Botanic Gardens Kew, pers. comm., 1992). The University of Illinois at Chicago collaborates with the Philippine National Herbarium and, in conjunction with the Arnold Arboretum of Harvard University and the Bishop Museum in Honolulu, with the Bogor Herbarium in Indonesia and the Forestry Research Institute of Papua New Guinea at Lae. In performing worldwide collections for industry, however, Illinois deals with "professional collectors"—that is, individuals who receive spot payments for samples—as well as appointed consultants to the University of Illinois. For the National Cancer Institute collections, Illinois prefers to send collectors from U.S. institutions to work with local collaborators, who are usually affiliated with or have access to local botanical research institutions and in most cases have set up separate private enterprises to collect plants for industry (Soejarto, University of Illinois, pers. comm., 1992).

Biotics, a private British for-profit company acts as a broker between companies and in-country collectors and employs local collaborators from both the private and public sectors. In Malaysia, Biotics collects through the Forest Research Institute of Malaysia; in Costa Rica, through the private company Polybiotica; and in Ghana, through a "private" taxonomist who also works at the Herbarium in Legon (Thomas, Biotics Ltd., pers. comm., 1992).

As a developing-country institution that negotiates directly with large multi-national companies, The National Institute of Biodiversity (INBio) in Costa Rica has collected for a variety of extra-tropical entities, such as Cornell University, Strathclyde Drug Research Institute, and Merck Research Laboratories. *(See Chapter II.)* INBio's Director, Rodrigo Gámez, claims that INBio's approach stands apart from that of others: Many companies go "in independently, not through a national organization like ours, and don't leave any direct benefit. They may contract with a country's botanical gardens, pay $75 for a sample, and that's it. Merck decided to go through the main gate" *(Business and the Environment, 1992).*

Advance Payments and Royalties for Sample Supplies

The supply of samples by a collector to a company for use in research forms the basis of biodiversity-prospecting contracts between those parties. A plant sample may consist of bark, leaves, fruit, wood, or roots. Most companies initially request samples of 0.5 to 1 kg each, though significantly less may be needed for initial testing. Up to 50 kg of fresh herbaceous plant material must be collected to obtain 5 to 10 kgs of dry plant material—enough to produce 50 milligrams (mg) of pure chemical substance. For most woody plants, the dry weight yield of roots, bark, or wood is much higher, sometimes as high as 75 percent (McChesney, 1992; Dhawan, Central Drug Research Institute, pers. comm., 1992). The Asian Symposium on Medicinal Plants and Other Natural Products, however, developed a "Code of Ethics for Foreign Collectors of Biological Samples" in February 1992 that advises collectors to not supply more than 500 grams (dry weight) of material for initial screening (ASOMPS, February 1992), though most companies now require more.

Depending on how difficult a particular species is to collect, collectors generally receive between U.S. $50 and $200 per kilogram (kg) sample. In exceptional cases, up to $1,500 (including collecting, travel, and shipping costs) has been paid for particularly desirable samples (Soejarto, University of Illinois, pers. comm., 1992). Payments for extracts can range between $200 and $250 per 25-gram sample (compared to $20 per soil sample). These payments, determined on a case-by-case basis, can include the costs of shipping from the field to the collector institution and then to the company (depending on the nature and number of samples shipped), confirming initial field identifications, curating voucher specimens, processing data, conducting literature searches, and maintaining staff and administrative infrastructure.

Collaborating in-country collectors usually receive approximately half the sample fee paid by companies to contracted collectors, but this share may be as low as one fifth, depending on such factors as the difficulty of acquiring the sample, the value added by in-country collectors to the samples, or the in-country collector's expertise. Contracting companies may also request exclusive rights from the collector to the samples supplied (though another collector in the same country may collect a sample of the same material under another contract) for a set period of time (usually six months to two years). (*See* article 10 of the Draft Contract in Annex 2.)

Companies and collectors do not decide on the size of advance payments arbitrarily.[5] Merck didn't make its US$1,135,000 payment to INBio until the two had agreed upon shared goals and a workplan. (*See Box IV.3.*) Other factors influenced Merck too: the University of Costa Rica has good facilities staffed by qualified personnel trained in extractive techniques; it's easier and cheaper to transport and import extracts than raw samples; and building research capability at INBio and the University of Costa Rica would cost Merck less than employing similar resources in the United States. Merck supplied chemical-extraction equipment to the University of Costa Rica but has exclusive commercial use of these facilities while the collaborative research agreement is in force.

Since the Merck-INBio contract and workplan served both institutions' objectives, why have so few other pharmaceutical companies been willing to make large advance commitments to collec-

Box IV.3. INBio's Use of Merck's $1,135,000 Payment

Contribution to the Ministry of Natural Resource's National Park Fund (conservation "overhead")	$ 100,000
Training for Costa Rican scientists	$ 120,000
Payment to the University of Costa Rica for extracting samples	$ 80,000
Equipment for chemical extraction at the University of Costa Rica	$ 135,000
Salaries for chemists, laboratory assistants, etc.	$ 100,000
Contribution to parataxonomists' work on the national biodiversity inventory	$ 60,000
Automobiles, fuel, oil, laboratory supplies, field supplies, per diem expenses, etc. for collectors	$ 120,000
Equipment for the Biodiversity Inventory— hardware, cabinets, solvents, computers, etc.	$ 285,000
Administration and overhead	$ 135,000
TOTAL:	$1,135,000

Source: Sittenfeld, 1992

tors? At Bristol-Myers Squibb and SmithKline Beecham, for example, researchers consider it unlikely that they could come up with a million dollars for a collection program in the first place. Even if they could, many would rather receive samples from geographically diverse collectors than spend their entire collections budget in one place. With numerous collectors agreeing to payment by sample and royalty provisions alone, holding out for significant advance payments like the one INBio received from Merck might prove difficult. Then too, the odds of commercializing compounds from any one biological sample are so low that few collectors can expect to receive advance payments from companies looking to minimize their risk.

However, royalties, rather than advance payments, have become the rallying point for many who question the equity of company-collector contracts and the rights of collectors to sell the samples they collect.[6] Jack Kloppenburg, a rural sociologist at the University of Wisconsin in Madison, considers the 5-percent royalty he believes Merck will pay should a drug be developed from INBio's collections "meager." Other observers have suggested that INBio's true royalty is closer to 40 percent, and still others say 1 to 3 percent. (Kloppenburg and Rodriguez, 1992; *Nature*, 1992). The size of the INBio-Merck royalty has never been publicly confirmed, however, and neither have the royalties built into contracts between other collectors and companies. But standard industry practices in related areas can provide a rough sense of the range of possibilities. *(See Box IV.4.)*

Royalties are based on net sales and depend upon the parties' relative risks and contributions to the development of the final product. Generally, the larger the advance and up-front payments a party receives, the smaller its share in the royalty.

Collectors come in on the low end (early research phase) of the royalty range. Although royalties can be structured to reflect the

---

Box IV.4. Typical Royalty Rates By Product Category

Product category supplied	*Percentage of revenue to supplier*
Early research	1–5%
Pre/clinical data	5–10%
Identified product/efficacy data	10–15%

Source: Harvard Business School Case Study, 1992.

closeness of the relationship between the final drug and the material and information provided by a collector to a company, most companies and collectors favor using a simpler average (1 to 3 percent for any derived product), which requires less legal counsel to agree upon and poses less potential for conflict. Some contracts provide for two levels of royalties—higher if the final drug is sold as it comes out of the plant, lower should modifications prove necessary (Balick, NYBG, pers. comm., 1992).

A royalty reflects the value of the biological and intellectual information provided by a collector, balanced by the relative amount of intellectual and financial investment a company must make to develop a useful product. For example, a soil sample usually receives less in royalties than a plant sample because microbiologists must isolate dozens or hundreds of organisms contained in the soil, culture them, and then test the extracts (Cragg, NCI, pers. comm., 1992). Royalties might be higher (closer to 5 percent) if ethnobotanical data supplied by the collector provides a direct clue for laboratory researchers.

Even in the best of relationships, monitoring is needed to ensure that the agreed-upon royalty payments are made—a common practice in the pharmaceutical industry. INBio codes samples sent to Merck & Co. which, in turn, maintains an extensive database that links all potential drug compounds with their sources. Another incentive for companies to live up to their side of a supply contract has been suggested: those that renege on agreements with suppliers or misrepresent the origin of commercial compounds may jeopardize their patents on new compounds.

The tendency to overstate the importance of genetic and biochemical collections to companies' R&D programs and, hence, to demand large royalties has incensed some in industry. As Richard Godown of the Industrial Biotechnology Association, which represents 80 percent of the biotech companies in the United States, put it: "It's as though you buy wool from a sheep farmer and then he insists on a 50-percent share in the price of the Gobelin tapestry you wove from it. It's not free enterprise, and it's a lousy deal however you look at it" (Browning, 1992).

112

Royalties have only recently been included in collecting contracts, despite obvious resistance by some in industry. As they gain in importance, it is useful to trace the path by which collectors return a portion of royalties to source countries, conservation programs, and local peoples who contribute to the collection effort. NCI, for instance, now signs a letter of intent with in-country collaborators stating that it will "make its best effort to negotiate with the company [that develops and commercializes a compound from the collection] for inclusion of terms in the licensing agreement requiring payment of a percentage of royalties accruing from sales of the drug" to the in-country collector institution (NCI, 1992, p.3). A collector signing a contractual agreement directly with a company seeking samples can usually expect a royalty and the discretion to determine who in the collecting country gets a share of the funds. In most cases, no legal side agreement is made between the collector and its in-country collaborators, though most collectors agree to "negotiate in good faith."

The New York Botanical Garden is developing a policy to set and apportion a percentage of royalties to in-country collaborators (Balick, NYBG, pers. comm., 1992). The Royal Botanic Gardens Kew (RBG) states in its *Memorandum of Understanding*, that "any net profits derived by RBG from...collaboration will be shared equally between RBG and the Supplier" (Royal Botanic Gardens Kew, 1992). Biotics' contracts with in-country collectors also earmarks 50 percent of Biotics' royalty for in-country collaborators (Thomas, Biotics Ltd., pers. comm., 1992).

As of late 1992, the University of Illinois has a written intention to return 10 to 50 percent of any royalty to in-country collaborators. It also encourages its contracting companies to sign third-party agreements directly with local collectors and pledges to "make its best effort" to negotiate with companies for additional royalties for the country of collection. When working with NCI, Illinois relies on the NCI Letter of Intent for guidance, but its policy for industry collaborations is determined case by case (Soejarto, University of Illinois, pers. comm., 1993).

The Missouri Botanical Garden eschews royalties. As a private scientific non-profit institution, Missouri finds it inappropriate to negotiate or distribute royalties. It "wants to be on the highest possible moral ground" and to thus avoid compromising other research activities it considers far more important than commercial collections (Lowry, Missouri Botanical Garden, pers. comm., 1992). Like the University of Illinois, the Missouri Botanical Garden recommends that companies work out royalty agreements directly with institutions in the countries providing samples.

Collectors hope that revenues received by in-country collaborators will be used to build institutional infrastructure, support conservation projects, compensate for the use of traditional knowledge, and benefit local forest communities, but specific stipulations rarely exist.

Non-Monetary Compensation and Technology Transfer

Advance payments and royalties are only part of a package of potential benefits that biologically rich countries can receive through contractual agreements with commercial or non-profit collectors and through the relationships expressed in these agreements. Non-monetary forms of compensation,[7] most of which could not be bought at will, can include: provision of health care and medicine, education and related material, training in collection and specimen-identification techniques, screening and other aspects of drug discovery, sharing of lab results, opportunities to be co-authors of publications, herbarium specimens for national and local herbaria, contributions to institutional infrastructure, development of field guides and databases, field equipment, botanical literature, academic exchanges, research exchanges with contracting companies, research on source-country diseases, and the distribution of drugs at cost in countries of collection. *(See Chapter V.)*

Many of these non-monetary benefits grow out of the more informal relationships between collectors and in-country collaborators and so may not be explicitly defined in a legal contract between collectors and companies. As a result, the most immediate non-monetary gains for countries of collection tend to be in sciences and institution-building related to collectors' objectives.

114

This is not surprising, given the typical objectives of collecting institutions: to "increase the knowledge and capacity to obtain information about plants, particularly from tropical regions" (Lowry, Missouri Botanical Garden, pers. comm., 1992), "discover leads for drug development" (Soejarto, University of Illinois, pers. comm., 1992), or collect and broker samples for profit (Biotics, 1992).

However, some non-monetary benefits can be included in collecting contracts; the Draft Contract featured in Annex 2 includes provisions for scientific collaborations and exchanges, research on developing country diseases, and the sharing of lab results.

Screening for tropical diseases

Companies looking for biological samples generally concentrate their research on particular diseases and rarely have screens for diseases found only in the tropics. At present, few companies are likely to bear the heavy expense of developing a screen (which requires basic research to determine a biochemical target) merely to get biological samples. Collectors could, however, negotiate to retain a portion of the samples collected with funds from the collector-company agreement to be used for screening for tropical diseases.

Research exchanges and support

Through research exchanges and advance payments that include technology transfer, a developing-country laboratory can tap contracting companies' expertise to build up its in-house skills in drug development. Shaman Pharmaceuticals, Inc., collaborates with research laboratories throughout the tropics, including the University of Nigeria at Nsukka and the Medicinal Plants Research Center in Mexico. Such collaboration between industry scientists and developing-country researchers benefits both parties and thus helps ensure a project's long-term success. As Lynn Caporale of Merck said of its relationship with INBio, "This is not something we have to do for the developing world. There are trained scientists there who need resources so they can do this for themselves.

115

We see potential partnerships as true collaborations and we do not see Costa Rica becoming dependent on this collaboration to move forward" (Caporale, 1992).

Distribution of drugs

Like disease screening, the distribution of drugs at cost in the country of collection is a provision industry is unlikely to accept. Merck & Co., Inc. has been praised in the press for distributing Mectizan in Africa for the treatment of river blindness.[8] But Mectizan is used as an animal anti-parasitic so the manufacturing capacity is already in place, the dose is small and inexpensive to ship, and Merck receives tax incentives for its donation (Harvard Business School Case Study, 1992; WSJ, 1992). The free distribution of most other drugs would be far more difficult and expensive.

Some firms have discounted drug prices in exchange for access to markets, such as HMOs or countries like Mexico with rapidly rising demands for pharmaceuticals. But few developing countries would qualify under these terms, and drugs distributed to developing countries at cost could potentially wind up in the black market. But source countries should have easy and affordable access to drugs developed from their genetic and biochemical resources, and contractual agreements can stipulate that companies license to the collector or their collaborators the right to manufacture a drug for use in that country.

From an equity standpoint, these and other non-monetary forms of compensation seem a minimal *quid pro quo* for collectors' collaboration with industry. By their nature, however, contractual agreements can provide only limited direct benefits outside of the intended purpose of the agreement and can reflect only what each party feels it can offer. A company-collector contract represents the parties' mutual understanding of the market value of the products, service and consideration exchanged. Collectors who are dissatisfied with the terms to which companies will agree and with the value placed on their products or services must look outside the limits of contractual agreements to national or international law and policy.

116

Future Supplies of Raw Material

Collector-company contracts often require companies to look in the country where the sample originated for the raw materials needed to manufacture a drug before looking elsewhere. Further, companies must under such contracts obtain these materials through the collector or a subcontractor of the collector, and doing so on a continuing basis is generally seen as a constructive way to generate income for developing countries and, in some cases, to promote conservation.

NCI's Letter of Intent has extended this concept. If a company licensing a drug does not wish to use source-country raw materials, or if the collector or its suppliers "cannot provide adequate amounts of raw materials, the licensee [company] will be required to pay the collector an amount of money (to be negotiated) to be used for expenses associated with cultivation of medicinal plant species that are endangered by deforestation, or for other appropriate conservation measures" (National Cancer Institute, 1992). But is the cultivation of medicinal plant species, even those endangered by habitat destruction, necessarily a significant conservation measure? Is supplying raw materials to developed countries a positive development activity? Indeed, are monocultures of medicinal plants any different from cash crops of bananas and coffee? And what happens when the task of "sustainably" producing supplies of raw materials falls to governmental or other agencies with poor track records in monitoring natural resource use or to countries where medicinal plants already are harvested nearly to extinction? These questions require attention.

Although source-country provisions like that of the NCI Letter of Intent and Shaman Pharmaceutical's commitment to drawing two-thirds of its raw materials from a "primary raw material supplier" seem to represent a genuine effort to transfer funds from industry to conservation and local development, other companies are less receptive to this concept. "Given the number of patients involved and the large development cost, it is unrealistic to expect a company to agree to one location for the future supply of a billion-dollar-a-year drug," said Lynn Caporale of Merck. "If there's only

117

one source of a drug, then a natural disaster could put at risk not only the company's profits but an important life-saving drug" (Caporale, Merck, pers. comm., 1992). Gordon Svoboda's description of Eli Lilly's search for *Catharanthus roseus* (over 1,000 tons of which are used in the United States every year for the manufacture of vincristine and vinblastine) reflects a similar viewpoint:

"My original crude drug came from India, followed by the Philippines, Australia next and finally Madagascar, plantations being established therein by the French. The crude drug happened to be of the highest quality which we had received to date. The natives eventually became restless, threw the French out, and took over the plantations. Drug quality became questionable, supply deliveries unreliable. This could not be tolerated: lives were at stake. So, Texas became our source of supply and still is. The cost factors of labor and farmland were overcome by the use of proper planting and fertilizing methods, along with harvesting mechanization. I hasten to add that in each case Lilly paid for all supplies received, thereby contributing to the economy of the country of origin." (Svoboda, Eli Lilly, pers. comm. 1992).

Additionally, the development and implementation of well-managed sourcing strategies for raw materials can prove difficult. For over a decade, E. Merck Company of Darmstadt, Germany has struggled to acquire reliable supplies of pilocarpine from the domesticated shrub jaborandi.[9] Jaborandi with a pilocarpine content warranting industrialization is known to occur only in Amazonian Brazil, but due to logging, slash-and-burn farming, and the over-harvesting of selected species, it is becoming a scarce commodity. E. Merck has tried to domesticate jaborandi with "interesting" pilocarpine content for over ten years and, as they have said, "This was by no means an easy task!" They will harvest their first commercial crop from 3,000,000 bushes planted in the Brazilian state of Maranhão in 1992 (E. Merck Industries, 1992; Elisabetsky, Federal University of Rio Grande do Sul, Brazil, pers. comm., 1992).

In general, the need for reliable supplies makes the prospect of synthesizing commercial compounds in the lab more appealing than that of culling them from the wild. But, eventually, the ex-

118

pense of synthesis must be balanced against that of obtaining raw materials. Of the 119 plant-derived drugs on the market today, fewer than a dozen are synthesized commercially or produced by simple chemical modification of the active chemicals; the rest are extracted and purified directly from plants (Farnsworth, 1990).

Collectors and source countries can take advantage of this demand and in doing so build up in-country expertise and agricultural research institutions. Negotiating for contract provisions may not always be the best way to do it, however, since companies may be reluctant to agree to provisions stipulating the source of raw materials. Moreover, if a collector is receiving royalties from a company, the most efficient sourcing strategies are in the collector's best interest; in some cases, the collector could lose in royalties what it makes from sourcing. "Instead of paying people to grow the rosy periwinkle, the countries and collecting organizations can train scientists," said Lynn Caporale of Merck (Caporale, Merck, pers. comm., 1992).

Traditional Knowledge and Rights of Local Peoples

Ethnobotanical Data and Industry Research Programs

Communities living in or around biodiversity-rich areas possess a wealth of accumulated knowledge that has played a significant role in drug discovery and development.[10] Norman Farnsworth of the University of Illinois at Chicago's Program for Collaborative Research in the Pharmaceutical Sciences estimates that at least three-fourths of the plant-derived drugs in use today were identified by chemists investigating plants used in traditional herbal medicine (Farnsworth, 1990). Accordingly, Michael Balick, Director of the New York Botanical Garden's Institute of Economic Botany, supports the use of what he calls the "ethnobotanical filter" of indigenous knowledge as a starting point in the search for new drugs. A preliminary test of plants Balick collected in Honduras and Belize for an NCI *in vitro* anti-HIV screen showed that of 18 species collected randomly only 6 percent showed activity, compared to 25 percent of the 20 ethnobotanically collected species (Balick, 1990).

119

Paul Cox of the Department of Botany and Range Science at Brigham Young University found that 86 percent of the plant species used in Samoan traditional medicine showed pharmacological activity in broad *in vitro* and *in vivo* screens (Cox, 1989).[11]

Some companies and non-profit institutions are acting on findings like those of Balick and Cox. Many companies, such as Merck and Co., Inc., SmithKline Beecham, Glaxo, Bristol-Myers Squibb, and the NCI collection often receive ethnobotanical data with samples. Biotics, which supplies ethnobotanical data to SmithKline Beecham, collects "common knowledge" from markets or provides SmithKline with the results of literature searches on natural products databases. The University of Illinois at Chicago provides detailed ethnobotanical information to companies through its database NAPRALERT, and, as with the Missouri and the New York Botanical Gardens, provides the NCI with ethnobotanical data on the samples they collect. At a March 1991 workshop organized by NCI and three other U.S. agencies, participants recommended that "an immediate priority need is for the completion of species and traditional-knowledge inventories, which should include information dissemination. These inventories need to be developed using electronic databases with wide access" (Schweitzer et al., 1991). Further proof of the potential economic viability of pharmaceutical R&D into traditional medicine can be found in the $42 million raised by Shaman Pharmaceuticals when they went public in January, 1993 (S. King, Shaman Pharm., pers. comm., 1993).

Still, the pharmaceutical industry as a whole remains to be convinced of the primary value of ethnobotanical data. Although many companies review ethnobotanical literature and data collected for their screening programs once an interesting compound has been isolated, initial research based on receptor and enzyme screens is so specific that companies do not generally find ethnobotanical data to be particularly relevant at that stage. Also, some in industry believe that while traditional medicine may lead researchers to bioactive compounds, the health problems they are used to treat are of limited interest to pharmaceutical companies or have existing, more effective treatments in industrial-country medicine.

120

Collectors' Obligations to Local Communities

Many of the cultures from which traditional knowledge is collected are more endangered than the ecosystems in which they reside. When their local knowledge and information is published or supplied to databases, industry, or the general public, a unique opportunity exists for these communities to receive economic or nonmonetary benefits from its use. If this opportunity is missed, their knowledge, once published, becomes part of the public domain and no longer their own to monitor and control. Yet, ethnobotanical information is often recorded without fully explaining to communities how it will be used or how local rights to control its use might be affected. Similarly, biological samples are sometimes collected from indigenous reserves without local communities' full consent (McGowan, Cultural Survival, pers. comm., 1992).

Recognizing this problem, the Kuna Indians in Panama have initiated a program to manage their forest reserve and the activities of visiting scientists. Program guidelines call for such benefits as copies of reports in Spanish, photographic materials, plant and animal specimens, training of Kuna researchers, and hiring of Kuna guides and informants (*Cultural Survival Quarterly*, 1991). But the Kuna are unique in their enterprise, and in most places the collector will bear the responsibility of equitably sharing benefits with collaborating communities.

As A.B. Cunningham points out in *Brokers, Botanists and Biodiversity*, "Researchers work at the interface between the social and biological sciences and at the interface between traditional and urban-industrial cultures. To obtain data, these researchers often place themselves in a position of trust, recording information which may [otherwise] be shielded from non-specialists within that community by initiation rites and taboos" (Cunningham, 1992). Most collectors return a percentage of royalties from all collections, including ethnobotanical, to their in-country collaborators, who are then responsible for returning some portion of these funds to communities that contributed their knowledge and expertise. But rarely are the details of this arrangement worked out ahead of time or local communities asked what they want as payment.

Few collecting institutions have detailed policies regarding sample collection and the allocation of benefits to and within countries of origin, and few have a formal institutional process for determining that policy. These institutions seem to rely on academic traditions to guide them, and advances in this field have often outstripped their ability to deal with resulting ethical and process considerations. But these traditions may now be changing. Staff at many of these institutions have established committees to debate the ethical and practical issues related to plant collection and to develop institutional policy.

The Return of Benefits to Local People

The return of benefits to local communities involves difficult decisions about the nature and proper recipients of the benefits. How does a collector determine the recipients of monetary and non-monetary benefits within a region where medicinal plants are widely and similarly used or where appropriate recipient individuals or groups within communities are difficult to determine?[12] What is the most effective form of compensation? Monetary payments for information might encourage respondents to provide "nonsense" answers (Cunningham, 1992). Should compensation thus take the form of education and training, health care, or the sharing of lab results and publications? Do these benefits answer communities' needs and desires?

A comprehensive policy for compensating communities for their intellectual property would be difficult to achieve (and probably unworkable). The scope of most professional collector society principles and codes of ethics tends to be general (and thus removed from practical application) in order to address the many and varied experiences of their members. But compensation policy can be determined by collectors case by case. Based on his experience, Cunningham suggests that collectors provide regional non-governmental organizations with legal resources, primary health care, medicinal plant nurseries for overexploited or endangered species, or educational bursaries (Cunningham, 1991). The New York Botanical Garden's Belize Ethnobotany Project has supported the Belize Association of Traditional Healers, and Shaman

Pharmaceuticals works with indigenous organizations on the sustainable production of forest products, providing multi-lingual publications and health care (King, Shaman Pharmaceuticals, Inc., pers. comm., 1993).

Region-specific relationships such as these can be built into contracts without waiting for legislation creating new intellectual property rights. In contracts between collectors and companies, suppliers and keepers of traditional knowledge can be named as collaborators. Alternatively, collectors can sign side agreements with communities (as described in Appendix C of the Draft Contract) outlining the company-collector relationship, the communities' role in collection, and the benefits that will accrue should a product be developed from traditional knowledge. Even where formal legal agreements may not be appropriate—as in many communities without access to legal and technical expertise—collectors should still clearly specify beneficiaries in written institutional policy before any ethnobotanical information is published or supplied to databases or companies.

As a prerequisite for any system in which local people will be compensated for biological or genetic materials removed from their lands, these communities must have rights to the land and its resources. As Steve Tullberg of the Indian Law Resource Center has warned, if communities do not own the natural resources on their lands (as is often the case in developing countries) or if the national law does not recognize such communities' right to make contracts and take legal action on their own behalf, contracts may "help the North-South flow of funds, but will not help the Indians" (Tullberg, Indian Law Resource Center, pers. comm., 1992).

Conservation Provisions

The creation of incentives for conserving biodiversity is often valued as a significant product of contracts between industry and collectors for the supply of biological samples. Through fees for samples, advance payments, and royalty payments, these agreements can generate direct income for conservation-related science (such as ethnobotany, inventories, or curatorial work); applied conservation programs with local communities; or park-management programs. Once formulated, contracts also constitute hard proof to policy-makers and debt-burdened governments in developing countries that, over time, low-impact uses of standing forests can pay higher dividends than, say, cattle ranching or uncontrolled logging.

Most existing contractual agreements between companies and collectors, however, include few explicit provisions for the conservation of biodiversity. Instead, companies rely on the mandate of their collectors to address the conservation implications of their agreements. From the collectors' perspective, however, contract provisions for applying funds to conservation programs may further several interests. While not publicly available, contracts are circulated to government officials and described to the press and general public. A conservation provision provides a guarantee, often sought by individuals in countries of collection, that funds are being generated for stated conservation and development objectives. Such a provision also insures that down the road ten years (the estimated minimum time required for a drug to hit the market), funds earmarked for conservation will not be applied elsewhere.

If not contained within a contract, collectors' conservation objectives can be written into institutional policies. Such a policy could specify, for instance, that 40 percent of all royalties would go to the collecting institutions for their scientific research and infrastructure, 30 percent (perhaps targeted to scientific training and education) to collaborating collectors and indigenous communities that supply ethnobotanical data, 20 percent to conservation programs in the collecting areas, and 10 percent to health care and community-development work in such areas. This sort of breakdown should be determined case by case, and the decision-making process should involve local organizations working in conservation, development, and health care.

Even if detailed provisions are made for conservation programs, however, questions about collectors' working definition of conservation will arise. While national inventories, scientific training, and the building of botanical institutions' infrastructure contribute significantly to conservation programs in developing countries, they represent the vision of only one category of conservation professional. As Jack Kloppenburg of the University of Wisconsin said of INBio: "even if (the) intent is to foster sustainable development, the problem is that contractual income would be channelled to the support of INBio's concept of sustainable development" (Kloppenburg, 1992).

Modifications in governmental policy as a result of company-collector agreements can help conserve a country's biodiversity and scientific research funded through collecting agreements is obviously a key component of any conservation program. But translating collector-company contractual relationships into critical conservation incentives for rural communities in and around forested areas has proved difficult. It is when benefits from the commercialization of biodiversity are captured by a range of communities within a country, including rural people as well as scientific and governmental institutions, that contracts will most effectively contribute to conservation.

Conclusion

Contracts between companies and collectors reflect well-defined relationships based on an agreement to exchange and screen samples for the commercialization of natural products. Alone, they cannot produce new leads for drug discovery, provide for complete national inventories of biodiversity, guarantee scientific research and training, provide incentives for conservation, increase the use of traditional knowledge in drug discovery, vertically integrate a pharmaceutical industry in a developing country, or ensure the equitable distribution of benefits to all affected parties. Although contracts can significantly contribute to all of these goals, many will be achieved only in conjunction with fundamental changes in international and national law and policy.

As an increasing number of companies become involved in natural products research, the demand for samples is increasing, and with it the prospects for unrestrained and inequitable collection of biological samples. Not only can contracts between collectors and companies guarantee firms a well-identified, reliable supply of samples; they can also provide a framework for ensuring that significant immediate and long-term benefits accrue to collectors and countries of collection.

Notes

1. This chapter is based largely on conversations, interviews, and written correspondence with the following individuals: **Michael Balick**, Institute of Economic Botany of The New York Botanical Garden; **Bradley Bennett**, Institute of Economic Botany, New York Botanical Garden; **Jorge Caillaux**, Sociedad Peruana de Derecho Ambiental; **Lynn Caporale**, Merck, Sharp & Dohme Research Laboratories; **Gordon Cragg**, National Cancer Institute; **Afranio Craveiro**, Laboratory of Natural Products, Federal University of Ceara, Brazil; **Douglas Daly**, The New York Botanical Garden; **John Devlin**, R&D Administration, Boehringer-Ingelheim; **B.N. Dhawan**, Central Drug Research Institute, Lucknow, India; **Donald Duvick**, Former V.P. for Research, Pioneer Hybrid; **Elaine Elisabetsky**, Federal University of Rio Grande do Sul, Brazil; **Linda Fellows**, Biochemistry Section, Royal Botanic Gardens Kew; **Pradhavathi Fernandes**, Microbial Molecular Biology and Natural Products Research, Bristol-Myers Squibb Pharmaceutical Research Institute; **Dan Harder**, Missouri Botanical Garden; **Christopher Joyce**, Washington, D.C.; **Joseph Kelly**, Sociedad Peruana de Derecho Ambiental, Peru; **Steven King**, Shaman Pharmaceuticals, Inc.; **William Lesser**, Cornell University; **Peter Lowry**, Missouri Botanical Garden; **Janet McGowan**, Cultural Survival; **German Sarmiento**, Fundacion Para La Defensa del Interres Publico (FUNDEPUBLICO), Bogotá, Colombia; **Claudine Schneider**, Artemis Project; **David R. Simpson**, Resources for the Future; **Ana Sittenfeld**, Instituto Nacional de Biodiversidad (INBio), Costa Rica; **Doel Soejarto**, University of Illinois at Chicago; **Yuri Stercho**, SmithKline Beecham; **Gordon Svoboda**; **Robert Thomas**, Biotics Limited; **Steven Tullberg**, Indian Law Resource Center; **Varro Tyler**, Purdue University; **Renata Villers,** Instituto Nacional de Biodiversidad (INBio), Costa Rica; **John Westley**, SmithKline Beecham; and **Chris Wille** and **Diane Jukofsky**, Tropical Conservation Newsbureau, Rainforest Alliance, Costa Rica.

2. Collecting-related issues are generally the same for biotechnology and pharmaceutical companies, and there is a significant overlap between their research programs. As Donald Duvick of Iowa State University said, "...surely every pharmaceutical company has a strong biotech department by this time. Of course, boutique biotech companies likely cannot do pharmaceuticals, but the boutiques are very thin on the ground, nowadays" (Duvick, pers. comm., 1992).

3. Despite any underlying awareness of conservation and development issues, company investments in biodiversity-rich regions are coming out of R&D budgets, not philanthropic foundations. Indeed, company foundations are legally prohibited as non-profit institutions from supporting projects that would benefit the company.

4. The complexities of industry-collector relationships, and the minefield of issues raised by them, argue against companies' participation in plant-collecting programs just to offset widespread criticism of their pricing and patent policies.

5. Advance payments support an agreed upon workplan and are applied to operations costs and conservation "overhead." They differ from "up front" payments, which—in agreements between small biotech firms and pharmaceutical companies, for example— are paid *prior* to the initiation of the workplan to recover the expense of work already carried out by the biotech company.

6. *See* Article 6 of the Draft Contract.

7. *See* Articles 5, 6, and 7 of the Draft Contract.

8. Mectizan, incidentally, is based on a microorganism that was found on a golf course in Japan.

9. E. Merck Co., based in Germany, is not affiliated with Merck and Co., Inc., based in the United States.

10. *See* Articles 6 and 8, and Appendix C of the Draft Contract.

11. With an average range of 8–15 percent for positive hit rates at the first level of random screening, these are impressive figures.

12. Brad Bennett describes the difficulty of assigning ownership when communities have exchanged germplasm and ethnobotanical lore for centuries: "The Quijos Quichua name *chiri caspi* (*Brunfelsia grandiflora*) becomes *chini kiasip* in Shuar. Both groups use the plant similarly. The Canelos Quichua probably served as the mediators between the Quijos and Shuar. Who then should be compensated for

a drug discovery based on this plant—the Canelos, the Quijos, or the Shuar? Or all of them?" (Bennett, pers. comm., 1992). Shaman Pharmaceuticals recently received the written consent of no less than 120 delegates of the Aguaruna Indian Federation in Peru for a collaboration involving the sourcing of a promising product.

Bibliography

Asian Symposium on Medicinal Plants, Spiced and Other Natural Products (ASOMPS VII). February, 1992. *Manila Declaration.* Manila, Philippines.

Balick, Michael. 1990. Ethnobotany and the identification of therapeutic agents from the rainforest. Pp. 22–39 *in*: Chadwick, D.J.; Marsh, J. (ed.) *Bioactive Compounds from Plants.* John Wiley and Sons, New York, N.Y.

Biotics Limited. 1992. Phytochemical Training Courses. Unpublished manuscript, June, Sussex, U.K.

Browning, Graeme. 1992. Biodiversity battle. *National Journal* 24(32):1827–1830.

Business and the Environment. 1991. Merck Deal with Costa Rica's INBio Offers Model for Future. 2(21)(8 November):1–3.

Caporale, Lynn. 1992. The Merck/INBio Agreement; A Pharmaceutical Company Perspective. Paper presented at the Rainforest Alliance *Tropical Forest Medical Resources and the Conservation of Biodiversity* symposium, New York, January 1992.

Cox, Paul Alan. 1990. Ethnopharmacology and the search for new drugs. Pp. 40–55 *in*: Chadwick, D.J.; Marsh, J. (ed.) *Bioactive Compounds from Plants.* John Wiley and Sons, New York, N.Y.

Cultural Survival Quarterly. 1991. How the Kuna Keep Scientists in Line. Summer:17.

Cunningham,. A.B. 1991. Indigenous Knowledge and Biodiversity. *Cultural Survival Quarterly.* Summer 1991: 4–8.

Cunningham, A.B. 1992. Botanists, Brokers and Biodiversity. Paper prepared, in conjunction with the WWF-International "People and Plants" programme, for the International Society of Ethnobiology Congress, Mexico City, 10–14 November, 1992.

DiMasi, J. and R. Hansen, H. Grabowski, and L. Lasagna. 1991. The cost of innovation in the pharmaceutical industry. *Journal of Health Economics.* 10:107–142.

E. Merck Industries. 1992. Pilocarpine: Activities of E. Merck in Brazil. Darmstadt, Germany.

Farnsworth, Norman. 1990. The role of ethnopharmacology in drug development. Pp. 2–21 *in*: Chadwick, D.J.; Marsh, J. (ed.) *Bioactive Compounds from Plants*. John Wiley and Sons, New York, N.Y.

Glaxo Group Research Ltd. 1992. Policy for the Acquisition of Plant Materials, Greenford, Middlesex, U.K.

Harvard Business School Case Study. 1992. A case on the Merck/INBio joint venture. Harvard Business School, Boston, MA.

Kloppenburg, Jack, and Silva Rodriguez. 1992. Conservationists or Corsairs? *Seedling* 9(2–3): 12–17.

McChesney, James. 1992. Biological Diversity, Chemical Diversity and the Search for New Pharmaceuticals. Paper presented at the Rainforest Alliance *Tropical Forest Medical Resources and the Conservation of Biodiversity* symposium, January 1992.

National Cancer Institute. 1992. The Letter of Intent and Material Transfer Agreement, Frederick, Maryland.

Nature. 1992. If biological diversity has a price, who sets it and who should benefit? 359(6396):565.

Royal Botanic Gardens Kew. 1992. Memorandum of Understanding; Conditions of acceptance of plant material from external collaborators for collaborative studies in the Biochemistry Section of the Royal Botanic Gardens Kew.

Schweitzer, J., F. Gray Handley, J. Edwards, W. Franklin Harris, M. Grever, S. Schepartz, G. Cragg, K. Snader, and A. Bhat. Summary of the workshop on drug development, biological diversity, and economic growth. *Journal of the National Cancer Institute* 83:1294–1298.

SCRIP World Pharmaceutical News. 1992. Redistributing discovery's profits—the Schwartz commentary. No. 1733 (8 July): 15–16.

Sherblom, James. 1991. Ours, Theirs or Both? Strategic Planning and Deal Making. Pp. 213–224 *in*: Dana Ono (ed.) *The Business of Biotechnology: From the Bench to the Street*. Butterworth and Heinemann, Stoneham, MA.

Sittenfeld, Ana. 1992. Tropical Medicinal Plant Conservation and Development Projects: the Case of the Costa Rican National Institute of Biodiversity (INBio). Paper presented at the Rainforest Alliance *Tropical Forest Medical Resources and the Conservation of Biodiversity* symposium, New York, N.Y., January 1992.

Vromen, Galina. 1992. Europe drug firms say bio-diversity pact harmless. Reuters News Service, London, June 22.

The Wall Street Journal. 1992. Merck's `River Blindness' Gift Hits Snags. 23 September.

The Wall Street Journal. 1992. Eli Lilly & Co. Investing in Rain Forest Research. 23 October:B1 & B7.

Williston on Contracts. 1957. 3rd ed. edited by Walter H.E. Jaeger. Baker Voorhis & Co., Inc.

V.

RESEARCH MANAGEMENT POLICIES: PERMITS FOR COLLECTING AND RESEARCH IN THE TROPICS

Daniel H. Janzen, Winnie Hallwachs, Rodrigo Gámez,
Ana Sittenfeld, Jorge Jimenez

Countries reap benefits from their wildland biodiversity, but they also pay both direct management and opportunity costs to maintain it. Field research can yield major benefits, and a national system of permits for field research helps allocate both these benefits and research costs within and between countries. Such a system also helps insure that research does not destroy its own raw materials.

Properly designed, research permits can facilitate the work of *both* the wildland custodian and the researcher. They also influence inter-institutional relations. To the extent that they determine researchers' and managers' time budgets and opportunities, they can also prompt researchers to choose one country or part of a country instead of another to work in. This choice, in turn, influences the overall advance of scientific and managerial understanding, nationally and internationally.

With so much at stake, the traditional view of the raw materials used in research on tropical wildland biodiversity—whether data, samples, or specimens—as "free goods" must be abandoned, and permit guidelines expanded to cover ecotourists, school groups, private collectors, taxonomists, collectors for pharmaceutical and biotechnology research, wildland managers, national developers, and many other kinds of users. In one sense, all of these people are participating in biodiversity prospecting, so the term "research agreements" as used here includes collecting permits but also covers other inter-related management activities and other non-destructive uses of wildlands and their biodiversity.

Traditionally, permits for research on biodiversity information have been granted on the basis of cost-benefit analyses, whether implicit or explicit. But collecting permits, research regulations, hunting licenses, tourism concessions, export permits, export taxes, national patents, and the like have tended to minimize either the costs or the benefits of a given research (or sampling) program. If society is to fully realize the benefits of wildland biodiversity, a full accounting of both costs and benefits is essential, and the potential value of wildland research must be considered in conjunction with the direct impact of that research on the organisms of a conserved wildland.

In response to this need, the structure of research agreements is rapidly evolving. "Codes of ethics" for tropical gene collectors, ethnobotanists, phytochemical samplers, etc., rest on philosophical positions and traditions that have been made largely obsolete by recent international agreements, advances in biodiversity technology, changes in our understanding of biodiversity information (or products), and new development policies in tropical countries. A simple lack of research experience throughout the tropics also all but guarantees that current guidelines will be interim guidelines only. In fact, major groups of wildlands users still largely ignore research permits, and beneficial collaboration among wildland managers, researchers, collectors, and other users is in its infancy.

At the same time, the basic concepts and rules governing biodiversity prospecting are changing extremely rapidly. For example, the simple recognition that traditional taxonomy is biotechnology "know how"—that, for instance a field guide to the moths of Costa Rica can be an essential tool for the biodiversity prospector—will give taxonomists more power when research contracts and permits are negotiated. This phenomenon is directly reflected in the recent funding of INBio's inventory process as a national development activity by bilateral aid agencies. Equally disruptive to the "balance of power" in the wildland biodiversity marketplace is the recognition that all tropical lands and climates are suitable for agriculture if biotechnologists put their minds to generating crop plants and technologies for them. With all tropical wildlands thus becoming potential agricultural zones, wildlands conserved for their biodiversity (and other) products must produce even more and their production must be valued correctly if biodiversity conservation and managed use are to be viewed as economically legitimate land uses.

Custodians of tropical wildlands must understand the basic issues and general principles behind the concept of the biodiversity research agreement and use them for guidance. In today's dynamic environment, specific collecting recipes or "codes" may be of little use. The guidelines presented here do not dwell on specific legislation either, because each country's approach to law and law-making differs. How relevant various countries find the Costa Rican experience distilled here also depends on which kinds of research, researchers, and users of research results are involved.

Key Considerations in Granting Wildland Biodiversity Research Agreements

Whether individual contracts, government regulations, or laws, research agreements can have a bewildering array of primary and secondary repercussions on current wildland management, academic collecting and research, commercial collecting and research, and financing for all three. Such agreements will produce significant new responsibilities and power shifts in the countries rich in wildland biodiversity, as well as create ample opportunities for corruption. The social consequences won't be the same in every country; rather they will be experienced as part of the broader changes now sweeping through the centuries-old relationships between "developed" and "under-developed" countries. Here, we consider some aspects of research agreements. *(See Box V.1.)*

1) Collecting Permit vs. Research Agreement

The word "permit" or "collecting permit" should be eliminated from the research management vocabulary and replaced with

Box V.1. Elements of a Biodiversity Research Agreement

At least eight elements should be included in any kind of research agreement between researchers and in-country biodiversity custodians (national park managers on site, national forest services, private reserve owners, national museums, ministries of natural resources, universities, conservation NGOs and other in-country custodians of biodiversity).

1) A clear and unambiguous description of the research itself. The researcher needs to specify:
   a. Who (individuals and institutions, with roles indicated and attached CVs of the individuals);
   b. Where, when, and how;
   c. Why the research is to be conducted;
   d. What kinds of information are to be extracted (recorded, collected, photographed, observed, etc.) and in what format (notes, specimens, photographs, computer entry, human memories, etc.);
   e. What the anticipated intermediate and final destination of this biodiversity information will be;
   f. How the information to be obtained will be used both initially (e.g., in a national inventory collection) and subsequently (e.g., in drug exploration, field guide preparation).

"agreement" or "research agreement." *(See Box V.2.)* The word "agreement" emphasizes the social partnership between the researcher and the custodian and de-emphasizes the "finders-keepers" rule on which "collecting permits" are based.

This need for a shift in thinking has a history. For many years, collecting has been viewed by conservation administrations with suspicion because organisms in protected areas are often damaged or killed during the process. Even if no biological damage occurs, col-

) Copies of the funding proposals (with budget attached) or a description of the funding support if there is no formal proposal.
3) An analysis by the researcher of the foreseen impact on the biology of the subjects of the research and on the habitats in which they occur.
4) A context-dependent evaluation of 1) and 2) above by the custodian of the wildland, including an analysis of why the perturbation is not deemed significant, or alternatively, of what is needed to mitigate the perturbation.
5) A detailed description of the immediate compensation anticipated—whether in cash, barter, services, or specimens—to the wildland custodian.
6) A detailed description of how the wildland custodian is to be compensated over the long-term—whether sharing in future production possibilities from the research, cash royalties, services, equipment or goods.
7) A roster of the in-country entities likely to receive the various compensations spelled out in item 5 above and the legal and logical reasons for such a distribution.
8) Clear protocols that either party can use to break the agreement and a list of the acceptable reasons for breaking it. The court or mechanism for resolving grievances should also be specified.

lecting represents a confusing exception to the "no extraction" ethic generally applied to national parks and other strictly protected areas.

The bigger the object collected, or the more objects collected, the more anguish. However, size, visibility, and number usually have little to do with either conservation importance or economic importance. Context is everything. The collection of the last 100 wild grizzly bears in North America would be far less devastating to the ecosystem than the introduction of ten 1-kg male and female

Box V.2. Collecting Permits are Research Agreements

For two reasons, "collecting permits" should be considered to be "research agreements." First, all collection of ideas, data, and samples is part of some research program. Second, the impact and significance of this research program are of primary interest to society, not the actual act of bagging up a sample or writing down a number. "Collecting" should be evaluated in terms of much more than whether it may lower or raise the population of the target organism or whether the observer may perturb or preserve a fragile ecosystem. Equally important, the "researcher" (as used here) refers to anyone from a schoolchild trampling a rare flower to a collector of samples working for a gene technology company.

We can no longer afford to classify events by who conducted them rather than by their impact on biology and economics. The burning of fire breaks by national park personnel should be scrutinized as carefully and objectively as the harvest of those same plants for a pharmaceutical company.

mongooses to the mainland neotropics. A pocketful of seeds may contain more than 90 percent of the biodiversity information in a plant species; the next ten million seeds collected from that species matter much less. A group of schoolchildren trampling through a scarce habitat may do much more damage than a plant taxonomist taking 100 herbarium specimens.

Collecting can also violate national sovereignty. This form of research, in contrast to the many kinds of observation research, looks like robbery to many wildlife custodians, even if they had no use or plan for the specimens themselves. Accusations of robbery come particularly easily when the custodians are irritated about something else (lack of professional respect, cultural conflict, lack of a budget to pay national park personnel, etc.). The basic problem is viewing research as "collecting" or "taking," rather than as collaboration—a perception that makes it difficult to form normal contractual relationships between custodians and users. Taxonomists, ecologists, chemical prospectors, and others who take samples without a research agreement, and justify their acts on grounds that nobody was using the material, hurt collectors and custodians alike, as well as science and the environment.

Physical samples (genes, tissues, specimens, populations) and the information about them are becoming almost interchangeable. From the standpoint of research management, there is often no reason to distinguish between them. But since collecting generally refers to the accumulation of specimens or samples, the assumption is that a "collecting agreement" covers only the act. In fact, it's often much broader. For example, under one agreement, a caterpillar will be dissected to study its parasites and then discarded. Under another, it may be ground up and screened in a bioassay, and then discarded. In yet another, the caterpillar will be used to establish a permanent tissue culture in a foreign laboratory. Each of these "collections" of a caterpillar generates quite different kinds of biodiversity information, and each has different economic implications for the custodial country. Clearly, a research agreement can cover all these uses and activities, but a collecting permit cannot.

2) Biological Damage vs. Economic Benefits

Every research agreement potentially involves both biological damage and economic benefits (including intellectual and financial gains). Wildland custodians have traditionally been deeply concerned about biological damage by biodiversity researchers. Requests to harvest organisms within national parks for commercial purposes are often evaluated (and frequently rejected) on grounds of perceived biotic damage.

Biodiversity researchers may need nothing more than a few leaves or just the chance to observe wildlands, or they may need so many specimens or such free rein that local extinctions or massive interference result. To get a sense of what the casualties of research might be, national park officers, field station directors, and private owners of conserved wildlands must reach a level of "biodiversity

137

literacy" high enough so they can evaluate biological damage and oversee research on-site. Reciprocating, researchers should foster this technical capability, serve on wildland advisory committees, and become volunteer custodians themselves. Certainly, experience and training will make both conservation area staffs and researchers much more capable of such on-site evaluation.

That said, few custodians or researchers worry much about how to mitigate biological damage or how to realize national benefits from biodiversity research. Wildland custodians rarely analyze the benefits of biodiversity research, and even when they do they focus on such abstractions as "national patrimony" or national pride, or rail about political patronage, contradictory regulations (e.g., a flat rule against commercial harvesting in a national park where tourists and tour companies are allowed to "harvest" information for only a token fee and to trample fragile habitats), or the motives of scientists working in their areas—real enough issues, but by no means the last word on either costs or benefits. Then too, custodians may not have any incentive to clearly identify benefits since doing so may intensify competition for these resources.

A further difficulty is that many benefits are hard to capture. For example, the fees charged by a national park may well go into the national treasury or fall under the control of distant politicians: why then should park staff raise fees or go out of their way to collect them if the parks don't benefit as a result? As a second and quite different example, planned culling of elephant family groups and the subsequent sale of ivory may be the best way to sustain biodiversity in a specific African conservation system, yet wreak havoc with international efforts to halt illegal trade in ivory. Such situations are probably best handled by an institutional structure flexible enough to work with wildlife custodians, the research community, and business, to optimize benefits nationally and internationally. To what degree such an institutional structure should be national or local, and private or governmental, depends totally on the context. A pilot project that is functioning in Costa Rica is INBio, a private non-profit organization that advises government on biodiversity, collects and distributes biodiversity information, and facilitates biodiversity use by all sectors. *(See Chapter II.)*

Within research agreements, the inclusion of more benefits in the cost-benefit calculations is definitely desirable. Cash grants for management, an increase in the size or diversity of the area conserved, public good will, information and technology transfer, and contributions to GNP, etc., should all be considered as benefits of research. The amount of biodiversity damage acceptable in a given research project can also be negotiated and mitigated. This way, the survival of tropical biodiversity hinges on a social contract, not a futile wish for 100-percent protection.

3) Who needs a research agreement?

A research agreement should be required for any research in any wildland conserved or used for its biodiversity. The terms for private and public holdings will differ with (1) national and international laws, (2) biodiversity prospecting rights, and (3) agreements in technology transfer, etc. Other kinds of users (e.g., fire crews, school groups, ecotourists) should be granted or denied access to wildlands on the same basis as conventional researchers. Just as a research agreement with a biodiversity prospector can insure that a conservation area is appropriately compensated, a very similar agreement can be made with an ecotourism company having a stake in the conserved wildland. Similarly, a taxonomist may easily compensate a wildland by providing identification services. In any case, sound biodiversity management may require trading severe damage to a hectare of vegetation or very light damage to a thousand hectares, for enough cash, training opportunities for nationals, technology, or jobs, to, for example, manage a conservation area adequately or even add another 1,000 hectares to it.

When a tropical research agreement is constructed, international scientists and commercial researchers are often treated differently from their national counterparts. The distinction rests on fact: many foreigners have comparatively little stake in the society's future, and they are inclined to export their earnings, and to pay low or no taxes. However, they also provide foreign currency and technology. But what about the many national scientists trained in developed-world universities? Although such scientists may have an international perspective on the user impacts of biodiversity, foreign universities aren't the best place to acquire a rounded sense of national (home-country) interests. Then too, exploitative commercial biodiversity research and contempt for research regulations are by no means restricted to foreigners.

The question of who serves the national interest and who doesn't is tricky. In a developing country, it is rarely clear just what the national interest is and just what segment of the national population represents the country. In nascent democracies, governmental policies can take wild swings, owing to the absence of strong national research institutions that can weather political changes. In unstable situations, researchers may seek shelter within international organizations (which may or may not have their host country's very best interest in mind) and their institutional research agreements. Instability also invites the international researcher to keep his or her distance from the host government, including the government custodians of conserved wildlands.

Undergraduate, graduate, and post-doc research is particularly difficult to incorporate into a research agreement because it is, at least initially, often very unfocused, and the outcome is hard to predict. Its practitioners are also socially powerless and unsure of the importance of their research. The same applies to many taxonomists, though they contribute important information to a tropical country. So as not to dampen students' curiosity about tropical research, some kind of "learner's agreement" is imperative. Such licenses should be given only in conjunction with a regular research agreement or on the condition that someone with appropriate experience supervises the student. (Of course, students inside and outside of the tropics still need to learn the mechanics and philosophy behind research agreements. Indeed, to help tropical biodiversity contribute commercially to both GNP and scientific advancement, the contemporary tropical biodiversity graduate student needs to understand the complicated implications of patenting genomes, as well as the opportunity costs to tropical countries of making their biological diversity available for research.)

Like the student, the experienced researcher also needs a type of exploratory agreement. Such an agreement would be deliberately vague about the directions and exact nature of the research, but just as firm as a regular research agreement on the destiny, ownership, commercialization, etc., of the findings. Unadorned trust between researcher and custodian, essential in all research agreements, is especially important in exploratory agreements.

Establishing a research agreement will always cost the researcher and the custodian time, and a slow process can cause friction or tempt the researcher to skip filing a research application. For researchers, time is often scarce, whereas for many bureaucracies time is abundant and wrong decisions are heavily penalized. Moreover, the research community tends to base its action on logic rather than on appeal to higher authority while regulatory agencies may be more comfortable appealing to written rules. Reasoned and constructive governmental response to a defective research application will make the researcher a more willing negotiator than will an authoritative "no." In general, rapid, sensitive, and constructive responses to research applications, even to defective applications, will attract international researchers and make national ones more productive. Considering that tropical countries will be competing with each other for research agreements, market competition will serve as a not-so-gentle instructor for this lesson in applied psychology.

4) Who Signs Research Agreements?

At a minimum, a research agreement should be evaluated and signed by (1) the researcher, (2) the custodians of the wildland, and (3) the government institution that oversees the potential benefits and costs to society. The second and third signatory may or may not be the same party. In any case, the third signatory should be the highest level national custodian of natural resources. (In many instances, this person will be a representative of a Ministry of Natural Resources or Ministry of Science and Technology.) Each of these three evaluators and signatories may designate others to perform their functions. What matters here is high technical competence and policy awareness—backed up on-site by government, private, or outside-funded expertise in evaluating and managing biodiversity research. Either the government should bear the very great costs of training and keeping the appropriate specialists on staff, or it should subcontract this responsibility to responsible private non-profit institutions—a task requiring more flexibility than usually found in middle-management ranks in most tropical governments.

The researcher who signs the research agreement is making a commitment to try to generate certain types of information. But the researcher's work inevitably entails resource or opportunity costs for the custodians, so something should be given in return. This introduces into research an accountability factor beyond the experience of most academics, who at best feel indebted to the granting agency and to their peers. Yet, the conserved wildland is, in a sense, a kind of granting agency insofar as it sustains the cost of keeping the organisms alive and maintains the infrastructure that all researchers use.

At present, a researcher's failure to comply with the terms of the research agreement typically jeopardizes future research contract applications or receptivity to the research results, but does not entail direct penalties. Assigning penalties fairly is tricky, however. In some cases, damage to a researcher's personal reputation may count for more than a monetary penalty.

Conflicts over confidentiality and use have already erupted, and more can be predicted. For example, it is a tacit assumption that NSF-funded research (funded by U.S. taxpayers) will be put into the "public domain" through publication in scientific journals or entry into electronic networks. But what if the research agreement with a tropical conservation area specifies that biodiversity results cannot be made public until a National Biodiversity Board determines that publication will not jeopardize in-country commercialization efforts? Such a stipulation can, among other things, wreak havoc with the career development of an academic being considered for tenure—unless, of course, the academic evaluation scheme changes to take such events into consideration as it long ago did in such academic fields as chemistry and engineering.

Another question is whether the state can represent the private person as well as it can the custodians of state-owned conserved wildlands. The answer depends heavily on the national view of who owns national biodiversity. Pathbreaking new policies on this

142

issue are needed immediately. It is not obvious, for example, that "the state owns all" policies so often applied to subsurface minerals are appropriate in the case of biodiversity. On the other hand, it may be highly appropriate for the state to issue "biodiversity prospecting concessions" for its conserved wildlands or even for the entire country, as Costa Rica has laid the legal groundwork to do. In effect, the government may delegate custodianship for national biodiversity management to private groups, just as it currently does for many other public service sectors.

Biologists and biotechnologists in the developed world, as well as many national private land owners in developing countries, will protest loudly that such legislation transgresses individual rights. The howl will be even louder if a private contract must be approved by government on grounds that conserved wildlands are considered public goods. However, computer technology, military hardware, and other complex products are commonly covered by government-granted licenses, and government approval of specific contracts covering such goods throughout the developed world is required as a "national security" measure. In a tropical country rich only in biodiversity, the unrestricted and untaxed export of biodiversity-related information from the government or private sector can seriously threaten national economic security, especially when the area covered by wildlands drops below 20 to 30 percent. Currently, a tropical country can invest heavily in developing its biodiversity greenhouses only to discover that a private entrepreneur has meanwhile sold most or all of it to some foreign biotechnology company. Does this not undermine a nation's economy and, thus, ultimately, its security?

When the research and development of wildland biodiversity information becomes an affair of the state, it moves into the realm of big-time politics and national planning. Such socio-political considerations as industrial competitiveness, health, education, national security, etc., all come into play. Accordingly, the traditional staffs and administrative structures for departments of game and fish, national parks, refuges, endangered species, and the like will require major restructuring, greatly increased budgets, and novel departments so they can handle research agreements. Consider the case of

143

the professor who suddenly learns that his or her research on caterpillars represents a national secret and that conducting business as usual in the local university's biology department threatens national security. Even if there is good will all around, dealing with such problems will be financially and politically expensive.

As it contributes ever more to a nation's GNP, Ministries of Planning in developing countries will increasingly want a say in biodiversity research. Scientists and other kinds of biodiversity managers are not prepared for this, but a research agreement will help by making the aims of research projects clear and the projects themselves highly visible. The social benefits and impacts of research on biodiversity should become more visible. Certainly, all is not bleak for the researcher. To the extent that wildland biodiversity management becomes a money-maker, the public will offer it tax breaks, roads, electric lines, and funding—just as it does for other development activities.

5) Protecting Biodiversity Information

Confidentiality clauses will often turn out to be essential elements in research agreements between researchers and the custodians of conserved tropical wildlands. Certain classes of commercial collaborators will also demand confidentiality. A conservation area manager may require that a plant ecologist not divulge the locations of plants in a study of mineral accumulation by plants. An ornithologist may want the information on the location of an endangered species' nesting sites on private lands to be restricted, registered as confidential in the national biodiversity data base. Or a drug company may not want to purchase research samples collected in a conservation area unless it can be certain that the conservation area staff will not tell the drug company's competitors which species were sampled. Such guarantees, which help the country to protect its biodiversity as a commercial resource, are already commonplace in mining, biotechnology, chemistry, computer science, and other industries.

Even though applied academic and industrial science has a long-established system of patents, direct research compensation,

144

delayed publication, and employee-employer agreements designed to allow the person or organization sponsoring the research to protect a costly investment, university or museum-based researchers in whole-organism biology still feel that the free and unimpeded flow of information and the exchange of data through symposia, publications, discussions, etc., are essential to keeping their discipline alive. Even so, much of such information doesn't begin to "flow" until its initial possessors have extracted what they need for their own research. True unimpeded information flow, such as will occur when scientists and others begin to put their information freely into public domain electronic networks, will require the academic research community to rethink the concept of privacy as it applies to information. Also, this information is used as a form of barter for salary, research grants, prestige, professional advancement, and access to other information. Each researcher is in effect a tiny company, often in an unspoken joint venture with a university or other institution.

In the context of whole-organism biology, and especially of the study of wild tropical organisms, academic studies were long viewed as having no direct commercial value and involving no management costs that needed to be compensated. The public didn't consider itself an investor, and it didn't expect any immediate commercial returns. In this setting, confidentiality and other devices that maintain value in the open marketplace were scarcely issues.

In fact, maintaining tropical biodiversity requires a major investment by a tropical country. First, the management budget for a national system of conservation areas is in large part a biodiversity research budget (as well as an ecotourism budget and watershed management budget). Second, when as much as 10 to 30 percent of a country has been designated as conservation areas, these wildlands must contribute at least as much to a country's intellectual and financial capital as they would if used in other ways. If they don't, these areas will rapidly be put to other kinds of land use. Then too, biodiversity researchers from developed countries shouldn't forget that their tropical host countries simply don't have the tax base that their own countries have to cover conservation and wildland-management costs.

145

Considering how valuable an open information flow is to researchers, confidentiality—both temporary and permanent—should be accorded a high value at the negotiation table. Since stale research information loses value in many ways, any delays caused by meeting the requirements of confidentiality are expensive for the researcher (and other users). If combined with bureaucratic delays, they may prompt researchers to scrap a project or move it to another country.

What constitutes a pilfering, larceny, leak, sale, or possession of biodiversity from a conservation area, from private land, or from a country, etc., depends greatly on circumstance. The price of excessive possessiveness by biodiversity custodians is a debilitating isolation from the world of collaborators. The tropical country that plans to close its borders and re-invent biodiversity science for itself will lose out, and no nation can be made leak-proof anyway. On the other hand, the free-forage ethic followed in the tropics for the last several centuries offers the custodians of a conserved wildland very little in return for their investments.

Taxonomists will have great difficulty working in an environment where every taxonomic specimen that moves out of a country might constitute a genetic and chemical information leak. Simply by depositing a specimen in an international museum or someone else's private collection, the scientist can easily and unwittingly become a "mule" for pharmaceutical and biotechnology industries that still want to treat biodiversity information as a free good. The only practical solution is a thorough system of research agreements whereby taxonomic specimens and information are clearly destined for taxonomic purposes, and commercial sampling is identified as such, to the best of the researcher's ability.

Tropical countries must also come to recognize the work of the taxonomist as a very beneficial form of technology transfer to the developing world. In addition, these nations must realize that though they have an attractive product in their complex biodiversity, it is their responsibility to bring it to the bargaining table with the intention of making sales rather than simply complain when others develop an "unused" resource. And finally, institutions trying to establish institutional norms aimed at keeping biodiversity information in trust for tropical countries deserve encouragement and support.

Success will also depend on the conscientious consumer. Before long, consumers of biodiversity information will demand the same sort of source certification that many developed-world consumers of tropical hardwood timbers are now demanding. Producers of biodiversity-based drugs and other chemical products, for example, could easily increase their sales in competitive marketplaces by displaying certification that the product's source country receives a royalty on the sale. Except in the case of one-of-a-kind drugs, consumer choice can thus help to protect biodiversity information and return benefits to the source country.

In efforts to protect biodiversity, demands by major granting agencies (such as the U.S. National Science Foundation and the National Cancer Institute) that in-country research permits be obtained for all projects that they fund in tropical countries are critical. So is the U.S. Patent Office's requirement that an applicant provide the pedigree of all the raw materials used to make a new drug. A complementary need now in most developing countries is for a legal framework regulating access to biodiversity and establishing requirements for the management and transfer of biodiversity information.

6) Violating, Re-evaluating, and Terminating Research Agreements

The same parties that sign a research agreement must be responsible for evaluating it periodically and determining whether it has been violated. Unconscious violation is all too easy where the subject matter is so new, and where parties on both sides of the bargaining table have very different goals and mores. Prime considerations are the investments made by both the researcher and the wildland custodian, and such externalities as the duration of secure funding. (Few researchers will establish a research project costing hundreds of thousands of dollars under an agreement that a wildlands custodian can break capriciously.) Also,

147

the researcher's greatest concern is that the cooperating government is stable and reliable since no researcher wants to be buffeted by political change or to fall victim to inter-agency struggles for jurisdiction. For their part, wildland administrators don't want to construct facilities for researchers or conserve large wildlands for users, only to have the research funds suddenly taken elsewhere. And all parties should see the wisdom in the emerging principle that signers from the developing and developed worlds are equally responsible for their parts in an agreement.

In general, when two or more entities enter into a potentially risky activity, they commonly deposit some kind of collateral or purchase an insurance policy to cover repairs or compensation should a party default. Mining contracts and construction contracts and loans all call for such safety nets. (For the academic biodiversity researcher with a limited budget, professional reputation functions as a form of collateral.) If such a bond—whether cash or barter—became a standard budget item for many classes of research agreements, biodiversity prospecting research agreements would be taken much more seriously and their consequences more carefully planned.

Currently, the most that can be asked is that the researcher take all pains to avoid damaging conserved wildlands. This means collaborating closely with the managers and technical advisors charged with taking care of conserved wildlands and making a best effort to insure that the source country benefits from the income generated by contemporary research on wildland biodiversity. It also means avoiding unevaluated transoceanic introductions of species or genes (e.g., the African honey bee into the New World, Australian *Melaleuca* trees into Everglades National Park, Florida, Central American *Mimosa pigra* bushes and buffalo into Kakadu National Park, Australia), and not reintroducing animals to the wild after they have become infected with diseases in zoos or homes. Finally, it means willingly conducting research on the impact of users and on the comparative resilience of wildlands research sites at various levels of use. Such measures do much to eliminate concern about breaking research agreements.

7) Who Pays for Tropical Research and its Management and in What Coin?

Research generally benefits the host institution and society. Research budgets from government granting agencies and many private foundations typically include overhead for institutional support. Equipment purchased with grant funds also amounts to an institutional subsidy since it generally remains in use long after the grant expires. Many project personnel perform various services for the institution—whether teaching, advising, serving on committees, or providing psychological support for other researchers and management staff. Also, the research project itself eventually generates information products that can be sold to replenish the public tax base and other income streams that support the cooperating institution. And, finally, when a researcher in a developed country commercializes a finding, direct returns from commercialization presumably repay the various investors along the way.

While all of these "payments" theoretically apply to research in a tropical conserved wildland, many foreign researchers (academic or commercial) and even many national biodiversity researchers working in tropical countries seem to forget to make an explicit effort to compensate the custodians of the conserved wildlands that are so vital to their research. Even less thought goes to compensation for the *national* opportunity costs of conserving a wildland rather than converting it to some other kind of land use.

Explicit and direct contributions to the costs of maintaining tropical wildland biodiversity must be part of any research budget, whether the researcher is non-profit (government or private) or commercial. But if the contribution is forced, acrimony can poison negotiations, especially because traditionally biodiversity has been viewed as a free good. Researchers in developed-country institutions have long been taught by experience to scrimp, cheat, bend, twist, and otherwise modify their research budgets to extract the maximum for themselves or their project. In wealthy institutions, such behavior seems a small enough price to keep research staff happy. However, in a tropical biodiversity research system, at least at its current state of development and financial

149

security, the same behavior can do great harm to both the researcher and the system.

An even greater psychological impediment to including wildland maintenance costs in research budgets is that such monies usually disappear into cavernous general government budgets and have no visible impact on the wildland where the researcher works. Worse, if researchers put the funds directly into the management budget of "their" wildland, they often see them being misused or stolen. Most biodiversity researchers have generally grown used to working on tight budgets, so it hurts to see a significant percentage of hard-won funds wasted. The answer? Wildland conservation administrations can win many friends by using research contributions efficiently and demonstrating routinely how they were spent.

In developed countries, most researchers are trained to contribute to the institutions that support their work, especially those in their own countries. But today, the nature of such contributions is changing very rapidly, and both scientists and businesspeople seem unprepared to respond to new needs, especially in a foreign land. Friction and misunderstanding intensify when the developing country grudgingly views compensation by researchers as simply a partial repayment of a long-overdue debt rather than as a form of collaboration. But a little perspective is needed here: virtually the whole taxonomic system on which tropical biodiversity information management is based was transferred directly from developed countries, as was most of the ecological science and philosophy that has informed the construction of tropical national parks and other conserved wildlands.

Another problem is that the wildland manager may not recognize or value some of the many kinds of biodiversity information that the researcher passes on to the public. A national park manager in tropical Costa Rica has little use for an analysis of leaf chemistry published in German in a German journal, even though an alert biodiversity prospecting program in some other Costa Rican institution might be able to use it. Unfortunately, the kinds of payments most useful to present-day tropical wildland management—cash or time invested in in-country training—may also be those hardest for the international researcher on a two-week visit to give.

Mixed messages further frustrate attempts to compensate countries for use of, or access to, their biodiversity and related information. Biodiversity information is managed at many different levels within a country, and each may give a researcher different signals or harbor different expectations. For instance, for the Minister of Natural Resources sufficient payment may be public remarks by a researcher at international meetings on the virtues of doing research in the Minister's home country, or the researcher's help in evaluating priorities for resource allocation. However, to the biodiversity research administrator in the conservation area where that researcher works, such contributions are often invisible. Worse yet, the technically-oriented biodiversity research administrator may not agree with the politically-oriented Minister of Natural Resources on the decisions that the researcher helped the ministry make. Conversely, a researcher's many small direct contributions to management activities in a given conservation area may be ignored by the Ministry if the researcher fails to cultivate the right communication channels. To complicate things even more, some national and foreign researchers working in the tropics have manipulated the national research management process to impede their competitors.

Given the plentiful pitfalls of managing biodiversity research in general and of defining and allocating research costs in particular, government offices of biodiversity research management—both at the conservation areas and in central bureaucracies—clearly need diplomatic staff with a crystal-clear vision of national and international biodiversity management goals at many levels.

8) How Should Research Gains and Compensations be Distributed?

"To the investor goes the profits"? Yes, but tropical sources or custodians of biodiversity information have not been viewed as investors, and few custodians and academic researchers understand what the profit is, much less who gets it. Commercial researchers

151

have a clearer sense of where profits are to be made, but they aren't eager to acknowledge the investors or—on pain of losing stockholders—to pay more than the market forces them to. In other words, there is little incentive to pay for what appears to be a free good, and the easiest and most lucrative kind of distribution of gains and compensations is no distribution at all.

The recipients of the diverse gains and compensations from biodiversity research in public and private conserved wildlands need to be negotiated case-by-case, as will the kinds of gains, compensations, investments and evaluations to be made. On the one hand, the barter system ingrained in tropical biodiversity research and research management is highly subjective and variable. On the other, in the no-nonsense exchange of money, certain social "goods" are certain to be overlooked. For instance, the amount of conserved wildland in a tropical country is currently ignored when the World Bank gives a country a credit rating. In Costa Rica, it is far easier to take out a loan using a cattle pasture as collateral than using uncut forest.

If a rancher sells a cow to a slaughterhouse, he gets the profits (less any tax imposed by the government to cover public services to the rancher). But if the rancher sells the genes of a tree on his ranch, he has sold a piece of common national property. Shouldn't some of the returns from such a sale be distributed more broadly and be nationally regulated? And does a transaction tax represent a fair contribution to the enormous national cost of maintaining the whole tree population? (Recall that the genetic material on the individual's ranch might not be able to survive if other populations of that species and supporting species were not thriving outside the boundaries of the ranch.) The problem is that if the profits are broadly distributed, individual farmers may receive so little that they will not value the tree. The solution—at least in part—is for ranchers to sell *services*. Getting the sample and insuring the survival and health of the tree from which it came are part of these services. However, if these services require subsidy from the public sector, as is the case with the tree's genes, then the commercial agreement should insure a return to the public. The INBio-Merck and Co. agreement discussed below contains this element explicitly.

Since a biodiversity research agreement will not serve every landowner's needs, biodiversity information is probably best managed, commercialized, protected, etc., through networks of institutions or by complex companies that understand that the bulk of the market cost of a given bit of biodiversity information (and thus the compensation for the provider) is largely for excavating and manipulating or preserving the information rather than for the item itself. If this approach is taken, most biodiversity research agreements would be among institutions or individuals representing institutions, and most immediate national gains and compensations would go to the custodial institution—whether government or private, non-profit or profit.

In the well-known contract between INBio and Merck & Co., Inc., what is unique is not only that the company is paying something approximating the true cost of the samples it receives. Also unique is that all of the initial payments and all of the royalties go either directly into management budgets and endowments for Costa Rica's conservation areas as a whole or cover the actual costs of collecting the samples. (The administrative headache lies in determining which fractions should be used to cover such traditional conservation costs as land purchase, infrastructure, and staff salaries; which used for development costs, such as biodiversity inventories, facilitation of further biodiversity prospecting, and the distribution of information to the public and various other user industries; and which used as endowments for the conservation areas and INBio.) *(See Chapter II.)*

The question of how to distribute the pay-offs from biodiversity research raises the larger issue of how to distribute all of the income generated by a conservation area. History provides few precedents, but it is nonetheless now clear that a conservation area *is* simply another kind of productive land use, one with costs and benefits like any other sector. For this reason, the biodiversity researcher should be a major participant—along with ecotourism companies, water users, timber harvesters, education ministries, planning ministries, regular citizens, etc.—in any discussions over how to allocate the costs and the gains for a conservation area. In this context, a tropical conservation area has much in common with a highway system or health system.

153

9) Biodiversity Information in the "Public Domain"

With several centuries of biodiversity information collection behind us, and most of this information already made "public" in the libraries, museums, seed banks, gardens, greenhouses, zoos, and other information storehouses in developed countries, the widespread assumption is that most such information is also freely available to the tropical world. In fact, most of it is not and much of it is not even known by most people to exist. This sad fact is only too obvious to the national researcher returning home to the trop-ics—in an act of technology transfer—with a fresh degree from a developed-country institution. It is even more evident to the ad-ministrators of conservation areas far from national centers of higher education, research institutes, national museums, botanical gardens, etc.

In the cost-benefit analysis that is part of today's biodiversity research agreement, what value should be assigned to public infor-mation? And what ownership prerequisites? It is tempting to view this handed-down wealth as an ancient aqueduct established (and paid for) with the labor of some previous society and to declare the water flowing within to be a public good to be cared for and used like the water in a natural river. But even natural rivers have main-tenance costs, as any protector of a watershed can confirm. The problem is much like that confronting the large museums in devel-oping countries, museums that are storehouses are processing cen-ters for much of tropical biodiversity information.

INBio's policy is that all basic inventory information (what species are where, and their natural history) gathered by INBio has been extracted from the public domain. All new biodiversity in-ventory information is likewise harvested from Costa Rica's con-servation areas, which are also in the public domain. This informa-tion therefore belongs to the public domain and will be placed there. However, this decision entails substantial operating costs for INBio and other institutions, costs that are unlikely to be covered by the national tax base. Indeed, the only way to meet them is through international taxes—in the form of service fees charged to all commercial users, in the form of collaborative arrangements for identifications and other services with researchers, and in the form of the INBio endowment established through bilateral international government assistance.

To open the world-level "public domain" to developing countries, researchers can voluntarily serve as librarians and reference librarians for the huge amount of tropical biodiversity information already gathered. Taxonomists, ecologists, physiologists, natural products chemists, and other such wardens and traditional purveyors of this information can provide (as some now do) taxonomic services, ecological analyses, clues to biodiversity prospecting, literature searches, etc., as retroactive "payments" on a long-term debt. And there may even be cases where the researcher offers so much service to the biodiversity source country that he or she should be compensated from the national research budget. We are not far from the day when the administration of a tropical conservation area will pay a taxonomist a hefty consultancy fee to generate, for example, a field guide to the species of moths or mushrooms that the conservation area will then use to promote itself to pharmaceutical companies or ecotourists.

10) Market Forces and Research Agreements on Tropical Biodiversity

Every area rich in tropical biodiversity is gradually becoming more accessible to foreign and national researchers, thanks to new communication technologies, greater ease of travel, and increasing international collaboration. As a result, every biodiversity research opportunity in the tropics increasingly competes with every other one to attract international field researchers, biodiversity prospectors, taxonomists, etc.

This is not to say, however, that all tropical countries have equal opportunities to collaborate. Some tropical countries have almost nothing biologically unique and will therefore fare better by specializing in support services. Others are veritable supermarkets of species and specimens. While abiding by its own laws and cultural mores, each tropical country will have to find its own niche.

155

Since high-quality field research often amounts to a long-term investment in planning and in time spent in the biodiversity-rich area, the researcher may initially be able to pick from many venues. Once research is under way, however, changing locations can be expensive, if not disastrous. For this reason, capricious changes in policy or in a research-management plan can be lethal for research, and—so effective is the researcher grapevine—just a few such changes are enough to blackball a conservation area or country for a very long time. Conversely, tropical countries that predicate their national research management process on collaboration can count on recurring investments by researchers who find the socio-political environment comfortable.

Two pitfalls of the free market deserve the last word here. First, biodiversity information (including samples) can all too easily become contraband sold on international black markets. It is easy to foresee one painful situation in particular: two adjacent tropical countries share a large block of unique biodiversity, and one sells the resources' genes on the cheap or puts information on the genetic material into the public domain, thereby keeping the neighboring country from realizing any economic gains from developing the resource. A war over biodiversity is not as far-fetched as it might first appear.

Second, in a free market, unscrupulous businesspeople deliberately pick the least-protected or least-organized countries for their operations so they can quickly mine the nation's biodiversity and sell it to the highest or most convenient international bidder before the unsuspecting country can do anything about it. Motivated solely by personal profit, they will sell cheap with no concern about a "genetic leak" into the public or international private domain. On such economic "frontiers," even well-written research agreements won't stop the raiding. More effective for now would be an immediate regional and even pan-tropical consensus on the *need* for research agreements that address the kinds of concerns touched in this document. The end user of tropical biodiversity research can also help by deciding to accept only information from sources fully covered by adequate research agreements with the source country. This could amount to a self-imposed tax by the biodiversity user and consumer. In any case, developed country users should be encouraged to take this first step and bear its initial burden so as to help save the future treasures that tropical biodiversity can yield.

VI.

AN INTELLECTUAL PROPERTY RIGHTS FRAMEWORK FOR BIODIVERSITY PROSPECTING

Michael A. Gollin

It is the marriage of the soul with Nature that makes the intellect fruitful, that gives birth to imagination. (Thoreau, 1851)

Intellectual property laws, typically viewed only as engines of industrial and cultural progress, have recently received attention as tools for achieving the broader goals of conserving biodiversity while promoting sustainable development and the equitable sharing of the resulting benefits. It is therefore necessary to outline how intellectual property rights can be applied to the new technologies, commercial practices, and ethical standards of biodiversity prospecting, and to examine the merits of creating new biodiversity prospecting rights.

Intellectual property rights such as trade secrets and patents can help people define and retain rights to biological resources, foster innovation, and facilitate acquisition of biotechnology. Intellectual property laws alone, however, are no panacea. Intellectual property, environmental protection, and commercial laws must be harmonized to marry the goals of development and conservation, and to build a framework for sustainable biodiversity prospecting.

The Convention on Biological Diversity calls upon countries to establish such a framework. The specific mix of laws and institutions will vary from country to country, depending on local concerns and legal traditions. This chapter provides an overview of the practice and content of intellectual property laws around the world as they may apply to biodiversity prospecting, and provides some general recommendations for individuals, organizations, and countries seeking to promote a sustainable biodiversity prospecting trade.

Intellectual Property and Public Policy

The basic argument in favor of applying property rights to biodiversity conservation goes as follows: if those who control a habitat hold proprietary rights to develop its biological resources, then they have a means for obtaining economic benefits from those resources, and, consequently, an incentive to conserve rather than destroy them (Khalil et al., 1992; Roberts, 1992; Barton, 1988; Sedjo, 1988). This market-based approach may also promote equity because it allows local people to share the benefits deriving from their conservation and knowledge of genetic resources through biodiversity prospecting (Posey, 1990). A key issue countries must address, then, is whether their current property laws, in particular intellectual property laws, are adequate to promote a sustainable biodiversity prospecting trade, or whether reform is necessary. The answer may be different for each country.

There has been a tendency to lump many different doctrines under the acronym "IPR." For purposes of this chapter, intellectual property rights include traditional rights arising from innovation such as patents and trade secrets, as well as untried concepts such as discoverer's rights. Intellectual property rights do not include but have much in common with access restrictions, which are a hybrid of land use and natural resources laws. Access restrictions may derive from sovereign rights or private property rights.

Intellectual property rights are generally justified on grounds that they can (1) provide incentives to innovators, (2) establish a system that promotes public disclosure of new information, (3) reward people who create commercial or cultural value by the exercise of their intellectual abilities and "sweat of their brows," (4) satisfy principles of moral rights by allowing creators to control the

160

fate of their creations, and (5) facilitate technology transfer (Juma, 1989). Intellectual property laws have historically been directed to industrial and artistic progress rather than environmental values such as conservation of biodiversity, and there are advantages to keeping that separate focus (Gollin, 1991).

Intellectual property laws carve exclusive private rights for innovators out of the public domain. When the boundaries between private rights and the public domain are poorly drawn, several concerns may arise (Gollin, 1992). Critics argue that intellectual property laws may remove technology and information from the public domain; increase the cost of drugs and other important products; concentrate industry and agriculture on a few protected cultivated species or varieties; promote competition instead of cooperation; and conflict with moral views on the proper extent of property rights in plants, animals, and microorganisms (Abraham, 1989; Fowler et al., 1988; Doyle, 1985). Clearly, intellectual property rights are subject to many conflicting concerns.

Each country draws the boundaries between the public domain and intellectual property rights somewhat differently, based on the level of technology, domestic policy, commercial practices, and social norms. Over time, cultures evolve, and intellectual property systems do too (Barton, 1992). For example, copyright has been extended over the decades in many countries to include motion pictures, photocopies, and computer software; and patent law has extended from chemical compounds to microbes, and further to genetically altered plants and animals. In other countries, intellectual property rights are more limited, leaving relatively more in the public domain, as in India, where pharmaceuticals are not yet patentable (though the method of manufacture may be) (Section 5 of the Indian Patents Act, 1970).

Guidelines for Applying Intellectual Property Rights

A rigorous analysis of intellectual property in a particular rainforest or reef would require research and analysis of applicable local legislation, executive regulations, and judicial decisions. The cultural context of the law would have to be assessed as well since the rule of law counts much more in some countries than others. Here the more modest goal is to explore, in general terms, those intellectual property doctrines and strategies appropriate to and consistent with conserving the components of biodiversity in wild habitats.

Before addressing policy concerns as to the proper scope of intellectual property, it is helpful to understand the practicing lawyer's approach to protecting intellectual property. In terms of biodiversity prospecting, the better the system works in practice, the better the custodians of wild habitat can protect the genetic resources in the wilderness, and the more incentive they will have to conserve them. The practitioner first identifies and defines the subject matter to be protected and, second, selects those intellectual property mechanisms (such as trade secret, patent, trademark, and copyright) best suited to protect that subject matter. The practitioner then develops a strategy for obtaining these rights, taking into account their duration, marketability, and enforceability.

As defined in the Convention on Biological Diversity (Article 2), biological diversity "means the variability among living organisms including, *inter alia*, terrestrial, marine and other aquatic ecosystems and the ecological complexities of which they are part; this includes diversity within species, between species and of ecosystems." *(See Annex 4.)* Of particular interest to policy-makers and prospectors alike are those habitats with the highest diversity (e.g. tropical rainforests and coral reefs), and hence the most abundant genetic resources.

Biological resources, as defined in the Convention, include "genetic resources, organisms or parts thereof, populations, or any other biotic component of ecosystems with actual or potential use or value for humanity" (Article 2). We must assume that all biotic resources have at least *potential* use for future generations. Biological resources thus present a cornucopia of potential objects for intellectual property protection, but only some are presently protectable under existing laws.

These objects include: a particular ecosystem as a whole; the species comprising it; knowledge pertaining to the habitat and its

162

species; inventories of plant, animal, and microbe species and their time and place of collection; knowledge of the species' usefulness; compilations of such information in databases; extracts and purified compounds from the species; and the methods for preparing and administering such substances (Elisabetsky, 1991). They also include seeds, plasmids, and isolated genes from the species; purebred or hybrid crops or animals originally found in wild habitats; synthetic derivatives of the compounds or genes isolated from the species; and products prepared from such compounds or by use of such genes. Useful products may include drugs, crops, and such environmentally friendly industrial substances as biodegradable pesticides and microbes that digest oil.

A broad range of technologies rely on biological resources. Traditional healers use their knowledge of particular plants and primitive extractive techniques for their own purposes. Modern biotechnology laboratories employ sophisticated but random screening of thousands of samples for biological activity, and purify, synthesize, and genetically engineer useful compounds. In either case, only a minute percentage of living organisms may prove to be useful, but we cannot know which ones.

1. *Trade Secrets*

The law of trade secrets has broad applicability to biodiversity prospecting (Barton, 1991b; Rensberger, 1992). A traditional healer's knowledge of the medicinal use of a plant or extraction method handed down over generations might be protected as a trade secret. Taxonomic and ecological information, inventories, and biotechnology techniques may also be covered. The usefulness of trade secrets is limited, however since they are difficult to establish, protect, and enforce.

In the United States, trade secrets protect confidential information and know-how that give the owner a competitive advantage. Particular measures to maintain secrecy may be necessary to establish, define, and provide notice of a trade secret. For example, marking documents as confidential, preventing access to certain equipment or plantations, and obtaining confidentiality agreements can distinguish secret from non-secret material. Legislative or private measures restricting access to habitats, such as rainforests or reefs, might thus strengthen a claim of trade secrecy with respect to information about the habitats. At the same time, such measures may chill experimental research.

Trade secret protection can be justified under three theories: (1) a trade secret is intangible property, and its theft should be forbidden; (2) obligations of confidentiality arise under contracts, express or implied; and (3) misappropriation of the fruit of individual effort should be prevented and should give rise to a claim for damages. In the United States, government disclosure of secrets can be a taking of property without just compensation, in violation of the Fifth Amendment of the U.S. Constitution.[1] Some countries provide little or no legal protection for trade secrets, making physical security measures (like limiting access to a preserve) the only way to prevent loss of secrecy. The current round of negotiations under the General Agreement on Tariffs and Trade may recognize trade secrets at the international level.

A trade secret can endure forever provided that the formula, information, or device remains secret. In plant breeding, for example, the lines used to produce a hybrid may be protected as secrets indefinitely. The owner of a trade secret may license, disclose, or assign the right to use the trade secret, subject to an agreement to hold the information in confidence.

One who without permission uses a farmer's or a traditional healer's secret knowledge to produce a new drug or crop may be liable for resulting profits. But, as noted, enforcing a trade secret is difficult. Typically, disputes turn on the rigor of efforts to maintain secrecy and the extent of public disclosure.

For example, the concept of confidentiality may be elusive in a traditional culture that emphasizes common over private property. If an extractive technique is handed down from generation to generation of traditional healers, the information could be considered a trade secret by developed-country standards if it is kept from others both within and outside the traditional society. But once traditional knowledge (e.g., the identity and use of a species of fungus) is published by a researcher, government entity, or anyone in the world, the trade secret rights are extinguished. In the United States, publication of such knowledge without knowing agreement arguably could be considered a misappropriation, theft, or taking of trade secrets as long as the information was not innocently learned from a third party, or reverse engineered from a product.

The requirement of competitive value also makes it difficult to apply trade secrets to indigenous healers or traditional farmers, who may not be using their knowledge in a competitive market. However, if such knowledge is misappropriated for commercial gain, the competitive advantage requirement should be satisfied.

Trade secrecy can be criticized on policy grounds since secrecy undercuts the full and open exchange of information needed for cultural and technological progress. Patents, which require public disclosure, are preferable in this regard. Nonetheless, trade secrets may comprise important components of packages of technology transferred as part of biodiversity prospecting agreements; they can also provide at least some form of protection for information in countries where patents are unavailable. Thus, the law of trade secrets is one suitable tool for promoting the sustainable development of biological resources in wild habitats.

2. *Utility Patents*

Wild habitats and species themselves cannot be patented. However, the marriage of the intellect with Nature can lead to patentable products derived from *development* of biodiversity. Such patents can indirectly enhance the value of biodiversity conservation. Consequently, the more that source countries can employ biotechnology to develop products from biodiversity prospecting, the greater interest they will have in applying patent protection to their biological resources.

a. *Patent procedure*
A utility patent conveys from the government to an inventor the right, for a limited time, to exclude others from making, using,

or selling the invention in that particular country. From society's point of view, patent protection is superior to trade secrecy in that inventors disclose what they have invented so that others may learn from the invention. In addition, the protection is of limited duration (generally 15 to 20 years), and the technology reverts ultimately to the public domain. From the inventor's standpoint, patents are advantageous because exclusive rights are not lost if someone else learns the invention or discloses it. On the other hand, the term of a patent is limited, and once a patent expires exclusive rights are extinguished.

To obtain a patent in most countries, an invention must be useful and novel (not publicly known or used by others), and must satisfy the standard of inventiveness denominated in the United States as "non-obviousness." It is sometimes said that mere discoveries are not patentable. Patentable subject matter may include any useful process, machine, or composition of matter. In most countries, the inventor must submit an application that discloses how to make and use the invention, as well as its best embodiment. In many cases, the enablement standard may require an inventor to describe the source and location of the original sample. Alternatively, where the invention involves living organisms, they may be deposited in a culture collection from which others can obtain samples. A patent examiner is likely to favor the deposit approach, while an inventor may prefer to describe the source. The patent application is examined and either approved or disapproved by a national or regional patent office.

Depending on the stringency and duration of review, administering a patent system can be expensive—a significant obstacle for poorer nations. For example, the 1992 budget for the United States Patent and Trademark Office exceeded $400 million, much of which was paid for by applicants. In the United States, equity is served by charging small businesses and not-for-profit organizations one-half the fees that apply to a larger corporation.

Particular subject matter may be singled out for special treatment. In the United States, inventions protecting biodiversity may also qualify as enhancing environmental quality; if so, they are con-

166

sidered "special" and receive swifter processing.[2] In industries subject to a lengthy regulatory approval process, such as pharmaceuticals, however, delaying the patent grant may be preferable to hastening it since the patent's life is measured from the date of issuance.

A recurring problem for indigenous people and other suppliers of information on wild biological resources is tracking the derivatives and ensuring that the source is identified (Cunningham, 1991). Patent disclosure rules might alleviate this problem and help assure that those who provide material and information receive appropriate compensation and recognition. In the United States, inequitable conduct by an inventor renders a patent unenforceable. Increasingly, national laws regarding use of biological resources will require permission from the person providing the material, and use of traditional knowledge will require informed consent. Failure to obtain the requisite consents may jeopardize any patent based on such improperly obtained samples or information.

A failure to disclose all relevant information may also be inequitable in the United States. This rule could be interpreted to require an inventor to identify the source of starting material and to describe traditional knowledge (e.g. of a shaman) that is used in an invention, along with other information about the state of the art. Such information could well be relevant to patentability as it might establish that the invention was not novel or was obvious. A test case will arise when a patent is challenged for failure to disclose such information.

Patent examiners are heavily burdened already, and it seems unwise to add a general requirement that the origins of all biological resources and information be disclosed. Rather, a person providing information or biological resources should seek a contractual provision requiring such disclosure by the recipient. Analogously, federal grants often require the grantee to identify the grant in a patent application. If the agreed-upon disclosure is not made, any patent issued would be vulnerable. The contractual approach has the additional advantage that the source may elect to remain out of the public record, so as to protect the source habitat from poaching or other destructive harvesting.

167

b. *The scope of protection*

In the United States, the scope of patentable subject matter has kept pace with biotechnology. It includes not only purified compounds, but also genetically altered microbes,[3] plants,[4] and animals.[5] Products of nature are not patentable, but U.S. courts have held that such novel life-forms, manipulated by genetic engineering, are the patentable fruits of human ingenuity. They can thus satisfy the statutory definitions of "manufacture" and "compositions of matter" and the other requirements for patentability outlined above. Hence, a wild plant and raw extract are unpatentable, whereas a genetically altered organism, purified drug, recombinant drug, or method of using a plant can each be separately subject to patent protection (Gollin, 1992).

In many countries, subject matter restrictions preclude or restrict patents on inventions relevant to biodiversity prospecting, including living creatures and pharmaceutical or agricultural technologies. *(See Table VI.1.)* The rationale for such restriction does not withstand close scrutiny.

First, such restrictions, thought to ensure public access to inventions of critical importance, may instead reduce access to foreign technologies; the inventors may choose not to import them without patent protection (Lesser, 1991; Bijloo, 1991; Evenson, 1990). Second, patentable subject matter may increasingly be found within developing nations with genetic resources. A lack of patent protection in a developing nation, or its inapplicability to biotechnology there, can severely limit the value of biodiversity prospecting.

Third, some people find the extension of property rights to genetic material morally offensive. Others find no moral difference between breeding, buying, and selling livestock, grain, and seeds, on the one hand, and genetic property rights, on the other (Nott, 1992). In any event, as Chief Justice Burger of the United States Supreme Court stated in *Diamond v. Chakrabarty:* "[L]egislative or judicial fiat as to patentability will not deter the scientific mind from probing into the unknown any more than Canute could command the tides."[6] Likewise, a concern about adverse environmental impacts of biotechnology will not be alleviated in any meaning-

Table VI.1. Limitations on Patents

Countries which do not allow patents for pharmaceutical compounds or compositions.

Argentina	Iran	Poland
Brazil	Iraq	Portugal
Egypt	Kuwait	Syria
Ghana	Lebanon	Tangier Zone
Honduras	Libya	Thailand
Hungary	Monaco	Tunisia
India	Norway	Turkey

Countries which restrict patents for biotechnological processes and their products.

Brazil	Nigeria
Chile	Peru
Colombia	Romania
Denmark	South Africa
European Patent Office	South Korea
Finland	Spain
Great Britain	Taiwan
Hungary	Thailand
India	Tunisia
Kuwait	Turkey
Lebanon	Uruguay
Malaysia	Yugoslavia
Mexico	

Source: Baxter and Sinnott, 1992.

ful way by simply banning patent protection for genetic material and other aspects of biotechnology. Only a system of environmental regulation can satisfy such concerns.

Finally, exclusive rights to an *improved* species or trait are narrow and do not remove the *wild* species (or any further modifications) from the public domain. As stated long ago by Justice Douglas of the United States Supreme Court in *Funk Bros. Co. v. Kale Co.*, in rejecting a product patent for a mixture of naturally occurring nitrogen-fixing bacteria: "The qualities of these bacteria...are part of the storehouse of knowledge of all men. They are manifestations of the laws of nature, free to all men and reserved exclusively to none."[7] This sweeping analysis has been narrowed somewhat, but it is safe to say that wild species as they exist in nature would not satisfy current standards of patentability in any country.[8]

Likewise, one could not obtain a patent on a wild habitat. The purified sample or the genetically altered organism could be protected, while the raw material or the original organism remains part of the public domain available for others to use (Barton, 1991a).

Even in the United States, novel theories of property that are not subject to legislation are likely to be met with skepticism in the courts. For example, in *Moore v. Regents of the Univ. of Cal.*,[9] the California Supreme Court rejected a plaintiff's assertion that he had a property right in his own genetic material sufficient to preclude a biotechnology company from using a valuable cell line derived from his spleen. (The court did uphold the patient's right to withhold informed consent to the use.) The policies cited by the court included the fear that such property rights would restrict biotechnology research. More recently, the National Institutes of Health filed patent applications on DNA sequences from the human genome. The U.S. Patent and Trademark Office initially rejected the applications, but the applications are still pending. (BNA, 1992).

These examples raise novel questions as to the morality and legality of property rights in human beings and, by extension, other species. Consider, for example, a species of fungus containing a useful antibiotic. A person who owned the fungus itself, or the land from which it was taken, might claim ownership of any products of genetic engineering that express the antibiotic activity, but there is no legal precedent extending personal or real property law so far. Rather, an ownership interest in the products can only be obtained via an intellectual property right such as a patent.

3. *Plant Breeders' Rights*

Most countries, including until recently the United States, exclude living organisms from utility patent protection. Plant breeders' rights can fill the gap with respect to plant species. These rights encompass a variety of intellectual property laws. In the United States, plant patents for distinctive asexually reproduced plants were established in 1930.[10] Plant patent protection may even extend to the discovery of an unprotected wild or domestic plant, as long as it can be bred asexually.[11]

New sexually reproduced plant varieties may be subject to the 1961 International Convention for the Protection of New Varieties of Plants (UPOV). UPOV remains principally an instrument of developed countries (including the United States), but some developing countries and other non-signatories of UPOV have their own plant breeders' rights (Lesser, 1991). Under UPOV, a breeder may obtain exclusive rights to a novel plant variety if it is distinctive, uniform, and stable. The duration is comparable to that for a utility patent. Arguably, the rights would cover a plant cultivated for medicinal or industrial (e.g., wastewater treatment) as well as agricultural purposes.

The requirements for obtaining protection under UPOV are geared toward cultivars that breed true-to-type for the desired trait. This is a difficult standard for a wild variety that contains many heterozygous genes, but can often be met by several generations of breeding. Although some wild plants might possibly be protected, many could not be; nor could animals or micro-organisms. Plant breeders' rights are thus of limited use in providing exclusive rights to the entire range of components of biodiversity.

171

Historically, plant breeders' rights have been weaker than patents: they were encumbered with various forms of compulsory licensing, including a right for a breeder to use protected varieties in research to produce new breeds, and for a farmer to use seed in subsequent seasons. Moreover, breeders' rights relate only to the whole plant, not to its chemical components. For this reason, industry has found utility patent protection for a plant and its components generally to be preferable to a plant patent or breeder's right.[12]

Although generally perceived as weak, plant breeders' rights, like patents, may be too strong from a developing nation's or farmer's viewpoint. Recent revisions to UPOV narrow the breeders' and farmers' exceptions and extend the period of protection. Developing nations and small farmers may distrust powerful breeding companies. They may also fear the possibility of losing the right to use germplasm or of a few protected varieties dominating agriculture and replacing the attendant threat of genetic uniformity (Juma, 1989). The same result may arise, however, from public sector agricultural research and development practices.

In sum, plant breeders' rights do not provide a direct stake in the wild components of biodiversity. Like utility patents, however, they can add value to plant cultivars deriving from wild habitats. Countries engaged in biodiversity prospecting for crops, as either sample providers or recipients, should consider adopting plant breeders' rights to promote sustainable development of plant genetic resources. Practitioners should apply such rights where available.

4. Petty Patents

In Germany and many countries with intellectual property laws modeled after Germany's (not including the United States), a technical advance that does not rise to the level of invention required by a utility patent may nonetheless be protected as a utility model, sometimes known as a petty patent. Petty patents may be more relevant than utility patents to adaptive innovation in developing nations (Evenson, 1990), so they are potentially important for defining native rights in biodiversity in source countries.

For example, a method of extracting an active preparation from a particular plant in the Amazonian rainforest, and the extract itself, might be "obvious" given the international state of the art and, hence, unpatentable. The method and the extract may, however, be novel, useful in obtaining a purified sample of an active component, and an inventive step ahead of other methods, entitling the inventor—whether a shaman or an ethnobotanist—to a petty patent.

As with utility patents, an applicant for a petty patent must demonstrate novelty, industrial utility, and an inventive step (which is short of the higher standard of non-obviousness). The petty patent is intended to reward and provide incentive for less sophisticated developments, and the duration of exclusive rights is shorter than for utility patents, typically 7 to 10 years (Lesser, 1990).

A fundamental weakness of petty patents is that they are limited to the country granting them: they are not subject to reciprocal rights under any international convention. Therefore, although the inventor in a source country may exclude domestic competition, someone in another country may immediately copy the innovation without infringement. Clearly, recognizing petty patent rights internationally would help protect source-country materials. However, the political impetus for such a reform is lacking.

A policy alternative to relying on petty patents is to adapt the utility patent system by maintaining a low standard of inventiveness, and providing protection for minor advances. International reciprocity could thereby be achieved. The disadvantage of such an approach is that it would invite a flood of "garbage" patents removing technologies from the public domain.

5. Trademarks

Leaving secrecy and inventiveness aside, a product linked to the sustainable development of biodiversity can enjoy a competitive advantage among consumers around the world simply because it is perceived as "green." Consumers in the developed nations are often willing to pay extra for such products. Trademarks and certifications can protect the competitive advantage of the company providing the green product, and the revenues can be returned to the source of the product through licensing and other contractual arrangements. This approach has been effective in providing funds to indigenous people sustainably producing, for example, Brazil nuts and materials for cosmetic products.

The general principles of trademark law are broadly applicable to biodiversity prospecting. In market economies, the trademark for a product may be critical to its commercial success, and a company's trademarks can be among its most valuable assets. A trademark identifies the origin of goods or services, prevents deception and confusion in the marketplace, and protects goodwill; trademark law prohibits competitors from using confusingly similar trademarks on competing products.

Trademark laws are relatively simple to administer and trademarks can be protected without national registration in some countries. A trademark can last forever, but cannot be licensed or assigned apart from the goods or services it represents. In licensing a trademark, the owner must retain the right of quality control; otherwise, the exclusive right to the mark, and the goodwill associated with it, may be lost. Principles of fair competition also control the use of trademarks—unfair or deceptive statements about products may be illegal.

Certification marks and denominations of origin resemble trademarks insofar as they are affixed to goods and signify to consumers a certain quality. Examples include the French Appellation Controllee, the German Blue Angel environmental certification, the U.S. Underwriters Laboratory, the Good Housekeeping Seal, the Green Seal environmental certification programs, and sustainable timber certifications. These certifications differ from trademarks in that the certifying organization is not the entity marketing the product, but rather an independent public or private organization.

In the context of biodiversity development, individual regions or organizations can certify that particular products, such as timber or Brazil nuts from local forests or algae from a coastal region, were obtained in a sustainable manner. The same principle would apply to products of genetic engineering. In practice, it will be difficult to find objective standards for certifying products of sustainable biodiversity prospecting. Economic and cultural concerns vary widely among countries and habitats.

6. *Copyright*

Copyright law may indirectly protect rights relating to biodiversity, and its simple administrative scheme is a promising model for addressing such rights. Copyright law protects original works of authorship expressed in a tangible medium, but not the underlying ideas. Copyrights can cover artistic and literary work, computer programs, and commercial designs. Copyright protection is easy and inexpensive to obtain—placing a notice on publications preserves the right, though registration is necessary to commence a lawsuit—and has a long duration, typically 50 years beyond the life of the author.

Data now being collected regarding species, extracts, and their utility, and data to be collected under the Convention on Biological Diversity, may be subject to copyright protection when included in publications or data banks. The extent of copyright protection for mere compilations of data has been rolled back and is in flux, at least in the United States. Those compiling biodiversity data bases must take care to obtain whatever copyright is available.

Copyright law is flexible. It has even been proposed that genetically engineered DNA sequences could be protected by copyright, so as to prevent copying of the DNA or reproduction of organisms carrying it (Kayton, 1982). Apart from questions as to the legality and morality of such an approach the protection would not as a practical matter apply to naturally existing sequences, which are not a work of authorship (Roberts, 1987). Trade secrets, patents, and plant breeders' rights are more appropriate than copyright for protecting genetic resources themselves, as opposed to information about them.

175

7. Intellectual Property Management

a. Enforcement

How does the owner of intellectual property rights exploit them to produce revenue, in the context of biodiversity prospecting? An owner able to market a proprietary technology may derive revenues by excluding others from competing, thus obtaining a market advantage. But maintaining that advantage may call for legal enforcement.

Litigation to enforce intellectual property rights is expensive, time-consuming, and difficult to accomplish worldwide—in many countries, the judicial system may not be adequate to the task. Obtaining jurisdiction over the defendant can also present problems. Arbitration agreements between contracting parties simplify matters, but they offer no protection against an outsider who infringes a patent or misappropriates a trade secret.

b. Voluntary Licensing

A license is simply an agreement not to enforce exclusive intellectual property rights in exchange for payment of an up-front fee, a royalty, or a cross-license. Revenue from licensing technology to others contributes to the incentive and reward of intellectual property rights, and can therefore foster conservation. An owner of a patent, trade secret, or other right derived from biodiversity prospecting may lack the capacity to develop and market a related product, but can license someone else to commercialize it.

From the licensee's standpoint, obtaining a license allows exploitation of state-of-the-art technology without fear of liability for infringement. For example, a biotechnology company may purchase a license from a sample provider in order to use a trade secret or patented compound without fear of an infringement action. Reciprocally, a sample provider may seek a license from a biotechnology company to use advanced techniques for extracting and assaying samples.

In theory, a license is a purely voluntary agreement between two parties, and the owner has the absolute right *not* to license the technology to others. In particular instances, a source country may decide not to allow others to use protected samples found during prospecting, or a biotechnology company may decide not to permit another company in a developing country to use a process for assaying a sample. However, this right of exclusivity in intellectual property is limited by such provisions as antitrust law and compulsory licensing.

c. Compulsory Licensing

Compulsory licensing provisions restrict the owner's right to exclude others. For example, statutory provision in the United States[13] allows the federal government or its contractors to use *any* patented technology upon payment of a reasonable royalty. Likewise, the Plant Variety Protection Act allows for compulsory licensing to ensure an adequate food supply.[14]

Many countries have even more extensive compulsory licensing laws than does the United States, pursuant to a policy of ensuring domestic access to significant technology. The broadest laws provide anyone with the right to use an invention upon payment of a set fee and allow individuals in a source country to use patented biotechnology despite the owner's desire to the contrary. Narrower laws have a "working" requirement: in other words, if a patentee does not employ or "work" the technology in a given country within a specified number of years, other private parties can obtain a compulsory license. In its narrowest form, the working requirement can be satisfied if the patent owner merely imports the patented product, such as a drug, plant, or seed.

The most narrowly defined working requirement, together with a government licensing provision, such as the United States' section 1498, assures that a product is domestically available, either through importation or by government action (Lesser, 1991). Thus, if a patented biotechnology process proves essential to the development of biological diversity in a given country, that country's government may contract for a private entity to employ the technology by paying a reasonable royalty to the patent owner. The requirement of government involvement ensures that a license is only taken based on public need, and makes compensation of the patent owner more certain.

177

Sui generis Biodiversity Prospecting Rights

A number of models have been proposed for a special intellectual property right in biodiversity, but none is satisfactory by itself. Several international laws and covenants are predicated on some sort of intellectual property right or moral right attaching to cultural property and the knowledge of indigenous peoples, but such rights have not yet been enacted or employed in practice (Posey, 1991). A pioneering amendment to Kenya's intellectual property law specifically allows for a petty patent for traditional medicinal knowledge.[15] Such national laws can supplement trade secret protection for local knowledge.

Belcher (1992) and others suggest broadly that plant breeders' rights should serve as a model for rights in animal varieties, microorganisms, and their genes. Many practical problems confront these proposals, including how to define the scope of the right, who is entitled to it, the standards for obtaining it, and how it would be enforced. Nevertheless, in countries where patents on living organisms are not permitted, expanded breeders' rights might help provide incentives to conserve and sustainably develop biodiversity.

A system of farmers' rights has been developing since 1983 under the auspices of the United Nations Food and Agriculture Organization and the International Undertaking on Plant Genetic Resources. A fund was established by the Commission on Plant Genetic Resources as a mechanism for returning benefits to communities that have cultivated plants and bred animals incrementally over many generations (Bousquet, 1989). The farmers' rights concept is inherently limited to domesticated, not wild species. Its applicability as a biodiversity prospecting right is further limited by ambiguity as to what exactly would be subject to protection, and which states or groups would receive proceeds from the Fund. Farmers' rights, as yet, cannot be relied on to protect the components of biodiversity in wild habitats. Such a system may, however, ultimately facilitate the equitable sharing of benefits from using wild genetic material (Correa, 1992).

178

Barton (1988) suggests that if those responsible for conserving genetic diversity have a property right in the wild plant genetic resources they control, they could prohibit others from using the material without paying a license fee, thus creating a market for export of germplasm and financial incentives for conservation.

The biodiversity prospecting right based on access restriction cannot truly be called an intellectual property right because it does not involve any innovator or demonstrable innovation. It is a different kind of property right (Goldstein, 1991), based on the ability to "shut the greenhouse door," and requiring a government willing and able to prevent poaching. What is the scope of the right to restrict access? Should the state grant concessions to private prospectors, and if so, to whom, and on what terms?

The access restriction approach has been applied in Costa Rica, where the government has granted the private organization INBio a non-exclusive concession for prospecting. *(See Chapters II and III.)* Prospecting revenues are shared with the state for purposes of conservation. Other mechanisms would be necessary if the concessionaire, rather than the state, was given responsibility for applying revenues toward conservation and sustainable development.

How could property rights be fairly allocated among multiple sources of the same organism, genetic material, or extracts? And how could original sources be distinguished from progeny or copies? Barton suggests that the multi-source problem may be resolved through a blanket license such as the one ASCAP holds for musical recordings: (A set fee is paid to ASCAP each time a song is performed, with a portion distributed to the artist.) However, use of genetic material may be much more difficult to monitor than music broadcasts.

A related approach is exemplified by a system established under U.S. copyright law to handle the problem of music piracy using digital audiotapes: a fee is levied on sales of equipment and tapes, and is then distributed to artists, recording houses, and other copyright owners according to a pre-determined formula (instead of based on actual use). Such mass licensing schemes may become practicable with regard to samples of genetic resources when a consensus is reached as to who receives the fees and on what basis.

Sedjo (1988) points out that a system treating wild species as common property provides no incentive to conserve and does nothing to promote equity between developed and developing nations. He also notes that private ownership of newly discovered species and their genetic resources (as opposed to inventions) would be difficult to define, assign, and enforce, and proposes sovereign rights over wild species instead. This is essentially a natural resources model, akin to those underlying petroleum and mineral law: countries may prevent access for anyone who does not pay a concession fee and agree to other requirements. The principle of sovereign rights over biological resources has recently been recognized in Article 3 of the Convention on Biological Diversity.

Recognition of sovereign rights based on discovery rather than concession could promote contractual arrangements that provide local benefits from biodiversity prospecting, but discovery-based rights present many of the same problems that apply to existing intellectual property rights. Delegating sovereign rights to individuals based on their "discovery" solves nothing: if the discovery of the wild type species or genetic material, or its use, is novel and required the exercise of ingenuity, then some combination of trade secret, petty patent, breeders' rights or utility patent protection would apply. If novelty and ingenuity are not factors, a species or substance may have been "discovered" countless times over the ages, and many individuals around the world might assert competing claims. If the system were based on the first to assert the claim, a deluge of speculative claims on species of unknown utility could be expected. Analogously, the recent NIH patent applications on portions of the human genome (BNA, 1992) met with public disapproval in part because the utility of the gene fragments was unknown.

Some degree of novelty, ingenuity, and recognition of utility must be required for a system of "discovery rights" to work. And then such rights add little to the existing regime of patent law that covers inventions of compounds and processes. Indeed, a discoverer's right to a new species may be subject to the same moral criticism as patents on living organisms.

As a further caution, sovereign exclusive rights for discovery of naturally existing species would expropriate far more from the public domain than would patents or other conventional intellectual property rights in innovative derivatives of species. Finally, national ownership raises the possibility of bureaucratic inefficiency and perverse or draconian measures, such as displacing traditional cultures from preserves to promote the development of biological resources. (Of course, private ownership of prospecting rights could also result in such displacement if no laws prevented it.)

The policy of rewarding the discoverer of a species should not be confused with the desire to protect indigenous rights and to subsidize traditional cultures. The discoverer will frequently be an outsider.

One option for a simpler system of discoverer's rights that avoids many of these problems involves an award with a small flat fee to the first person who completes a taxonomic identification of a new species. Because identifications will frequently be made by foreigners, it may be best for the awards to be administered by an international body such as the United Nations.

The requirement of prior informed consent in Article 15(5) of the Convention on Biological Diversity suggests a mechanism for a system of discoverer's rights: if access to biological resources requires consent of the source country, then the country may impose a fee in consideration of the access, and pass that fee along to the person or group that discovered or traditionally used the species. This approach is a hybrid of the natural resources and intellectual property models. It is also reminiscent of the holding in *Moore v. Board of Regents*, discussed above, upholding a patient's right of informed consent to the commercial use of his cells.

Only intellectual effort can be protected as intellectual property—wild species or products existing in nature cannot. Hence no *sui generis* right can provide a direct economic incentive to protect wilderness biodiversity. Nonetheless, from the patents, trade secrets, and the other existing intellectual property rights discussed above, it should be possible to build a framework for protecting the biological components of biodiversity as they are used and developed and to provide adequate indirect economic benefits to reward those who foster conservation. This framework can then be strengthened with evolving intellectual property rights and linked with access restrictions and natural resources laws.

Recurring Problems with an Intellectual Property Approach

As we have seen in the specific cases above, many practical problems and policy questions arise in applying existing and proposed intellectual property rights to wild species and habitats— e.g. the establishment, ownership, and valuation of rights, allocation of benefits, and resolution of international differences in intellectual property policy. There are no simple resolutions to these problems and the questions remain open. They must be addressed by each involved person, group, or government seeking to build a framework for sustainable biodiversity prospecting. It will be a continuing challenge for intellectual property lawyers to find effective ways to satisfy the sometimes-conflicting imperatives of economic development, environmental conservation, equity, and ethics affecting biodiversity prospecting.

1. *Ownership*

Who should own a particular intellectual property right, including the right to protect it, develop it, enforce it, and profit from it? Consistent with the property rights approach inherent in sound biodiversity prospecting programs, the favored owner should be the person with the greatest potential for conserving habitat—the person closest to or with greatest control over the habitat. The owner may be the first to identify and taxonomically classify an organism, the first to use it, the first to purify an active component, or the first to clone the gene for a product. It has been suggested that a traditional community historically occupying the land should have an interest too.

Once an intellectual property right has been established, there are many possible ownership strategies for transferring, exchanging, pooling, and developing it. These include sole ownership by a vertically integrated corporation or a public agency, contracts between individuals and corporations, between collectives and corporations, between corporations in arms length or joint venture agreements, and between public agencies and private parties. The most inclusive approach is a consortium, a multilateral joint venture between public agencies, private corporations, conservation groups, academic institutions, and economic development agencies from various countries (Gollin, 1993). The feasibility of these arrangements varies from country to country. *(See Chapter IV.)*

How do intellectual property rights apply in wildlands historically occupied by a traditional community, wildlands held by private or public entities, privately owned and cultivated lands, or in marine environments? The simplest answer is that land ownership is unrelated to intellectual property rights. It may be more meaningful, however, to look for some kind of interest analogous to the "shop right" found in some countries, allowing the employer to use the employee's invention, or like the moral right of the artist under copyright law.

2. *The Complexity of Life*

Any attempt to establish a proprietary right to a wild species or habitat will likely founder on the very complexity of life. The diversity and flux of habitats, each with a unique mix of indigenous species, makes it difficult to do more than take a "snapshot" of the inventory of species, thus showing a given habitat at a given time. A species present in a particular habitat may be present in other habitats, in other parts of the planet, concurrently or later on. Fish swim, birds fly, seeds scatter. Moreover, species evolve over time and they can appear in many strains. Can an intellectual property law identify and distinguish different components and varieties from one another? If not, then owners will have trouble enforcing their rights.

183

3. Derivation

It is difficult to prove the source of genetic material used in a recombinant organism, the species from which a purified compound derived, and the habitat in which the organism lived (McNeely et al., 1990). Derivation can be monitored to some extent by recording the chain of custody of a specimen. But what happens when a company receives samples from several sources, and develops a single product based on all such samples? Can each source of a chemical claim rights based on derivation? This situation could arise, with, for example, the neurotoxin homobatrachotoxin, which is found both in such widely different species as a New Guinea bird called a hooded pitohui and the Amazonian poison-dart frog (Angier, 1992).

There is a continuum from a raw extract, to a purified compound, to structurally related, but different compounds, to products whose design was inspired by an idea derived from a natural compound, but whose particular structure is unrelated (Wegner, 1992b). The proper scope of derivative rights is a contentious issue. Sample providers will push for broader standards of derivation, while recipients will favor a narrow standard extending only to products directly extracted.

4. Valuation

Those who supply and receive biodiversity samples have little basis for placing values on the components and products of biodiversity prospecting or on intellectual property rights in them. Valuation should become easier with experience as a broader basis for comparison develops (Simpson, 1992). Barton has estimated that the maximum fees for biodiversity prospecting of unimproved agricultural seed material worldwide are less than $100 million (Barton, 1991b). Of course, pharmaceuticals provide a larger market, and revenue for improved samples could be much higher. Still, royalties and compensation will probably not be sufficient to fill the needs of conservation, and other sources of financing will be necessary (Touche Ross, 1991).

5. *The Limits of Intellectual Property*

There is an extensive literature on the pros, cons, and practicalities of intellectual property rights in plant genetic material *ex situ* (Juma, 1989; Cohen, 1991), but such discussions have only indirect relevance to wild species and ecosystems (in their undisturbed states). Here, the question is: can intellectual property rights apply to wild species and habitats? By definition, a wild habitat is free from human intervention and devoid of intellectual attributes. Only when a human being studies, samples, or alters a wild habitat or species can "intellectual property" be created. But such property is not the habitat, itself, but the human interaction. Thus, strictly speaking, when we consider property rights in wilderness, these are not *intellectual* property rights.

In general, as noted, intellectual property rights do not attach directly to a product of nature, whether a species or an ecosystem. Applying intellectual property rights to the development of biological resources in an ecosystem nevertheless increases the economic value of the wild habitat, indirectly, because the ecosystem can be viewed as a repository of the raw materials for biodiversity prospecting (Reid, 1992; Sedjo, 1992). However, this indirect connection becomes attenuated when owners have no relation to the habitat and no ability to control it. It therefore seems that the wilder the material to which trade secrets, patents, and other intellectual property rights can attach, the more effective they will be in adding commercial value to wilderness.

6. *Equity and Indigenous Rights*

Intellectual property laws do not necessarily promote equity. The principles underlying intellectual property law reward the person or party who worked to create the right, but may block others from using an important drug or other product. The laws provide no surefire mechanism for balancing the needs of innovators with those possessing longstanding, but unexploited, indigenous knowledge. Finally, the costs of obtaining a patent tend to favor the wealthy over the poor, the sophisticated over the inexperienced, and developed nations over developing nations. That cost may need to be reduced to promote equity.

7. Ethics

To some, the ethical rationale for preserving biodiversity is more important than practical, economic, or aesthetic concerns (Doremus, 1991). Indeed, biodiversity prospecting may devalue the relationship of humanity with nature. Hence it may be impossible to fully reconcile a market-based intellectual property approach with certain ethical systems.

8. International Legal Inconsistencies

Biodiversity prospecting is an international trade that involves a wide variety of far-flung activities. Moreover, each country recognizes a different mixture of intellectual property rights (Lesser, 1991). Such differences make it difficult to develop an invention internationally.

International treaties such as the Paris Convention, the Berne Convention, and the Patent Cooperation Treaty provide reciprocity and some consistency in international intellectual property practice. Nevertheless, no legal advisor in one country may confidently plan a global strategy for intellectual property protection without extensive help from foreign lawyers (Fox, 1991). In addition, international technology transfer arrangements are expensive and somewhat unpredictable, thus undercutting the confidence needed to invest in biotechnology R&D.

The concerns and limits raised above hamper development of an international approach that would support biodiversity prospecting through intellectual property rights. Great effort will be required to sort these problems out, find practical solutions, and harmonize intellectual property laws with conservation and development laws and policies worldwide.

Intellectual Property in a Framework of Laws

Ideally, the role of intellectual property in a legal framework for biodiversity prospecting should be to provide incentives for sustainable development and conservation of bio-resources and to generate benefits, including royalty payments and enhanced access to technology, that may then be equitably shared. Vice President Gore has argued that better protection for intellectual property rights is essential to improve environmental protection around the world (Gore 1992, pp. 320-321). Yet, the sort of incentives an intellectual property system creates may work against conservation and do little to promote an equitable distribution of benefits. Intellectual property mechanisms are thus only part of a sound biodiversity prospecting policy. Along with the access restrictions and pro-conservation contractual clauses discussed in other chapters, other important components of the legal framework necessary to support conservation and equity include national environmental protection and natural resources laws.

Some of these laws are intended to protect habitats and species absolutely, with scant regard for economic costs. In the United States, for example, the Migratory Bird Treaty outlaws killing or trading in certain birds. The Endangered Species Act mandates protection of wildlands inhabited by endangered species. The National Wilderness Act sets aside entire ecosystems for preservation. Portions of the Clean Water Act and state and local laws restrict the development of wetlands. Such laws, easily justified in moral as well as practical terms, may be essential to limiting the destruction of biodiversity. But they do not promote sustainable development of biological resources as do intellectual property laws and technology transfer policies. The distribution of costs and benefits of such conservation laws is likely to provoke substantial political opposition—witness the heated debate in the United States over the application of the Endangered Species Act to the habitat of the spotted owl.

Other environmental laws more explicitly recognize economic imperatives, and regulate development to minimize environmental damage. In the United States, the National Environmental Policy Act requires that environmental impacts of and alternatives to any federal project be analyzed in an environmental impact statement which must address impacts on biodiversity (Carlson, 1988). The Clean Air Act and Clean Water Act establish limits for pollution and thereby transfer costs from the public to private permit applicants. Such laws can require project developers to assess wild habitat de-

187

struction, to consider alternatives that mitigate destruction, and to balance them against potential economic gains from development.

Natural resources laws, such as those allowing restricted access to federal lands for forestry, cattle grazing, and mining, and those restricting the catch allowed in off-shore fisheries, provide a good starting point in developing a model for sustainable biodiversity prospecting. Such laws need not promote destruction of resources rather than their conservation, but often have that result because they underestimate the costs of extractive (as opposed to sustainable) development. Great care must be taken to avoid such mistakes because once a species is lost it is gone forever, and "useful products cannot be harvested from extinct species" (Wilson 1992).

Genetic resources may be managed like other natural resources, but their conservation is absolutely essential. A biodiversity management plan must recognize the importance of traditional knowledge, biotechnology, and intellectual property rights, and it must take into account and balance the many potentially competing interests of landowners, residents, sample collectors, international biotechnology companies, and consumers.

Requiring genetic prospectors to obtain extraction licenses, such as for forestry and fishing, would serve the goals of conservation, development, and equity. Doing so would allow governments to limit the rate of sampling and destruction of wild habitats for their genetic materials, provide a process for prospectors to use to gain access to biodiversity, strengthen the possibility of agreements on access control and trade secrecy, and generate revenue through license fees on unimproved materials that could be channelled back into the sustainable development of natural resources. Such measures will complement any intellectual property regime for protecting improved genetic materials (Barton, 1991b).

The Convention on Biological Diversity's Effect on Intellectual Property Law

Strengthening intellectual property rights in non-industrialized nations has been a prominent issue in recent years, and no consensus has yet been reached (Bijloo, 1991; Evenson, 1991; Lesser, 1991). The United States urges the adoption of uniform, strong intellectual property laws throughout the world to promote innovation and protect markets (Gore, 1992). Meanwhile, less developed countries maintain generally less extensive systems of intellectual property protection (Wegner, 1992a), and insist on the right to tailor them to local circumstances. Differential treatment creates friction under international trade laws (Housman and Zaelke, 1992, pp. 590–94).

The Convention on Biological Diversity has placed intellectual property rights on the agenda of decisionmakers dealing with the environment and its sustainable development. In essence, the Convention puts access to genetic resources on the same plane as transfer of biotechnology and establishes reciprocity as a principle of biodiversity prospecting. In other words, the Convention promotes transfer of genetic resources in exchange for technology transfer to build a biotechnology capacity in source countries.

U.S. opponents of the Convention focused on provisions affecting intellectual property, and argued that the Convention undercuts ongoing efforts by the United States to persuade all countries to adopt strong and uniform intellectual property laws. A particular concern was raised that the Convention would result in an improper taking of biotechnology through compulsory licensing (Porter, 1992).

The Convention includes troublesome language, but as a whole it does not warrant such opposition. A detailed textual analysis of the Convention is set forth in Annex 3; some general points are emphasized here. First, the narrow focus of the United States on intellectual property policy and the goal of technological progress failed to take into account competing or divergent interests that are also central to the Convention—the goals of conservation and development. By the same token, other nations went too far by emphasizing their own development needs exclusively. The Convention should be judged on the basis of its impact on all relevant policies, not just one or another (Reid, 1992).

Second, critics have overemphasized Article 16, "Access to and Transfer of Technology," and have underemphasized other sections much more favorable to an intellectual property rights approach (Wegner, 1992b). The much-negotiated language of Article 16 is not contrary to the property interests of United States industry. In addition, the provisions in Article 16 calling for access to and transfer of technology are balanced against Article 15, which calls on countries to increase access to genetic resources. It is unlikely that a developing country with genetic resources will pursue an interpretation of Article 16 that allows it to pirate patented technology when a parallel interpretation of Article 15 would allow foreign biodiversity prospectors free access to the country's preserves.

Moreover, Article 11 establishes the principle that intellectual property rights should be expanded, not diminished: it calls for each contracting country to "adopt economically and socially sound measures that act as incentives for the conservation and sustainable use of components of biological diversity." Such incentives clearly include intellectual property rights.

Other sections also support intellectual property rights. For example: Article 1, which covers both genetic resources and the intellectual property rights in them, includes among its objectives sustainable use, access, and technology transfer; Article 7 promotes the development of information and data bases subject to copyright and trade secrets; and Articles 8(j), 10(c), and 18(4) call for the protection of knowledge and innovation of local and traditional people and the use of such intellectual property. Agenda 21 also includes provisions emphasizing the importance of intellectual property rights.

The Convention was satisfactory to more than 150 countries and unsatisfactory (initially) only to the United States—based on concerns with maintaining competitiveness. The concern that Articles 16 and 19 are ambiguous is well-founded. The United States has now taken the more prudent approach of adopting the Convention while issuing an interpretive statement clarifying how the Convention would serve domestic interests, as well as those of other countries.

190

Intellectual property rights are supportive of the goals of the Convention (Duesing, 1992). Hence, in the long run, the Convention may actually promote the U.S. goal of strengthening intellectual property rights in developing countries. In particular, countries that are sources for genetic material have an incentive under the Convention's reciprocity principle to support the growth of a local biotechnology industry that will, in turn, facilitate the development of their genetic resources. Establishing such local industries will create markets for biotechnology equipment and demand for further technology, and thus benefit the biotechnology industry in developed and developing countries.

Historically, the evidence suggests that as countries acquire a basic level of technology, they reach a threshold where intellectual property rights become desirable to protect exported products and to facilitate technology transfer from other countries into the country (Fritschak, 1992; Bijloo, 1991; Touche Ross, 1991; Evenson, 1990; Primo Braga, 1990). Ultimately, then, the Convention may help the United States achieve its goal of expanding the scope of intellectual property protection around the world.

Increasing attention to biodiversity prospecting by multinational companies and developing countries only enhances the possibility of a "Grand Bargain" whereby developing nations would find it in their self-interest to expand and strengthen intellectual property rights, thereby profiting from their biological resources, while developed nations more readily concede that each nation may tailor its system to fit its own conservation, development, and equity needs. In sum, then, the Convention promotes technology transfer in a manner that is unlikely to disrupt intellectual property rights, but overall is more likely to promote free trade in genetic resources and associated technologies—a sustainable biodiversity prospecting trade.

Conclusion

The greater the range of intellectual property protection available in a country, the more choices the inventor and the practitioner have as they try to protect the fruits of research, development, and marketing. A developing nation seeking to promote biodiversity

191

prospecting, domestic innovation, and technology acquisition should have an intellectual property system including trade secret legislation, patent protection, plant breeders' rights, and utility models in a supportive economic and political climate (Lesser 1991). Trademark and copyright laws, as well as a petty patent system, also will facilitate biodiversity prospecting.

These laws can be tailored to balance rights between the exclusive private domain and the public domain. For example, countries may allow pharmaceutical and agricultural inventions to be patented without fear that monopoly rights would prevent use of critical technologies, *if* provision is made for limited compulsory licensing by the government. Compulsory licensing provisions in other countries along the lines of those already found in the United States are not likely to be strongly opposed by industry. The alternative of precluding protection of intellectual property related to biodiversity, which may seem politically attractive based on moral arguments as to property rights in genetic resources, may instead have catastrophic results on the development of a biotechnology industry and a biodiversity prospecting trade.

To specifically promote sustainable development of wild biological resources and equitable allocation of the resulting benefits, some countries may be tempted to consider enacting *sui generis* rights that would protect species as discovered in the wild. The theoretical and scientific underpinnings for such rights are weak, and so far no comprehensive proposal of how such a system would work has appeared. The details of discoverer's rights require extensive elaboration before these rights can be recommended in practice.

An intellectual property rights approach to biodiversity prospecting is necessary, but it is not enough to ensure conservation, sustainable development, and the equitable allocation of benefits. In each affected country, intellectual property laws need to be analyzed to determine whether they allow adequate protection of the products of biodiversity prospecting, maximize the benefits to those who preserve wild habitat, and complement laws for natural resources protection. Legal reform may be necessary to achieve these ends.

For now, there is no international agreement on the optimal interplay between biodiversity, biotechnology transfer, and intellectual property rights. Until a consensus or compromise is reached, unresolved disputes will impede efforts to rely on intellectual property rights as a tool for conserving biodiversity.

The Convention on Biological Diversity ensures that the role of intellectual property in the sustainable development of genetic resources will continue to receive attention. Future interpretations of the Convention and domestic laws around the world should help promote mechanisms that make habitat conservation worthwhile and ensure that those who conserve the habitat are properly rewarded for their efforts. A robust intellectual property system can provide such mechanisms and can support the other measures discussed in this report to provide a solid framework for biodiversity prospecting.

Notes

1. *Ruckelshaus v. Monsanto Co.*, 467 U.S. Reports 986 (1984).
2. Title 37, Code of Federal Regulations, § 1.102 (c).
3. *Diamond v. Chakrabarty*, 447 U.S. Reports 303, 309-310 (1980).
4. *In re Hibberd*, 227 U.S. Patents Quaterly (BNA) 443 (PTO Bd. App. & Int. 1985).
5. *In re Allen*, 2 U.S. Patents Quarterly 2d (BNA) 1425 (PTO Bd. App. & Int. 1987).
6. 447 U.S. Reports 303, 317 (1980).
7. 333 U.S. Reports 127, 130 (1948).
8. See *Diamond v. Chakrabarty*, 447 U.S. Reports 303, 309-310 (1980).
9. 271 Cal. Rptr. 146 (1990).
10. Title 35, U.S. Code, §§ 161-164.
11. Chisum, *Patents* (1992) § 1.05[1][a], p.1-253.
12. Chisum, *Patents* (1992), § 1.05[4], pp. 1-283 to 286.
13. Title 28, U.S. Code, § 1498.
14. Title 7, U.S. Code, § 2404.
15. The Industrial Property Bill, 1989. Kenya Gazette Supplement No. 92 (Bills No. 18):1399–1459.

193

Bibliography

Abraham, M. 1989. Some consumer and Third World concerns on the patenting of biotechnology products and processes. Pp. 53–54 *in: Patenting life forms in Europe, Proceedings*. International Campaign for Development Action, Barcelona, Spain.

Angier, N. 1992. Rare bird indeed carries poison in bright feathers. *New York Times*. October 30:A1.

Barton, J.H. 1991a. Patenting life. *Scientific American* 264:40–46.

Barton, J.H. 1991b. Relating the scientific and the commercial worlds in genetic resources negotiations. Paper presented at the Symposium on Property Rights, Biotechnology, and Genetic Resources, African Centre for Technology Studies and World Resources Institute, Nairobi, Kenya, June 10–14.

Barton, J.H. 1992. Adapting the intellectual property system to new technologies. Paper presented at National Research Council Conference on Intellectual Property Rights in the Global Arena, Washington, D.C., Jan. 8–9, 1992.

Barton, J.H., and E. Christensen. 1988. Diversity compensation systems: Ways to compensate developing nations for providing genetic materials. Pp. 339–355 *in*: J.R. Kloppenburg, Jr. (ed.) *Seeds and Sovereignty*, Duke Univ. Press, Durham, N.C.

Baxter, J.W. and Sinnott, J.P. 1992. *World Patent Law and Practice*, Matthew Bender, New York.

Belcher, B, 1992. Living inventions. *IDRC Reports*, July 1992, pp. 20–22.

Bijloo, J.D. 1991. *The impact of intellectual property protection in biotechnology and plant breeding on developing countries*. Study commissioned by the Stimulation Programme of Directorate General International Cooperation, Ministry of Foreign Affairs, The Netherlands.

BNA's Patent, Trademark and Copyright Journal. 1992. NIH gene application is debated at forum on human genome. 44:73–75.

Bousquet, J.P.C., 1989. Plant genetic resources: Protection of rights. *Pp. 43–47 in: Patenting life forms in Europe, Proceedings*. International Campaign for Development Action, Barcelona, Spain.

Carlson, C. 1988. NEPA and the conservation of biological diversity. *Environmental Law* 19:15–36.

Chisum, D.S. 1992. *Patents*. Matthew Bender, New York.

Cohen, J.I. 1991. *Ex situ* conservation of plant genetic resources: Global development and environmental concerns. *Science* 253:866–872.

Correa, C.M. 1992. Biological resources and intellectual property rights. *European Intellectual Property Rights* 5:154–157.

Cunningham, A.B. 1991. Indigenous knowledge and biodiversity. *Cultural Survival Quarterly*, Summer:4–8.

Doremus, H. 1991. Patching the ark: Improving legal protection of biological diversity. *Ecology Law Quarterly* 18:265.

Doyle, J. 1985. *Altered Harvest* pp. 300–321, 373–385. Viking, New York, N.Y.

Duesing, J.H. 1992. The Convention on Biological Diversity: Its impact on biotechnology research. *AGRO food INDUSTRY HI-TECH* 3(4), p. 19.

Elisabetsky, E., 1991. Folklore, tradition, or know-how? *Cultural Survival Quarterly*, Summer:9–13.

Evenson, R.E. 1991. *Intellectual Property Rights for Appropriate Invention.* The Economics of Technology, Working Paper No. 6, USAID Bureau for Program and Policy Development, Washington, D.C.

Evenson, R.E. 1990. Survey of empirical studies. *Pp. 33–46 In*: W.E. Siebeck (ed.) *Strengthening protection of intellectual property in developing countries: A survey of the literature*, World Bank Discussion Paper 112, Washington, D.C.

Fowler, C., Lachkovics, E., Mooney, P., and Shand, H. 1988. From cabbages to kings? *Development Dialogue* 1988(1-2):239–255.

Fox, B. 1991. An international charter for inventors? *New Scientist* January 19:33–35.

Fritschak, C.R. 1992. Harmonization vs. differentiation in IPR regimes. Paper presented for The Global Dimensions of Intellectual Property Rights in Science and Technology Conference, Washington, D.C. January 8–9, 1992.

Goldstein, J.H. 1991. The prospects for using market incentives to conserve biological diversity. *Environmental Law* 21:985–1014.

Gollin, M.A. 1991. Using intellectual property to improve environmental protection. *Harvard J. Law and Technology* 4:193–235.

Gollin, M.A. 1992. Carving property rights out of the public domain to conserve biodiversity. Paper presented at the Conference of the International Association for the Study of Common Property, Washington, D.C., September 18.

195

Gollin, M.A. 1993. Ownership strategies for conserving biological diversity. Paper presented at The Industrial Utilization of Tropical Plants and the Conservation of Biodiversity Conference, Enugu, Nigeria, February 18, 1993.

Gore, A. 1992. *Earth in the Balance*. Houghton Mifflin, Boston.

Housman, R. and D. Zaelke. 1992. Trade, Environment, and Sustainable Development: A primer. *Hastings International and Comparative Law Review*. 15:535–612.

Juma, C. 1989. *The Gene Hunters: Biotechnology and the Scramble for Seeds*. Princeton University Press, Princeton, NJ.

Kayton, I. 1982. Copyright in living genetically engineered works. *George Washington L. Rev.* 50:191–218.

Khalil, M.H., Reid, W.V., Juma, C. 1992. Property rights, biotechnology and genetic resources. *Biopolicy International*, African Centre for Technology Studies, Nairobi, Kenya.

Lesser, W. 1990. An overview of intellectual property systems. *Pp. 5-15 in*: W.E. Siebeck (ed.) *Strengthening protection of intellectual property in developing countries: A survey of the literature*, World Bank Discussion Paper 112, Washington, D.C.

Lesser, W. 1991. *Equitable patent protection in the developing world: Issues and approaches*. Eubios, Christchurch.

McNeely, J.A., Miller, K.R., Reid, W.V., Mittermeier, R.A., and Werner, T.A. 1990. *Conserving the World's Biodiversity*. IUCN, Gland, Switzerland; WRI, IUCN, WWF-US, and the World Bank, Washington, D.C.

Nott, R. 1992. Patent protection for plants and animals. *European Intellectual Property Rights*. 3:79–86.

Porter, G. 1992. *The false dilemma: The Biodiversity Convention and Intellectual Property Rights*. Environmental and Energy Study Institute, Washington, D.C.

Posey, D. 1990. Intellectual property rights and just compensation for indigenous knowledge. *Anthropology Today* 6:13–16.

Posey, D. 1991. Effecting international change. *Cultural Survival Quarterly*, Summer:29–35.

Primo Braga, C. 1990. The developing country case for and against intellectual property protection. Pp. 69–87 *in*: W.E. Siebeck (ed.) *Strengthening protection of intellectual property in developing countries: A survey of the literature*, World Bank Discussion Paper 112, Washington, D.C.

Reid, W.V. 1992. Genetic resources and sustainable agriculture: Creating incentives for local innovation and adaptation. *Biopolicy International* No. 2, African Centre for Technology Studies, Nairobi, Kenya.

Rensberger, B. 1992. Scientists search the land for disease-fighting flora. *Washington Post*, Aug.2:A1.

Roberts, L. 1987. Who owns the human genome? *Science* 237: 358–360.

Roberts, L. 1992. Chemical prospecting: Hope for vanishing ecosystems? *Science* 256:1142–1143.

Sedjo, R.A. 1988. Property rights and the protection of plant genetic resources. Pp. 306–314 *in*: J.R. Kloppenburg, Jr. (ed.) *Seeds and Sovereignty*, Duke Univ. Press, Durham, N.C.

Sedjo, R.A. 1992. Property rights, genetic resources, and biotechnological change. *J. Law and Economics* 35:199–213.

Simpson, R.D., 1992. Transactional arrangements and the commercialization of tropical biodiversity. Discussion Paper, Resources for the Future, Washington, D.C.

Thoreau, H.D. 1851. Cited in: R. Sattlemeyer et al. (eds.). 1992. *Journal*. Princeton University Press, Princeton, p. 3–4.

Touche Ross, 1991. *Conservation of Biological Diversity: The Role of Technology Transfer*. A report for the United Nations Conference on Environment and Development and the UNEP Intergovernmental Negotiating Committee for a Convention on Biological Diversity. Touche Ross & Co., London, U.K.

Wegner, H.C. 1992a. Patents to aid (or hinder) international technology transfer. Pp. 1057–1073 *in*: *Wege zum Japanischen Recht*, Duncker & Humboldt, Berlin.

Wegner, H.C. 1992b. Biotechnology law in the U.S.A. and the Nairobi biodiversity treaty. Paper presented at Biofair '92, Yokohama, Aug. 27.

Wilson, E.O. 1992. *The Diversity of Life*. Harvard Press, Cambridge, MA.

VII.

POLICY OPTIONS FOR SCIENTIFIC AND TECHNOLOGICAL CAPACITY-BUILDING

Calestous Juma with the assistance of Bernard Sihanya

Can policies on biodiversity prospecting contribute over the long term to economic development, conservation, and the equitable sharing of genetic resources? Yes, if they help the countries providing genetic resources develop national capacity in biotechnology, and no if they don't. Efforts that do not build such capacity will only perpetuate the traditional export of raw materials from developing countries, which has left their human capital and technological capacity underdeveloped.

Many policies and institutions emphasize the sharing of returns on the sale of products derived from biological material, thus giving developing countries an incentive to conserve biological diversity. But putting more emphasis on the role of technological innovation in long-term national development would serve all nations better.

National Innovation Policy and Biodiversity

Since colonial days, the global economic system and the national policies of developing countries have promoted the export of raw materials to the industrialized countries for processing. But over the last three decades, returns from the export of raw materials have dropped as technology has changed and production and utilization efficiency increased. Biotechnology itself may make a

199

wide range of raw material exports from developing countries redundant (Sasson, 1992).

Increasingly, developing countries are emphasizing downstream processing as a way of adding value to their exports. Thanks to such policies, machinery imports have been high and local industrial production and employment have grown. Indeed, much of the technological development in the developing countries has been associated with the acquisition of the equipment and machinery needed to extract raw materials. But most new plants have added little to national technological capacity. Experience has given the lie to the assumption that if machinery is installed, technological competence will automatically follow.

Biodiversity offers developing countries unique opportunities for linking the use of a raw material with technological innovation, not simply industrial production. Biotechnology is knowledge-intensive and developing it need not involve the massive transfer of mechanical equipment. The right technology policy can help developing countries capture future returns in both the pharmaceutical and agriculture industries while increasing local technological capacity. By empowering local people to know, use, and conserve biological resources, it can increase meaningful participation in the management and development of genetic resources.

Whatever superficial resemblances the technology policies adopted by various countries have, their underlying differences have enormous significance, especially with respect to international trade and competitiveness. The United States, for instance, emphasizes basic science, health, energy, agriculture, and defense. Japan and the Newly Industrializing Countries (NICs) of the Pacific Rim, on the other hand, tend to take a systems approach with a strong bias toward industrial research and development (R&D); then focus research and commercial activities on local and regional markets (OTA, 1991). Such differences in scientific and technological capability, industrial potential, as well as political and economic ideology, must be taken into account when examining the relevance and transferability of technology strategy to developing countries.

200

Technology policy measures came of age in the industrialized market-economy countries in the 1960s, when the role of science and technology in the growth of the U.S. economy over the previous 50 years became clear. In the Keynesian tradition, government intervention was considered necessary to compensate for factors inhibiting technological progress. Market and institutional imperfections that distorted the rate and direction of investment in R&D represented one such factor. The failure of firms to translate research findings into applicable technology was another. This failure largely arose from the weak linkages which existed between universities, research and other academic organizations, on the one hand, and industry on the other. This feature is still prevalent in developing countries (Pavitt, 1987; Ghai, 1974). In addition, risk, uncertainty, and the high costs of R&D were in some cases reducing the rate of investment, shifting research toward short-term goals, and reducing the social benefits of R&D. Policy-makers thus began to view government intervention as requisite to maximizing the social gains of R&D.

Against this backdrop, technology policy in the industrialized countries has followed three paths. The Japanese model is one. The role of Japan's Ministry of International Trade and Industry (MITI), which has been studied in depth (Johnson, 1982; Okimoto, 1989), has been to promote technological innovation as a tool for international competitiveness, not to simply promote trade in the context of comparative advantage. Japan's approach has been systemic from the beginning. MITI virtually ignored conventional economic theory and from the start adopted the practical goal of backing the most advanced technologies with the widest possible world market.

Another approach, adopted by the United States, has been to enhance international competitiveness through selective policy measures and government funding for new technologies. Specifically, government procures technologies at the early stages of their development. This approach was used extensively to develop the U.S. electronics industry and stimulate military technology. Other countries, especially in Europe, promoted innovation in renewable energy technology in the 1980s through public procurement.

The third approach to technology policy involves less direct financial support for innovation. Tax credits have been used in countries such as Japan, Canada, United States, and elsewhere to stimulate and promote innovation. In most industrialized countries, grants, risk-sharing investment, and loans are also used. In addition, a number of these countries provide special support to small and medium-size firms.

All of these approaches are currently being supplemented by policies and investments focusing on specific sectors and by international collaborative arrangements. The European Research Coordination Agency (EUREKA), launched in 1985, brings together industry, university, and government researchers working in market-oriented information technologies in a bid to compete against the United States and Japan. Other collaborative research measures include the Programme for Basic Research in Industrial Technologies for Europe (BRITE), the European Strategic Programme of Research and Development in Information Technologies (ESPIRIT), and the European Technological Community, approved by the European Economic Community in June 1985.

In some countries, including Japan, France, and Italy, technology policy furthers broad national development strategies. In others, such as Germany, Denmark, and the Netherlands, the technology policy goal is to create a suitable environment for economic change and international competitiveness. Few countries have integrated technology policies fully into national plans, but this may be changing. Countries such as the Netherlands are already starting to review the role of science and technology in sustainable development, set up a wide range of consultative and co-ordinating procedures along with institutions within government and industry, and introduce new institutional measures to create and galvanize links between industry and government. What remains conspicuously lacking, however, is any attempt to make industrial policies sensitive to environmental concerns.

Unlike their industrial counterparts, developing countries' technology policies have emphasized technology acquisition rather than technological innovation. This fourth approach has led to efforts to tie the transfer and acquisition of biotechnology to the exploration of and access to biodiversity. A few developing countries have also introduced fiscal incentives. For example, South Korea, Singapore, Malaysia, Mexico, and Peru all promote technological development through tax incentives. But the most common stimulus to technological growth in developing countries is direct financial assistance. Singapore, for example, has experimented with a number of R&D and product development schemes in the last 10 years that include direct financing.

In general, most developing countries have yet to come up with effective policies for technological development, and the few that have them haven't administered or managed them well. A case in point is Ethiopia, which worked hard to develop a comprehensive policy framework on science and technology only to have its implementation compromised by the internecine wars raging there and the related lack of funds allocated to science and technology activities.

Given the status and nature of technology policies in developing countries, it's not surprising that biodiversity prospecting is not yet seen as an integral part of technological development. Laws and institutions dealing with biodiversity have so far been based on conservation imperatives, and the economic value of these resources has been all but ignored. Agencies targeting biodiversity are being established in many countries, but most are adjuncts of environmental agencies or natural history institutions with scant experience in product development. Without significant policy changes, biodiversity and its potential for technological development will simply be exported to the developed world, retracing the flows of raw materials during colonial days. The result will be destruction of habitat, limited or inefficient development of resources, and unfair distribution of resulting benefits.

Linking Biotechnology to Biodiversity

Questions of technology transfer were closely linked to the issue of access to genetic resources during the negotiations for the Convention on Biological Diversity. *(See Annex 4.)* On the one

Table VII.1. Government Innovation Policy Measures

Measure	Examples
Procurement	Central and local government purchases and contracts, establishment of *public corporations*, science and technology R&D contracts, prototype purchases, setting of design criteria, and choice of priority technologies
International trade	Trade agreements, technology acquisition agreements, tariffs, foreign exchange regulations, export compensation, import subsidies, and licensing
Public enterprise	Innovation by publicly owned industries, the creation of new industries, pioneering use of new techniques by public corporation, and participation in private enterprises
Scientific	Research laboratories, support of research associations, learned and technical societies, professional associations, and research grants
Education	General education, universities, technical education, and retraining
Information	Information networks and centers, libraries, advisory and consultancy services, databases, technology monitoring, liaison services, and public awareness campaigns
Financial	Grants, loans, subsidies, financial sharing arrangements, venture capital, loan guaran-

	tees, duty and customs remissions, export credits, and provision of equipment, buildings, or services
Taxation	Tax allowances, depreciation allowances, tax exemption for private foundations, and company, personal, indirect, and payroll taxation.
Legal and Regulatory	Patents, utility models, plant breeders rights,environmental and health regulations, contractual arrangements, conventions, inspectorates and monopoly regulations
Political	Planning, regional policies, honors or awards for innovation, encouragement of mergers or consortia, public consultation, creation of new institutions, setting up of research funds, and initiation of legal reforms
Public services	Purchases, maintenance, supervision, and innovation in health service, public building, construction, transport, telecommunications, infrastructure; administrative guidance
External assistance	External aid, technical assistance, local and external training
International relations	Sales organizations, trade and diplomatic missions (science attachés), technical co-operation, and designation of research representatives

Source: African Centre for Technology Studies, Nairobi

hand, excessive restrictions on the flow of genetic resources—which states such as Malaysia support—will slow technological development in pharmaceutical and agricultural biotechnology, as well as conventional agricultural research. In many developing countries, for instance, Kenya and Zimbabwe, commercializing the diagnostic kit for salmonella and the low dose human alpha interferon (KEMRON), respectively, have proved tricky. The latter is regarded in certain medical circles as a palliative for AIDS. But, on the other hand, genetic resources are among the few strategic resources that developing countries still control, and ignoring their legitimate interest in obtaining some benefits from these resources would be a mistake.

While the links between biodiversity and biotechnology cannot be denied, several issues stand in the way of a reciprocal exchange of one for the other. First, institutions that safeguard intellectual property in the form of technological innovations are larger and stronger than those that protect the interests of local communities involved in conservation efforts. Indeed, most possess scientific, technical, and legal expertise available to few conservation groups. More generally, developing countries are not likely to benefit fully from the provisions of the biodiversity convention or other transactions involving genetic resources until new legal and institutional regimes are established. Accordingly, developing countries should establish public agencies to address intellectual property concerns within the framework of national legislation and use them as a basis for international negotiation (Reid, 1992).

Second, developing countries have limited national institutional and legal capacity for regulating access to genetic resources. Currently, only the assertion of national sovereignty over the resource can be used in negotiations over access to biodiversity and biotechnology. During the negotiations of the Convention on Biological Diversity, for example, the question of sovereignty arose during discussions of a proposed global list of habitats and species threatened with loss. By arguing that the publication of such a list would impinge upon national sovereignty, developing countries were able to keep it from being published. But unless legal and institutional regimes are established to assert and enforce that sovereignty, how can developing countries benefit fully from the provisions of the Convention on Biological Diversity covering genetic resource transactions?

Third, developing countries have tended to separate institutions involved in biodiversity management from institutions involved in biotechnology. In fact, ratification of the Convention on Biological Diversity could stimulate the development of effective biodiversity prospecting institutions by providing the policy, legal and institutional bases for linking biodiversity and biotechnology. Today, few of the key principles of this Convention are reflected in the character and organization of national and international biodiversity institutions.

The development of biotechnology represents a convergence of a wider range of skills and knowledge than any single institution or country is likely to possess. Thus, institutional cooperation will be critical to biodiversity prospecting's success. Clearly, the coordination of biotechnology activities, as part of the larger enterprise of science and technology, needs to be given legitimacy and impetus at government's highest levels.

Many developing countries have set up stand-alone institutions to promote biotechnology or biodiversity conservation. But such units—often established in anticipation of funding rather than out of genuine interest to promote the use and conservation of biodiversity—are unlikely to yield long-term benefits unless they play a coordinating role. New institutional arrangements aimed at promoting biotechnology development should be constructed with national goals in mind, not donor politics.

Institutional cooperation should also be extended beyond national boundaries—difficult for most developing countries since their institutional arrangements for technological cooperation are limited. There are two main ways of dealing with this issue. One is through multilateral arrangements. For instance, developing countries can use the facilities of such international institutions as the International Centre for Genetic Engineering and Biotechnology (ICGEB) to acquire technological skills. Another is through bilateral arrangements and such institutions as the U.S. Agency for International Development (AID) which can also provide access to such facilities.

Fourth, harmonizing the rights of the state and local people to a nation's biodiversity is difficult. Government interest in asserting national sovereignty over genetic resources in their territories should not override individual and human rights, especially those of local communities and indigenous peoples (*see* Bhalla, 1990:234–248). Similarly, international prospecting institutions may erode more meaningful rights already held by local communities and undermine farmers' attempts to conserve biological diversity. For this reason, any international bioprospecting activities should be carried out in concert with national institutions that will make sure that the rights of local communities are recognized and enforced.

The Convention on Biological Diversity now recognizes the contribution of indigenous knowledge and technology to sustainable development (*see* Preamble, Article 8(j) and Article 10(c) and (d)). This is an important step, but still needed are more specific and justifiable provisions that ensure that the rights of innovators at all levels are recognized and protected. Without them, local communities won't be convinced of the benefits of conserving genetic resources.

Finally, attempts to link biodiversity and biotechnology in international negotiations have so far excessively emphasized monetary compensation and the enforcement of intellectual property rights. Although these concerns are important, biodiversity prospecting will not contribute much to the developing countries unless it helps them accumulate technological capacity (through training programs) and technology development (through scientific innovation). To ensure that national biotechnology policies enhance biodiversity prospecting, far more attention needs to be paid to human resource development, technological innovation, legal and institutional reforms, biotechnology regulation, and intellectual property management.

Biotechnology Transfer

"Technology transfer" describes a complex process whereby the scale and type of flow of equipment, knowledge, and expertise among nations changes. As used in international debates, the term has come to mean "the transfer of systematic knowledge for the manufacture of a product, for the application of a process or for the rendering of a service" (UNCTAD, 1990, p.48) and not the simple sale of goods and services.

Implicit in this definition is the notion that the recipients in the transaction already have a critical minimum capacity to assimilate and operationalize the new technology—what Chapter 37 of *Agenda 21* calls human, scientific, technological, organizational, institutional, and resource capabilities. Effective technology transfer also requires prospective recipients to negotiate—to articulate their goals and choose wisely among alternatives. In the same chapter of *Agenda 21*, further prerequisites are sketched: "Skills, knowledge and technical know-how at the individual and institutional levels are necessary for institution-building, policy analysis and development management, including the assessment of alternative courses of action with a view to enhancing access to and transfer of technology and promoting economic development." This list boils down to the possession of a basic infrastructure and a good command of the issues involved.

In practice, though, most developing countries treat technology transfer as a process initiated and controlled by the holders of technologies for their own ends. Developing countries often contend that strong intellectual property rights in developed countries are the main obstacle to securing access to biotechnology (Juma, 1989) and that simply removing certain barriers will undam the flow of technology to the developing countries.

Although abiding by the strictures of intellectual property rights does increase the transaction costs of getting access to biotechnology, the intellectual-property and licensing restrictions are more scapegoats than major obstacles, and relaxing them will not necessarily lead to technology transfer. Developing countries have failed to fully utilize the technological information that is in the public domain—or whose patents have expired. Indeed, most of the biotechnologies that developing countries need are in the public domain and are based on conventional practices (UNEP,

1991). Moreover, countries that cannot utilize public domain technologies are not likely to use patented ones.

A genuine and effective technological partnership will require willingness to transfer the relevant technology. But technology cooperation must also involve efforts by developing countries to *acquire* technology. The measure of how well such a partnership works will be reflected in the developing country's capacity to absorb and assimilate technologies, as well as to develop local technological capability (Shariff, 1988). To make technology appropriate for local circumstances, indigenous contribution to technological development is crucial, and this depends on indigenous technological capability: how many technicians and technologies, how many laboratories, workshops; how effective are the assembly plants, factories, etc.

Key elements of a strategy to foster biotechnology transfer are training and access to information. Many developing countries have severely restricted the international flow of technical information or have failed to give the local scientific community incentives to exploit the information available internationally. If the communications infrastructure isn't improved and the research environment liberalized, developing countries will be hard-pressed to enter the field of biotechnology (OTA, 1990).

Better pricing of biodiversity goods and services is also essential. Royalties received on patented technologies represent only a sliver of the total cost of acquiring and operating imported technologies. Technology searches, negotiation, and user training cost far more—so does complying with the restrictive clauses in licensing agreements on the use of technology.

This is not to say that intellectual property rights are not important, especially since they are sometimes used as non-tariff trade barriers. Nor is the implication that additional resources to finance payments for proprietary technologies are unnecessary. But it is a mistake to think that biotechnology development can be boiled down to that of intellectual property rights. Indeed, for developing countries, most of the challenge in fostering the mutual growth of biotechnology and conservation of biodiversity lies in creating a political, economic, and institutional environment in which the provisions of the Convention on Biological Diversity can be fully realized.

Technological Capacity. Developing countries will not be able to develop biotechnological industries until they themselves have built up a critical minimum level of biotechnological competence. Among other things, "technological capability" means being able to control how a new technology is deployed for socioeconomic ends. Recent literature has emphasized technological capacity since most technology transfer mechanisms have failed to bridge the technology gap between rich and poor countries.

The acquisition of technological production capacity is associated with the flow of different kinds of knowledge and expertise. The first category includes the know-how needed to transfer and set up production facilities and all the various operational services associated with any investment project.[1] The second category includes the knowledge and expertise needed to operate and maintain the new system once it has been installed—both the codified knowledge in manuals, schedules, charts, and diagrams and the "people-embodied know-how" fostered through training, information services, and on-the-job learning. The third category includes the knowledge and expertise needed to implement technical change: an understanding of how the technological system itself works and the techno-managerial capabilities needed to evaluate and transform plants already operating to meet new conditions (Bell, 1986; Fransman and King, *eds.*, 1984).

In genuine technology transfer, developed countries help developing countries build up all three types of capacity, starting with the first working up to the third. The third category is what triggers technological dynamism and helps countries fully utilize both public domain and proprietary technologies; policies that merely help countries adapt to international trends won't reach critical mass in this regard. The policy keys are integrating legal provisions in technology transfer contracts (for example, on local content) that emphasize/underscore the development and utiliza-

211

tion of local resources, for instance, using national engineering, environmental, and legal consultancy companies at all stages of project planning; providing national facilities for research and technological services; and providing an adequate national training system for scientific, technical, and managerial manpower.

Access to Biotechnology. The most important factor in enhancing global competitiveness in biotechnology is a country's ability to bring available knowledge and expertise to bear on the development of specific products and processes (Clark and Juma, 1991). The entry barriers for biotechnology—mastering traditional techniques, such as tissue culture—are lower than in other frontier technologies, such as microelectronics, so developing countries have unique opportunities to enter the field. Moreover, such precedents as the development of diagnostic kits for tropical diseases in Africa confirm that a small group of well-trained scientists in the South can contribute heavily to biotechnology development.

But developing countries cannot fully benefit from the new access to biotechnologies provided for in the Convention on Biological Diversity unless they build a broad base of knowledge and expertise in complementary fields and make their institutions more amenable to research cooperation. Consider in this light the broad knowledge base needed to become a player in biotechnology. Article 2 of the Convention on Biological Diversity defines biotechnology as "any technological application that uses biological systems, living organisms, or derivatives thereof, to make or modify products or processes for specific uses." Not only do developing such applications require a deep grasp of molecular biology; commercializing them requires knowledge of a wide range of other technologies and processes—such as fermentation technology and process engineering—based on biological systems. Thus, training to meet the challenges of the knowledge-intensive industries of biodiversity exploration and biotechnology development must encompass genetics, taxonomy, molecular biology, biochemistry, and process engineering. Both basic bioscience training and that in the "applied" disciplines, such as biochemical engineering skills from biochemistry and microbiology, should be emphasized.

212

Concerns over financing, access to genetic resources, and access to and transfer of technology, tended to dominate negotiations for the Convention on Biological Diversity. But because biotechnologies are science-intensive and their economic application relies largely on the available technological capacity, the Articles promoting training (Article 12), information exchange (Article 17), and technical cooperation (Article 18) are just as crucial to the transfer of biotechnology and the consequent improvement of developing states' ability to conserve and sustainably use biodiversity.

Negotiating Power for Technology Transfer. How successful a country is in negotiating for favorable contractual arrangements with foreign firms or governments often determines its ability to promote its technology development programs. Further, countries that explicitly recognize technology development as part of their long-term goals are less likely to be blinded by financial concerns.

Developing countries often seek to legislate the terms of technology transfer and assume that such legal provisions will protect them against unfair business practices. Some, following the trend toward increasing economic liberalization, have also reduced restrictive regulations. But developed-country firms entering into technology transfer agreements may include a wide range of clauses that restrict the importing countries' ability to acquire the relevant technological competence. Importing countries inexperienced in this type of contract negotiation thus face a dilemma: "[I]f restrictive clauses are rejected outright, access to the desired technology may be refused. If on the other hand such clauses are too rapidly accepted, the value of the technology may be seriously undermined" (Luedde-Neurath, 1988). Competent negotiation is key.

In some biotechnology transfer negotiations, approaches formulated for other forms of technologies, such as those embodied in the Montreal Protocol on Substances that Deplete the Ozone Layer (1987) and the London Amendment to the protocol, have been used. But two categories of technologies covered in these agreements differ fundamentally from biotechnology. First, ozone-related technologies are clearly identifiable products and processes; in contrast, biotechnologies represent a set of techniques that can't be applied without expertise in a wide range of other sectors. Also, the scope of application of the ozone-related technologies is fairly obvious and easy to determine before they are employed, unlike that of generic biotechnologies.

Technology Assessment

Technology assessment has emerged as an important discipline for evaluating the prospects and risks associated with particular technologies.[2] As a generic concept, it has now become part of the administrative language of many institutions in the industrialized nations and a few developing countries.

The first reason for technology assessment is to provide a basis for safe long-term development policy. A second is the need, amid ever more complex modern socioeconomic systems, to rely on more than economic policy to cope with rapid and unpredictable structural shifts. Too much modern economic theory details static assumptions about costs and prices while ignoring dynamic aspects of ecological change, development, and linkages in the wider socio-cultural setting. Technology assessment is beginning to play an important role in filling this analytical gap.

The resurgence of the environmental agenda in the 1980s and the growth of analytical techniques for technology assessment have led to renewed interest in what is now called "environmentally sound technology assessment" or "ecotechnology assessment." This technique takes on added importance in light of radical technological change, especially in biotechnology, which has witnessed the development of products and processes whose environmental ramifications are not yet sufficiently understood. As noted in *Our Common Future*:

"Technology will continue to change the social, cultural, and economic fabric of nations and the world community. With careful management, new and emerging technologies offer enormous opportunities for raising productivity and living standards, for improving health, and for conserving the natural resource base. Many will also bring new hazards, requiring an improved capacity

214

for risk management" (World Commission on Environment and Development, 1987, p. 217).

The issue of biosafety is a controversial regulatory theme. Some believe that biotechnology poses no particular threat to the environment and that stringent regulation would stifle biotechnology R&D. Others believe that it should be closely regulated. Better than either of these approaches would be making safety guidelines *part of* broader policy on biotechnology and drawing an expert line between these poles only on a case-by-case basis.

At the moment, the regulatory environment for biotechnology development in most developing countries remains uncertain. As biodiversity prospecting and technological development matures, close monitoring and regulation will be needed to ensure that the new technology does not compromise the genetic resource base. Here the actions of industrialized countries may provide guidelines for developing country policies.

The idea of technology assessment was first put forward in the United States in the late 1960s. Stemming from a growing awareness of the adverse effects of some new technologies, it was devised to help bring the development of large-scale, complex, and extremely expensive technology into conformity with social goals. The focus then reflected the view that technological change was the main source of ecological problems.

Technology assessment found statutory expression in the Office of Technology Assessment (OTA), established in 1972 in the United States as an advisory agency to the U.S. Congress. Since then, OTA has published report after report attempting to "assess" the likely impacts of new technologies. Measurable costs and benefits are only part of the story, and OTA gives equal weight to environmental impacts, political acceptability, learning effects, and other factors that conventional economic analysis has often side-stepped.

Like INBio in another context, OTA might be a useful model for other countries. Such institutions can insure that ecological standards are met in the utilization of biodiversity, particularly in the

Box VII.1. INBio: A Pilot Technology Transfer Project

At INBio in Costa Rica, the establishment of an institution was closely linked to training of technical personnel, as well as the local residents. INBio thus serves as a pilot project, demonstrating one way to accumulate the scientific and technological capacity needed to get into biodiversity prospecting and biotechnology development.

The INBio experience emphasizes the importance of developing countries adding value to resources. Since developing countries can't expect to collect large sums simply for conserving their biodiversity resources, they must increase their returns on conservation by investing in efforts to understand and characterize the genetic composition of the conserved material. Through such science-intensive activities they can attract commercial resources to support conservation and technology transfer (Sasson, 1992).

INBio's "production process" starts with basic research and development and moves through the stages of product development. This approach could provide some developing countries with a new base from which to leapfrog into the next wave of technological innovations based on biotechnology and genetic engineering.

Even very small countries with limited industrial capacity can move to biotechnology's frontiers in specific fields by enhancing their human resource capability (Clark and Juma, 1991). Besides investing in training and improving the environment for access to information, (especially to specialized databases), they must also try to add value to their genetic resources through screening and characterization. This expanded approach paves the way for the development of new products, such as bio-pesticides, from biological resources (*see* van Latum and Gerrits, 1991).

INBio's experience suggests that the choice of partners in prospecting efforts should be guided by the foreign firm's ability and willingness to strengthen the scientific and technological capacity of the developing country institution, and this element of partnership should be spelled out clearly in the prospecting contract. Mechanisms for assessing whether the required training has been conducted must also be specified, though it is up to developing countries to ensure that the trained personnel are fully utilized. (Frequently, the training offered is underutilized because developing countries don't have the institutional infrastructure needed to support the personnel.)

INBio has scored high on all these counts, but how feasible is replicating the INBio experience in other parts of the world? To the extent that INBio represents a unique convergence of historical and institutional factors that makes acquiring scientific and technological capacity, as well as the required managerial and organizational skills, easier than it will be in many developing countries, it can't be readily replicated, and its "learning-by-doing" approach may be glacially slow in many countries of the South. There is also the danger that an INBio for each country which houses biological resources may lead to competition among the source countries and lower the benefits. Still, several generic lessons about technology transfer can be learned from the experience. First, the high degree of international cooperation that has characterized INBio right from the beginning enables it to maintain links with experts and other sources of support. Second, at INBio international cooperation builds on a strong base of national competence, especially in institutional management. Third, the political and legislative support that INBio receives from the Government of Costa Rica is critical to the functioning of the institution. As a private nonprofit institution, INBio enjoys the institutional autonomy needed to pursue its scientific endeavors, but its genesis through a parliamentary statute gives it the legitimacy necessary to do its work.

As a pioneer in this field, INBio is already sharing some of its experiences with other countries seeking to establish similar institutions. (As one example, INBio has already signed a statement of cooperation with the Indonesian Institute of Sciences and the Ministry of State for Population and Environment of

217

Box VII.1. (Continued)

the Republic of Indonesia.) Arguably, INBio is undermining its competitiveness by helping other countries to establish similar institutions, but it is also likely that INBio would be losing income-generating opportunities by not commercializing its first product—INBio, the institution itself. It is, of course, up to INBio to decide how to market its institutional services, though other developing countries must hope that it continues in the spirit of generosity that it has already demonstrated. (*See Chapter II.*)

---

area of prospecting and exploration. Meanwhile, since many transnational corporations, (some of them are already at work on matters related to prospecting) have little regard for the ecosystem, and since few developing countries have the capacity to utilize available technologies fully, national and international institutions like OTA are needed to assess technology with environmental criteria in mind.

Blind Alleys and Windows of Opportunity

The policy of establishing unfocused across-the-board biotechnological expertise is bound to fail. All that would result would be a rigid scientific bureaucracy isolated from economic production, poised to consume large quantities of scarce resources, and unable to produce research closely related to developmental needs.

Conversely, biotechnology policy targeted at specific "windows of economic opportunity" could give rise to the technological dynamism necessary for long-term economic development, conservation, and equity in resource management. With such an approach, links between research and production can occur faster and more naturally. Technological capabilities in biodiversity prospecting can also serve other areas of economic output and environmental management. (For example, funds derived from prospecting or investment aimed at facilitating prospecting may improve infrastructure—roads, water facilities, etc. Funds from prospecting could, ideally, be applied to strengthen community-based and other conservation groups; through training of para-tax-onomists, one would hope that the knowledge, use value, etc. of biochemical resources would be enhanced.) At the same time, national research policy can be targeted more explicitly and given a greater chance of success. Those working in science and technology will find their work more directly valued, their own resources thereby enhanced, and, ultimately, their morale increased. Finally, the science and technology system as a whole will be able to promote economic development conservation, and equity more efficiently.

Training local communities and establishing or strengthening institutional capability will become increasingly important and will require developing states to invest in science and technology research and information dissemination and to resist the ingrained temptation to put such activities at the mercy of donor politics.

Notes

1. These include feasibility studies, plant commissioning and start-up services, design engineering and training.
2. For a more detailed application of technology assessment to biotechnology, *see* Clark and Juma (1991).

Bibliography

Bell, M. 1986. *The Acquisition of Imported Technology for Industrial Development: Problems of Strategy and Management in the Arab Region.* United Nations, Geneva, Switzerland.
Bhalla, R. S. 1990. The Effect of Modernisation on Acquisition of Property and Rules of Compensation: A Kenyan Case. *African Journal of International and Comparative Law* 2:234–248.
Clark, N. and Juma, C. 1991. *Biotechnology for Sustainable Development: Policy Options for Developing Countries.* African Centre for Technology Studies, Nairobi, Kenya.
Fransman, M. and King, K. (eds.) 1984. *Technological Capability in the Third World.* Macmillan, London, U.K.

Ghai, D. 1974. Social Science Research on Development and Research Institutes in Africa. Discussion Paper No. 197. Institute for Development Studies, University of Nairobi, Kenya.

Johnson, C. 1982. *MITI and the Japanese Miracle: The Growth of Industrial Policy, 1925–1975*. Stanford University Press, Stanford, California.

Juma, C. 1989. *The Gene Hunters: Biotechnology and the Scramble for Seeds*. Princeton University Press, Princeton, New Jersey.

Juma, C. and Ojwang, J.B. 1992. Technology Transfer and Sustainable Development. *Ecopolicy* No. 2. African Centre for Technology Studies, Nairobi, Kenya.

Juma, C. and Ojwang, J.B. (eds.) 1989. *Innovation and Sovereignty: The Patent Debate and African Development*. African Centre for Technology Studies, Nairobi, Kenya.

Luedde-Neurath, R. 1988. State Intervention in 'Outward-looking' Development: In South Korea. *In* G. White (ed.) *Developmental Studies in East Asia*, Macmillan, London, U.K.

Okimoto, D. 1989. *Between MITI and the Market: Japanese Industrial Policy for Higher Technology*. Stanford University Press, Stanford, California.

OTA. 1990. *Critical Connections: Communications for the Future*. Congress of the United States Office of Technology Assessment, Washington, DC.

OTA. 1991. *Biotechnology in a Global Economy*. Congress of the United States Office of Technology Assessment : Washington, DC.

Pavitt, K. 1987. The Objectives of Technology Policy. *Science and Public Policy* 14(4):182–188.

Reid, W. 1992. Genetic Resources and Sustainable Agriculture: Creating Incentives for Local Innovation and Adaptation. *Biopolicy International* No. 2. African Centre for Technology Studies, Nairobi, Kenya.

Sasson, A. 1992. *Biotechnology and Natural Products: Prospects for Commercial Production*. African Centre for Technology Studies, Nairobi, Kenya.

Shariff, M.N. 1988. Problems, issues and strategies for S&T policy analysis. *Science and Public Policy*, 15(4):195-216.

UNCTAD. 1990. *Transfer and Development of Technology in Developing Countries: A Compendium of Policy Issues*. United Nations Conference on Trade and Development, United Nations, New York, N.Y.

220

UNEP. 1991. *Description of Transferable Technologies Relevant to Conservation of Biological Diversity and its Sustainable Use.* United Nations Environment Programme, Nairobi, Kenya.

Van Latum, E.B.J. and Gerrits, R. 1991. Bio-pesticides in Developing Countries: Prospects and Research Priorities. *Biopolicy International* No. 1, African Centre for Technology Studies, Nairobi, Kenya.

World Commission on Environment and Development. 1987. *Our Common Future.* Oxford University Press, Oxford, UK.

Annex 1

THE ROLE OF THE PARATAXONOMISTS, INVENTORY MANAGERS, AND TAXONOMISTS IN COSTA RICA'S NATIONAL BIODIVERSITY INVENTORY

Daniel H. Janzen, Winnie Hallwachs, Jorge Jimenez, and Rodrigo Gámez

INBio's national biodiversity inventory—slated to begin in 1993—is described at length in Chapter II. Here the all-important role of the parataxonomist is described, along with that of the inventory managers and taxonomists with whom they work.

The Parataxonomists

Costa Rica does not have many decades and many millions of dollars to train a large number of university graduates to the Ph. D. level to inventory its biodiversity. Nor can it expect the international science community to drop everything and to conduct Costa Rica's inventory.

But the inventory is urgent, so INBio decided to tap an abundant underutilized resource—Costa Rica's rural populace—to collaborate with Costa Rican university graduates in biology and the taxonomic community to get the job done within a decade at a reasonable cost. The move makes sense from several perspectives. Rural Costa Rica is flush with highly capable under-employed adults, the international scientific community has long overestimated the training requirements for persons participating in a thorough biodiversity inventory, and Costa Rica's extraordinary biodiversity both makes the job inviting and attracts the international technical and training assistance needed to gradually empower Costa Rica to do much of the job itself.

A Chronological History of the Parataxonomists

A look at the historical roots of parataxonomy in Costa Rica reveals how parataxonomists differ from the "collectors" and "biological technicians" with whom they are frequently confused, and which factors are vital to their success.

From 1974–1979, Gerardo Vega worked as a field assistant with Daniel Janzen to help with NSF-supported ecological field experiments and insect collecting in Corcovado National Park and Santa Rosa National Park. In his checkered career, Vega had been a Costa Rican farmer, hunter, gold miner, squatter, liquor-smuggler, and national park helper. His parents had been coffee pickers, and he had three years of formal education. His employers in the national park system were eager to be rid of him because he always felt he knew how to do things better than his bosses. After Vega returned to gold mining, Roberto Espinoza was hired for the same job, which he held from 1983 to 1989. He came from the small fishing town of Cuajiniquil in northern Guanacaste Province, where he had been a machete swinger, cowboy, and fishing boat helper. His parents were ranch employees—cowboy and housewife—and he had six years of formal education. Both Vega and Espinoza were chosen for their extensive experience in the field, great curiosity, strength, and whole-hearted involvement in the task at hand.

It quickly became evident that Vega and Espinoza could accept even more responsibility and learn even more complex tasks than those given. Furthermore, in the field they were more helpful and enthusiastic than were Costa Rican university students (volunteers and employees) and more logistically competent than were any but the most exceptional U.S. graduate students working in field biology in Costa Rica.

While this realization was dawning, the NSF-supported "Moths of Costa Rica" project began in 1978, initially to scientifically name the adults of the caterpillars being reared in the dry forest of the Guanacaste Conservation Area. Two employees of this project Isidro Chacon and Maria Marta Chavarría (both exceptional students from the University of Costa Rica) spent a year collecting and spreading moths (he at SPN Estacion Carillo and she at the OTS La Selva Biological Station, both in the Cordillera Volcanica Conservation Area). Isidro also taught his brother Abelardo Chacon the necessary skills, and all three worked very well unsupervised, even under very trying field and administrative circumstances. These initial successes in proto-parataxonomy came to mind years later when, in early 1986 the idea of the donor-supported Guanacaste National Park Project took root. It was evident that an insect inventory of this 100,000 ha area of dry forest, cloud forest, rain forest, and intergrades could shed considerable light on insect migrations, seasonality, micro-distributions, and other ecological parameters bearing on resource-management decisions. Accordingly, in 1986–1988, local rural adults living near the Guanacaste Conservation Area (GCA) were hired and trained with the help of several Costa Rican biologists to collect specimens with minimal supervision. Participants taught each other, and visiting foreign researchers taught them as well. The evolution of the parataxonomist was in motion.

The First Parataxonomist Course: January–July 1989

In the fall of 1988, the GCA was suffering the anguish of attempted integration with the rest of the Costa Rican National Park System. The need for staff from other Costa Rican national parks to observe and understand the micro-revolution in administrative structure and philosophical attitudes that characterized the GCA was becoming clear. Meanwhile, US-AID had volunteered to support any GCA environmental educational effort aimed at helping Costa Ricans become more involved with the other parks. To capitalize on the opportunity, the GCA quickly formalized efforts to train people to inventory the GCA and other Costa Rican proto-conservation areas. A six-month full-time course (January–July 1989) was instituted for ten Costa Rican national park system employees: one from the GCA and nine from Corcovado, Amistad, Carara, Tortuguero, and Braulio Carrillo national parks (now the core parts of Costa Rica's Conservation Areas). Five more GCA non-governmental employees brought the course membership to 15.

Under the basic agreement, the $120,000 US-AID course would provide training, supplies, equipment, and supervision (field liaison and coordination from INBio) for a year of work, and the graduates' employers would provide salaries and office/living space

225

for the six-month course and the following six months. Administrative and moral support, as well as use of its buildings, vehicles, and field stations, was donated by the Guanacaste Conservation Area. No formal contract spelled out the employer/training relationship. Instead, various explicit and implicit verbal agreements were made with directorate of the National Park Service, the Ministry of Natural Resources, and the directors of the individual national parks.

The INBio course contained many aspects of "old-fashioned" university courses (ornithology, herpetology, entomology, cryptogamic botany, field botany, algology, etc.) of use in conducting an inventory. Collecting and preparation techniques, basic natural history, basic taxonomy, basic evolution, and the principles of ecology were all covered, along with the rudiments of genetics, math, natural products chemistry, physiology, anatomy, etc. The course also touched on the definition of administration, the structure and content of environmental legislation and conservation propaganda, research funding, personal relationships with government and NGO (non-governmental organization) administrators, teaching skills, and self-confidence. Theory was mixed with such practical skills as how to drive a car, operate a chain saw, care for and use horses as pack animals, use a computer and a topographic map, use a field guide in a foreign language, manage a budget and petty cash fund, and fathom and tolerate foreigners. More personal matters were covered too. Some participants needed eye-glasses and pointers on how to use them. Others needed to learn how to work alone at night in the forest without fear, how to lose weight, and how to absorb constructive criticism.

To recruit participants, a brief notice describing the course and the parataxonomist's vocation and responsibilities was circulated among the headquarters of the Costa Rican national parks in late 1988. A response form asked for standard biographical information and a short essay about why the applicant wanted to become a parataxonomist. For the first course, only NGO personnel of the GCA (legally, employees of the Fundación de Parques Nacionales) and government employees of the National Park Service could apply. Twenty-eight applications were completed, and 22 of the best candidates were invited to come to the GCA by bus for individual interviews with the course faculty, the coordinator, and at least one GCA Administrator. Ten new people and the five GCA insect collectors were selected for the course once their employers approved—an essential imprimatur since the employer basically "donates" a valued staff member to the program and gets in return a much-changed person occupying a new type of position.

Final selection was admittedly subjective. Enthusiasm, basic intelligence, eagerness to move on from their current jobs, independence, and robust health all figured in the choice. (Later, it came out that many of the successful candidates were previously viewed by their employers as "problem persons," famous for balking at unchallenging civil service work within the National Park Service.) Two women, both from the GCA, took the first parataxonomist course, and both have since proved to be outstanding parataxonomists. No other women applied for either of the first two parataxonomist courses. Although a few parataxonomists go on to more complex training, from the beginning the intent was to prepare people for a highly independent lifetime vocation, not help them take the first steps toward advanced degrees and university-level employment.

The term "parataxonomist" was borrowed from "paramedic." For good reason the parataxonomists are not called "barefoot taxonomists": they are *not* barefoot, and a certain lack of respect is implied by that term. Nor are parataxonomists technicians, though civil service evaluations call them so. The emphasis is on the ability to work independently and to understand the philosophy behind the work—neither of which are characteristic of technicians in Costa Rican society.

This kind of course works only if all involved are totally immersed. Formal lectures, discussions, lab work, and field activities were thus opportunistically intermingled continuously from 7 a.m. to 6 p.m. (with one hour for lunch) for 10 to 15 days, followed by 3- to 4-day breaks to visit family and attend to personal affairs. Many nights were also spent in the field collecting specimens.

The aim of this melange of activities was to prepare parataxonomists to understand and answer such questions as the following:

1. How can one use an identified reference collection of the species of moths, beetles, wasps, butterflies, etc., occurring in a conservation area? How does one use other kinds of biodiversity information (e.g., on the numbers and kinds of

227

habitats and climates, numbers and kinds of plants, locations of populations)? How does biodiversity information help in the conservation, management, and development of a conservation area?

2. When is it time to stop collecting one group and work on a different group? How many specimens of a "species" should be collected?

3. How can one know if a sample of species is representative of the species of the area? How does one decide where to collect?

4. How can one encourage professional taxonomists and other kinds of biologists to work on the specimens one is collecting?

5. How does one justify rapidly producing local field guides for conservation areas when the emphasis in taxonomy is on painstaking revisions of all the species in large geographic areas? How is a field guide produced? What material is needed? What does the public want in such a guide?

6. How can one determine if a particular collecting technique will damage the biota of a conservation area? How does one integrate collecting and other biodiversity-survey activities with other kinds of research and management?

7. How are scientific names produced? Why do we have them? And how can they be used to locate other scientific information? What is a species? What is a population? What is a research collection? A national museum?

8. What are the basic natural histories of the various groups of animals and plants in an area? How do these histories relate to a biodiversity survey?

9. How can biodiversity information best be coordinated with a conservation area's management needs?

10. Why should specimens be viewed and treated as international property and distributed broadly among responsible users? How does one integrate one's collecting activities with the activities of other users, including other collectors?

11. What are the collector's responsibilities to a questioning public? Should specimens be displayed in a conservation area? Who should take care of them? How?

12. Why are conservation areas critical for the maintenance of biodiversity?

13. Why is it important to conserve and maintain a very large portion of the diversity of the earth's organisms and habitats?
14. Why should Costa Rica be particularly concerned about the conservation of its biodiversity? And how does the country's natural wealth relate to the biodiversity of the remainder of the world?

Insects and higher plant species received the heaviest emphasis during the course because both their numbers and their potential novel uses are so great and they so readily exemplify evolution, ecology, development, mimicry, protective chemistry, complex life cycles, etc. Then too, the inventory of all Costa Rican vertebrates except small reptiles and amphibians is essentially completed. Parataxonomists need further training after the basic course if they are to work on micro-organisms, fungi, nematodes, diatoms, etc.

Taxonomists and Costa Rican university and museum personnel were opportunistically invited to visit and to discuss their specialty and their collection methods.

As soon as the first course was under way in early 1989, the parataxonomist trainees began to generate huge numbers of high-quality mounted specimens—far more than the Museo Nacional could store or process. Meanwhile, the INBio concept was taking shape. The first INBio building was opened in Santo Domingo in the suburbs of San José in May 1989, just in time to shelter the collections and curators of the Department of Natural History of the Museo Nacional, which had been evacuated during museum remodeling. To the still-wet floor of the new INBio building also came the first bulk deliveries of insects and plants from the first parataxonomy course.

After two months, the students were sent back to their "home" conservation areas to work independently for a month, practicing what they had learned. They then returned to the GCA for two more months of intense training. Upon graduation, they were supposed to return again to their source conservation areas, establish Biodiversity Offices, and go to work—which they did.

Since then, less formal training in scientific and practical matters has continued, particularly through the field liaison, the INBio inventory managers and staff, and some visiting scientists. Also formal short courses on groups of organisms have been taught by taxonomists, many of them world authorities on one taxa or another.

229

The Second Parataxonomy Course: May through August 1990

In May–August 1990, a second and quite similar parataxonomy course was taught, financed again by US-AID, but administered by the Biodiversity Support Program, a consortium of World Wildlife Fund-US, The Nature Conservancy, and the World Resources Institute. The Course Coordinator and Teaching Assistant this time was a graduate of the first course. The second course, like the first, was taught entirely in the GCA, making use of field stations located in almost every type of habitat represented in Costa Rica's conservation areas. Yet, by this time it had become clear that the parataxonomists have an institutional home at INBio, regardless of where they work or who pays them.

As in the first course, 7-to-10 day periods of study and fieldwork were broken up by 2-to-4 day vacation periods. After two months of this pattern, each parataxonomist returned to his or her "home" park to work for a month alone. The first class of parataxonomist graduates had set up Biodiversity Offices in the conservation areas during this mid-course trial, and the parataxonomists of the second course used them in mid-1990 while their regular occupants were taking an advanced parataxonomy course in Microlepidoptera in the GCA and in INBio. The students of the second course then returned to the GCA for another month of intensive study. At the end of the second course, all parataxonomists from both courses participated in a 3-day field workshop in marine invertebrates on the Islas Murciélagos in the western end of the GCA.

In the second course, the student source pool was broadened to include employees of the National Forest Service and of two conservation-oriented NGOs. A private logging company was also invited to support a parataxonomist, but voided its contract after three months when it discovered that the parataxonomist (later hired by INBio to work in the Tortuguero Conservation Area) would answer to INBio rather than to the company.

In retrospect, three major errors were made with the second course. First, it was two months shorter than the first, mainly because of administrative disagreements about how much "release time" the government-employed students selected for the course would get and because chaos in Costa Rica's conservation efforts reigned after the ruling political parties changed in early 1990. Second, the course relied too heavily on the course coordinator for too much of the teaching: a second-year parataxonomist, no matter how extraordinary, lacks the pedagogical stamina and a sufficiently strong grasp of the basic material to carry a major teaching burden. Third, persons outside of INBio were allowed to select three of the participants, and all three dropped out of the program after graduation. This error in candidate selection presumably occurred because non-INBio personnel find it hard to grasp what characteristics matter most in a candidate and what is expected of the graduates.

The Third Parataxonomy Course: January–June 1992

For four reasons, no course was offered in 1991. First, funds for a third course had to be raised. A pledged donor withdrew support, and it takes three years for the INBio-Pew Teaching Endowment to generate enough interest income to cover most course-related costs. Second, it was decided to give the first parataxonomists time to function, and then to use feedback from their experience to modify the course. Third, the faculty needed a break. A fourth, more circumstantial factor, was that an intensive NSF-supported two-month advanced course in Hymenoptera was taught to the parataxonomists during the first half of 1991.

In late 1991, INBio received a grant from the Liz Claiborne and Art Ortenberg Foundation to cover three years of salary and operations costs for ten female parataxonomists. Eight more women and three men were also recruited for the 1992 course, which was supported by the National Fish and Wildlife Foundation in the U.S., the Moriah Fund, the Swedish International Development Authority, the Conservation, Food and Health Foundation, and INBio's Pew Teaching Endowment. This successful course will be discussed in a different report in detail. Suffice it to say here that women have now been brought more fully into the ranks of parataxonomy, and a parataxonomist course constituted largely of women involves new challenges and opportunities.

Questions Commonly Asked About Parataxonomists

1. What are the parataxonomists' goals?

A parataxonomist's current local goal is to initiate and conduct an inventory of the fauna and flora in the vicinity of his or her respective Biodiversity Office. The emphasis is on taxa selected by the inventory managers and through INBio. Administrative input is essential in the choice of groups because certain taxonomic groups are already well inventoried, parataxonomists can't collect or observe various others without additional training, and INBio does not yet have the facilities to handle certain groups of specimens (e.g., small reptiles and amphibians, spiders, marine invertebrates, microbes, and living cultures). However, all taxa will eventually be covered. *(See Box 1.1.)*

For more than a century, superficial collecting sprees have been the basis of most tropical inventories. In contrast, each parataxonomist is posted at a single site to insure that sampling takes place year round and that species that can be collected only in certain years can be found. Parataxonomists thus get familiar enough with fauna and flora so they don't collect redundant samples but can find additional specimens later if INBio needs them. Also, parataxonomists acquire first-hand a substantial knowledge of natural history and species behavior that INBio and other biodiversity managers are beginning to tap for biodiversity prospecting, conservation management, ecotourism, education programs, etc. They do collect substantially more material than would be needed by only the taxonomic function, in great part because there are many different users for the specimens and because multiple specimens are needed to understand variation in many species' traits.

The last two decades of intensive collecting at various Costa Rican sites reveal that almost all of a major habitat's fauna can eventually be found at one site *if* the site is studied year round and for several years. For example, a single light placed strategically in Santa Rosa National Park in the Guanacaste Conservation Area will attract at least 99 percent of the entire macro-moth fauna of this 10,500 ha park in about five years. Such a survey can be conducted even faster if there are multiple light sites. Fifteen carefully chosen sites of about 10,000 ha each in Costa Rica's conservation areas could yield samples of 90 percent of the country's fauna and

---

Box 1.1. INBio's Inventory Criteria

INBio bases inventory decisions primarily on five factors:
1. the perceived needs and logistic availability of particular conservation areas;
2. individual parataxonomists' varying circumstances and abilities;
3. taxonomists' and other INBio collaborators' special needs;
4. the species richness of the area; and
5. the number of person-years already invested in a particular Biodiversity Office. For example, during any Biodiversity Office's first year, all groups of insects and plants are collected, as will be the case for other groups as their inventory begins.

---

flora in ten years of collecting. As a site becomes well-inventoried, the parataxonomist can range farther afield to locate species not yet collected—more efficient and engaging than waiting for the species to drift into one small site.

Finally, the growing expertise on the fauna and flora of a site helps parataxonomists stay interested and engaged—simply picking up unknown specimens quickly becomes boring—which makes it easier to work alone at a field station and to find further biodiversity employment once the inventory is completed. Long-term residence in an area is also essential to knowing, developing, and managing the many social mechanisms that help the parataxonomist work with the administration and survive in the microsociety of the Conservation Area. It's also the best way to influence the surrounding community and to share knowledge. Indeed, more and more of the parataxonomists will spend major portions of their lives in these areas and raise their children there.

A second, more subjective but equally important goal of parataxonomy is to legitimize the study and understanding of wildland biology and to promote biological literacy. Whether indirectly or directly, parataxonomists can influence their associates in the park service and their families, as well as school groups, tourists, ecotourists, businesspeople, apprentices, and neighbors. Such constant informal contact is the best way to reach a rural populace that has long been on the attack in the age-old human war against wild tropical nature.

The current parataxonomist has a third goal: to illustrate the problems and strengths of INBio's approach to a national inventory of a very large and complex biodiversity. When the ten-year national inventory officially gets under way in 1993, the parataxonomist staff is expected to gradually grow to one hundred or more working throughout the country. Many of the parataxonomists trained in the first three courses will no doubt serve as examples, teachers, coordinators, and facilitators as people are trained, hired, or replaced.

Parataxonomy represents a giant experiment in training, institution building, and goal-directed science. The methods of teaching and guiding these 100+ (mostly new) parataxonomists will be shaped by experience gleaned from 1989–1992. This is what INBio means by "planning by doing." The public and scientific community view the millions of specimens and thousands of species accumulated to date by the parataxonomists as a marvelous product, even though the work is just beginning.

2. What is the goal of the inventory?

The two-fold goal of the inventory is to get the taxonomic nomenclature of Costa Rica's biodiversity as "clean" as possible and to get at least a rough sense of where various species and groups can be found. Simultaneously, the inventory is the first step in beginning to accumulate enough natural history information to be able to use biodiversity without destroying it. With a reliable nomenclature established, biodiversity information can be organized and managed at the species level. Also, taxonomy can be brought into the service of biodiversity prospectors and managers, as well as many other users. INBio can thereby gain access to the vast amount of information on Costa Rican biodiversity in the international scientific literature and freely distribute the information accumulating at INBio. This goal is reinforced as the Costa Rican public begins to value specific conserved wildlands for the species they contain. Already income is flowing into Costa Rica in return for "natural" goods and services, and someday biodiversity will attract to Costa Rica industries that are based on the use of biodiversity materials.

234

3. Are collecting agreements necessary?

Each parataxonomist carries an I.D. card that identifies him or her to any authority as an INBio employee and parataxonomist, allowed to collect inside a national park, conservation area, wildlife refuge, etc., and to transport biological specimens.

By formal agreement, INBio and MIRENEM are collaborating on the national biodiversity inventory (and the biodiversity prospecting activities). As national biodiversity legislation and regulation become more ordered, as they are in Costa Rica, such formal understanding is critical. Without it, INBio is open to the charge that it is privatizing a public good—the biodiversity of a Conservation Area.

4. What will happen to the parataxonomists when the inventory is completed?

Experienced parataxonomists will always be in demand in Costa Rica. Their high level of biological literacy makes them ideal for positions within agricultural, wildland biodiversity and forestry industries in the government, and for jobs as teachers, ecotourist guides, environmental educators, and environmental consultants.

As INBio grows, its needs for increasingly specialized biologists happy to work in the field also increase. If it had the funds, INBio itself could easily hire all the parataxonomists it trains—either for the inventory or work on biodiversity prospecting. Ten years from now, as the inventory nears completion, many parataxonomists will have moved into other areas of biodiversity management (some within INBio and many within the Conservation Areas), become paraecologists, obtained higher degrees, or even moved on to work and advise in other countries.

Each conservation area needs someone to manage its research program, and some of the older and more experienced parataxonomists have become administrators. Each such area also needs field personnel familiar with large groups of plants, insects, birds, etc., to work with the other conservation staff and to provide on-site taxonomic services for users of the conservation areas.

5. What are a parataxonomist's obligations and benefits?

It costs approximately U.S. $15,000 to train a parataxonomist and support his or her operations for the remainder of the year.

Although Costa Rican conservation efforts and society at large would benefit mightily from a continual turnover of trained parataxonomists who leave to take other positions, it might be more effective to train a certain number of people initially and directly for these other positions. Certainly, if all parataxonomists depart shortly after they are trained, the inventory will take much longer because it will be conducted primarily by relatively inexperienced persons.

From the start, the parataxonomist is expected to stay involved in the national biodiversity inventory for many years. Successful applicants for the program make a moral commitment to work at least three years as a parataxonomist. Also, INBio makes a serious effort to convince parataxonomists tempted by other opportunities to stay on as parataxonomists. However, if an amicable break occurs, INBio encourages departing parataxonomists to stay in touch.

The parataxonomist's work schedule is 22 working days per calendar month. He or she receives a monthly salary, two weeks of paid annual vacation, an extra month of pay on 1 December, social security benefits, health insurance, free medical services, and other social benefits typical of those received by any Costa Rican employee. A "working day" tends to be 6 to 16 hours, distributed through the night and day. Exactly which hours and days the parataxonomist works is his or her choice, though the biological characteristics of the focal organisms are very much taken into account.

A parataxonomist costs his or her employer 1.46 times the annual salary. In late 1992, a beginning parataxonomist earned roughly U.S. $3,000 annually, while the most experienced parataxonomists received approximately U.S. $4,100. In Costa Rica this is a good but not outstanding annual salary for a rural person of 20 to 35 with a grade-school or high-school education.

6. How has the academic community responded to parataxonomists?

The response of the academic community to parataxonomists and the concept of parataxonomy has varied. Academic and museum administrators generally say "of course, why not?," but do not automatically include parataxonomists in their actual field operations. Many older international Ph.D. taxonomists initially view them as mediocre field collectors incapable of specialized collecting. On the other hand, once these doubters get to know the

236

parataxonomists or work with their collections, their attitude changes. Once they begin responding to the parataxonomists as individuals, scientists typically begin teaching them how to do their particular kind of specialized collecting. Most younger foreign Ph.D. taxonomists would like to work with the parataxonomists in the field if they had the chance.

Latin American Ph.D.s and university professors have often greeted the parataxonomist with a mixture of fear, contempt, and resentment. While many are sympathetic, some ask why some poorly educated rural person is offered such a good job when Latin American university students and graduates in biology don't have jobs. But any Costa Rican university graduate who wants to become a parataxonomist can do so if he or she can come with a salary and want to live and work in a rural environment. (Most parataxonomists come to INBio with their salaries paid by a government agency or NGO, a commercial interest, or a grant.) But the fact remains that a rural person with less than a university education is nearly always more capable and more comfortable in the field than is the (usually urban) university graduate. Also, most rural people share their knowledge with others in rural areas more effectively.

Of course, the appearance of rural parataxonomists who can understand and do much of the work of university-level faculty and senior institutional representatives has been highly threatening to some Costa Rican professors and mid-level government administrators. Careful politicking by INBio staff and INBio supporters in other institutions has only partially defused this bomb, and the strongest support for the parataxonomist and parataxonomy comes from *upper* level government and university officials.

More philosophically, parataxonomists represent a form of affirmative action essential for the further development of a country like Costa Rica, where 80 percent of the power, trained intellect, and decision-makers currently resides in greater San José. If there ever was a government sector that is by nature decentralized, it is that for managing the conservation and use of wildlands. Costa Ricans will never succeed at either conservation or biodiversity use while being absentee landlords. What better caretakers than people whose social, psychological, and financial roots are in the very area to be protected?

7. Why are only Costa Ricans allowed to be parataxonomists?

INBio itself is a Costa Rican national institution, and "pride of ownership" generates *esprit de corps*. As such, it would be highly inappropriate to fill parataxonomist slots with foreign volunteers or employees. They might initially speed the inventory, but they would also slow the all-important acceptance of conservation areas—and indirectly, biodiversity's importance—by Costa Ricans.

Still, INBio will no doubt gradually grow into something like an "Instituto Mesoamericana de Biodiversidad" and work with the INBio-like Biodiversity Commission established by Mexico in February 1992. Already, INBio is prepared to admit parataxonomist students from other Central American countries if there are sufficient funds to cover their support. Of course, this readiness raises the question of what "parent institution" will receive and process the material collected from, say, Nicaragua and Panama or provide constructive feedback for these parataxonomists. It is not enough to simply receive their material, as if they were professional collectors delivering boxes of samples. INBio is willing to consider incorporating material collected elsewhere in Central America, but a massive increase in funding would be needed. The administration and legislative aspects of biodiversity management would also have to change since Costa Rica's experience will not necessarily take root "as is" in other Mesoamerican countries.

8. How are parataxonomists and their work evaluated?

The parataxonomist's performance can be evaluated in two relatively distinct ways. One is how the parataxonomist responds to professional feedback from INBio inventory managers, international scientists visiting INBio and the Biodiversity Offices, professors in parataxonomy courses, and field liaison officers on the quality of material, the choice of taxa, collecting techniques, sampling patterns, etc. Since feedback measures both how well parataxonomists can handle the many interpersonal dimensions of their work and how much support they are getting, the parataxonomists' responsiveness reflects on the quality of their training and of the basic course.

Most parataxonomists leave a long-established friendship circle to enter a new social and technological world when they begin their careers. This is a difficult move, and only substantial contact with other parataxonomists, other biologists, and biodiversity users will keep recruits from feeling isolated in their new vocation. They also need to be treated as professionals, even when there are unfortunate vestiges of their previous behavior as wage-earning employees in an autocratic administrative system or as workers in an unstructured home environment. It is hard to suddenly become a professional who designs daily and monthly activities within a goal-oriented framework. With some very notable exceptions, communicating with taxonomists accustomed to working with university and graduate students has also proven hard for the parataxonomists.

Much of the feedback to parataxonomists occurs during a three-day period every two to three months when all parataxonomists gather at INBio so inventory managers and visiting taxonomists can inspect recently collected material. An evening lecture of general interest is given and group discussions of policy and techniques are held. But parataxonomists also visit INBio opportunistically to leave specimens and get supplies or information. (Parataxonomists can stay at INBio's small 32-bed dormitory and meeting facility whenever they come to San José for any purpose.)

INBio is currently developing a program to involve the parataxonomists more directly in managing the inventory in the INBio facility. Since the inventory managers are themselves still defining and developing their own non-conventional *modus operandi,* most have been slow to grasp the many ways that they can manage their interactions with the parataxonomists to the benefit of all. However, it has been very striking to watch the inventory managers change from bystanding observers of parataxonomists in 1989 to being their true leaders. One-on-one feedback about the specimens that the parataxonomists bring in has catalyzed that change.

In the field, opportunistic, pointed, and strategic feedback from INBio's parataxonomist liaison is vital. The liaison delivers messages and materials to remote Biodiversity Offices and views the parataxonomist's work firsthand. For this reason, the liaison person is often the first person to flag a potential problem with a parataxonomist. Besides understanding with absolute clarity the specific goals and general strategy of the inventory and INBio, the liaison has to be an individual and group psychologist, skilled in defusing personal conflicts and able to cope with irregular hours and long difficult trips, miserable living conditions, and crises.

The second aspect of evaluation is that of determining the parataxonomists' salaries. The liaison's subjective impressions of how well the parataxonomist gets along with administrators, neighbors, apprentices, and others help the INBio administration determine merit pay raises and the automatic pay increases associated with inflation and seniority.

But the matter is far more complex. Many parataxonomists have worked for many years as civil servants. When they move into this more professional job climate, questions of merit, the quality of individual work, soft money, intangible benefits (e.g., full access to INBio facilities, real training programs, independence in the workplace, opportunities for advancement) are new and confusing. In contrast, they understand immediately about the value of INBio's health insurance, especially since INBio had to struggle with government unions to get it.

Since different parataxonomists have different employers and different employment histories, two parataxonomists who work side-by-side and do exactly the same tasks commonly receive quite different salaries. INBio has no direct power to change this, but has a very large responsibility to try. As a stop-gap measure, it reached a temporary agreement with the government whereby it can give a "sobre-sueldo" (salary add-on) to a government worker to get him or her up to the INBio salary for parataxonomists. INBio also suggests to directors of the conservation areas what their parataxonomists should be paid, especially those in positions funded by NGOs. INBio's initiative here is very important since most conservation area staffs are not yet technically capable of evaluating the parataxonomists' monthly contribution to the inventory.

As parataxonomists gain experience, they become exposed to the lifestyle, thoughts, issues, and analytical styles of Costa Rican decision-makers. They bring all this to bear on their own work and soon naturally want their new skills reflected in their monthly paychecks. (For perspective here, U.S. $20 to $50 additional pay per month can strongly affect performance.) And if a parataxonomist is doing fieldwork normally done by a university graduate, why not pay accordingly? INBio tries, but as a result it is continually searching for funds to increase parataxonomist salaries. This struggle to stay ahead illustrates a more general truth about the economics of tropical conservation development: initially low management costs increase very rapidly as a country begins to develop.

Many parataxonomists have never worked for a salary or an employer before coming to INBio. These people tend to accept the pay structure as a fact of life. But the degree to which these newcomers to the workforce accept responsibility in exchange for a salary varies widely. Some work 18-hour days until they drop from exhaustion but are perplexed when they aren't allowed to take off for several days during the dark of the moon—a particularly important time for collecting with lights—for a family birthday. Some also balk at criticism of their work, accustomed as they are to simply shrugging off any problem as "my way of doing things."

9. What is the function of the short courses for the parataxonomists?

The short courses are taught both in INBio, and in one or more conservation areas. The basic six-month parataxonomist course gives an overview of how to conduct an inventory and gets the parataxonomist to the point at which continued on-the-job training will be enough. Highly specific knowledge in the basic course is generally imparted only to illustrate a process or technique. The intent is not to try to pass on everything one needs to know to collect and understand a particular large taxon. That said, many species-rich groups of organisms would baffle parataxonomists unless they had a short course in collecting and preparation techniques, methods of distinguishing among species, natural history, etc. To date, short courses of two to sixty days have been held on marine invertebrates, beetle families, Chrysomelidae, microlepidoptera, Hymenoptera, spiders, Tachinidae and Syrphidae, higher plants, ferns, aquatic insects, and mites. Obvious candidates for additional short courses include mites, Diptera, families of small beetles, lower plants, protozoa, fungi and small reptiles and amphibians.

The short courses also give parataxonomists the chance to work together, to see how international scientists work and think, and to stay in direct contact with INBio for weeks. Course participants converse at length with the inventory managers, look up things in the collections, and generally get a feel for what a central information clearinghouse is.

The short courses also expose parataxonomists to taxonomists (and vice-versa) in both field and lab. Some of these collaborators have been so deeply impressed by the parataxonomists that they have been willing to cut into their field research time and, with their administrators' approval, deviate from their more traditional taxonomic pursuits to teach the advanced courses.

The length and location of short courses depends strongly on which group is studied and which taxonomists are teaching. For large and diverse groups, such as Hymenoptera and microlepidoptera, the most satisfactory structure seems to be to have three faculty members teach two three-week sessions, with one faculty member present throughout and the other two each visiting for three weeks each.

10. How does INBio get taxonomists to cooperate in training parataxonomists?

Taxonomists who want to help train parataxonomists in Costa Rica need some kind of clearance from the directorate that pays their salary and evaluates their performance. Thus, a major INBio task is convincing that directorate of the value of the work, or helping the taxonomist do so.

Of course, only a select subset of the taxonomic community will want to come to Costa Rica and spend time teaching in Spanish what amounts to a high school class. The trick is to find and reward those few. An upshot is that the particular groups of organisms emphasized will be the favorites of the participating taxonomists and not necessarily a thorough systematic coverage. So be it. Over time, other kinds of specialists will get involved. As word spreads that Costa Rican parataxonomists are ready to be told how to collect, say, mirid and lygaeid bugs, and that they have already collected thousands of specimens of them, someone is sure to decide that Costa Rica's mirid and lygaeid bugs are more interesting than the pentatomid bugs of the United States on which he or she works. When taxonomists with no interest in working with the parataxonomist come to Costa Rica to collect specimens of one group or another INBio should welcome them with open arms anyway and "accidentally" leave specimens belonging to the collectors' group, collected by the parataxonomists, in plain view.

In the future, INBio should offer to find inventory managers for taxonomists on the condition that they teach these new inventory managers about their group. This approach, however, will cost

INBio money (for more Costa Rican inventory managers) that it does not now have. (Today's INBio inventory managers are barely surviving on "soft money" from U.S. NSF and AID grants and private donations.)

11. What are the parataxonomists producing today?

A representative unspecialized parataxonomist generates each month 20 to 30 plant collection numbers (each number consisting of one to many specimens of a species), 1,000 to 3,000 properly pinned and mounted insects, and large uncounted numbers of insects in alcohol from Malaise traps, interception traps, yellow-pan traps, etc. When the parataxonomist is instructed to focus on particular groups, the overall number of specimens declines to some degree, but the needs of the inventory are met more strategically.

All specimen preparation is done in the field: pinnable (or point-mountable) insects are delivered to INBio mounted and ready to be labeled. The parataxonomists are trained to discard material if there is no time to mount it in the field. Such a philosophy represents a dramatic departure from the time-honored tradition of preserving large samples in the field during a collecting "expedition," and later slowly mounting them in the home institution at great cost in technician time. Samples in alcohol from traps are sorted at the Biodiversity Offices to whatever degree the INBio insect-processing team requests, and then delivered to INBio for freezing until a specialist sorts them further. An INBio-University of Costa Rica sorting center is currently planned for large bulk samples from insect traps.

The parataxonomists are now also "producing" apprentices too. Drawn from either school groups that visit their biodiversity offices or enthusiastic individuals living in the immediate area, these persons already collect specimens (with an associated cost in minor equipment, supplies, and time), and, more important, many will one day become parataxonomists. (Three former apprentices to parataxonomists recently graduated from the third parataxonomy course.)

12. How much will the parataxonomist component of the Costa Rican biodiversity inventory cost?

Getting the specimens and associated information for Costa Rica's half million species into a standard inventory format and into the front door of INBio will cost about U.S. $22 million spread over ten years ($2.2 million per year). This calculation is based on the actual costs and experiences during the past 30 months of program operations and on salary increases and other non-inflationary cost rises in Costa Rica. This comes to $44 per species, for roughly 4 percent (500,000) of the world's species. Once the material and information have arrived at INBio, the further processing, identification, and information management cost is roughly half the cost of obtaining them. Thus, a safe estimate for the total is U.S. $30 to $32 million in today's dollars. (The largest uncertainty associated with this figure is the cost of locating and isolating tens of thousands of species of microbes.)

13. Why expend funds on parataxonomists, instead of taxonomists?

First, this is not an "either or" situation. A body of inventory managers, taxonomists, and other kinds of information processors are needed to handle the parataxonomists' output. Second, taxonomists (systematists) have had centuries to get the nomenclature of the world's biodiversity in order. While they have made great strides, at the current pace, current style, and current funding, many centuries more of work will be needed. Clearly, a partial shift from a taxonomist who spends an entire lifetime monographing a group from Alaska to Argentina, to one who also guides the regional or local work on the fauna and flora is needed, since there are many users who urgently need regional or local information and will support its collection. Likewise it is clear that there should be a massive infusion of funds into the support of taxonomists to do taxonomy, rather than have them doing the multiple tasks that parataxonomists and inventory managers can do.

To use Ph.D. taxonomists for the basic muscle and brains of the inventory locally or regionally is to ask a mouse to gnaw down a tree instead of using a beaver colony. Even if there were funds enough to train a large cohort of Costa Rican Ph.D.s in systematics to handle first Costa Rica and then the rest of Central America, it would take many decades that we just don't have. And even these Ph.D.s would quickly decide that their time was better spent on detailed and background-demanding systematics and cladistics, leaving the time-consuming field inventory work to the equivalent of parataxonomists.

244

Second, putting the very populace that threatens tropical biodiversity to work inventorying it is an important step toward saving it. Indeed, biological literacy among the general populace is probably the only really long-term solution to tropical conservation problems.

14. Why do some parataxonomists drop out of the program?

Of the 32 parataxonomists in the first two courses, 13 have left the program as of late 1992. The reasons given for leaving include the desire to return to a former life style (3 persons), to get a university degree (1 person), or to take another kind of biodiversity-management position (biological illustrator, INBio inventory manager, education program, conservation administrator) (5 persons). A few poor performers have also been asked to leave (4 persons). The 19 remaining experienced parataxonomists are almost certain to stay in biodiversity management. Perhaps as many as half, however, may eventually move upward or laterally into higher education, administration, taxonomy, or teaching.

15. What major problems are anticipated with the parataxonomist program?

At present, INBio in general and the parataxonomist program specifically depend on much financial and some political support from the government of Costa Rica, international aid agencies and from foundations and private donors in the developed world. The more a program builds itself up and the more it narrows the socioeconomic gap between the donor and the recipient, the less outside funding sources can be expected to help. On the one hand, individual park guards that have become parataxonomists have been denied pay raises because they have "received the enormous freedom of work bestowed on the parataxonomist"; on the other, funding for operations has been denied by the donor community because the program is not "grass roots agriculture" but, rather, "scientific." INBio walks the razor's edge by demonstrating both extreme need and considerable success.

INBio Inventory Managers and Collections Management

Traditionally in tropical taxonomy and inventory, taxonomists collect specimens in the field and then take the material back to their (usually) developed world museums and universities. Duplicate samples are sometimes, but not always, deposited in tropical national collections. Additional material is purchased from a few independent local commercial collectors. Only a few neotropical countries (e.g., Mexico, Costa Rica, Venezuela, Brazil, and Peru) have national scientists who carry out a substantial amount of this taxonomic work on their own. Collection, curation, and the taxonomic activities of an inventory are conducted at a pace that is determined by the budgets, personal interests, commercial interests, and academic traditions of a handful of developed world countries. Through this approach, a substantial taxonomic foundation on which to build a tropical biodiversity inventory has been laid over the centuries. However, the main output has consisted of monographs on major taxonomic units throughout their whole geographical range and a large number of isolated species descriptions. The time for regional or national field guides, focused identification services, regional or national centers of specimen and taxonomic management, and the creation of local taxonomic ability has now come.

Tropical ecologists, agriculturalists, medical entomologists, etc., depend on the international community of taxonomists to identify specimens—usually a relatively small number of focal species. It even appears that this identification is done free of charge, but of course the "charge" is in the form of the taxonomists' salary and support from the tax base. But a new kind of user is appearing today, one concerned with huge blocks of biodiversity in which no particular species is sufficiently central to attract major taxonomic effort or funding at the time of identification.

INBio quickly realized that its parataxonomists could all too easily generate enough material to swamp the developed world's taxonomic service capacity for Costa Rica, an estimated 365,000 species of arthropods and millions of specimens. It also realized that Costa Rica is not the only biologically rich and interesting country in the world requiring taxonomic service. Accordingly, INBio set out to facilitate the work of any taxonomist eager to work with Costa Rican specimens, to train large numbers of Costa Ricans with undergraduate degrees in biology to do as much of the inventory management (and in some cases taxonomic) work as possible, to attract taxonomists to INBio to process specimens, and to define and realize a new kind of product-oriented profession as inventory managers. As will be evident below, the inventory manager is similar to a curatorial position, yet this person has a substantially broader institutional responsibility.

The Demands of the Job

As the four goals mentioned above imply, a successful INBio inventory manager must be able to juggle many activities and prioritize competing demands, taking overall institutional goals into account. Clearly, each of the activities listed below could be a full-time job, and may eventually become so. But for now, funds to hire enough people to specialize in this way aren't available. Moreover, many of these responsibilities need to be carried out only occasionally, in spurts.

Within this context, nine curatorial duties are paramount:

1. *Make sure incoming specimens from the parataxonomists are correctly labelled and sorted.* This process is normally the responsibility of a single person at any given moment.

2. *Oversee and conduct the taxon-oriented batching of specimens needing further work by the inventory managers and taxonomic specialists, or sending them off to the latter.*

3. *Provide organized feedback to the parataxonomists, at INBio and at the Biodiversity Offices.* This feedback is focused on the taxa for which the inventory manager is responsible, but also on the choice of groups to be collected, the techniques to be used, natural history, logistics, the parataxonomists' taxonomic ability, and the parataxonomists' solidarity with a larger system. Inventory managers must also help the parataxonomist accept broader responsibilities in administration, taxonomy, or public service, or acquire further formal education, etc.

4. *Curate specific taxa in the INBio reference collections.* The inventory manager must insure that the computerized databases for the taxa are as up-to-date as possible, with respect to specimen data, name data, and information management.

5. *Collaborate with taxonomists* working on his or her assigned or chosen taxa to facilitate their work, attract their interest to these taxa, extract from them taxon-specific and Costa Rica-specific information and understanding, and encourage the

development of Costa Rica-specific products. An inventory manager is likely to specialize on some major taxon for a number of years.

6. *Conduct direct identification services for INBio users.* Such services range from producing electronic and hard copy field guides to teaching users how to use the reference collections to making an identification to sending a specimen off to a taxonomist and getting its name back to the user. In-house identification of biodiversity prospecting samples is a major activity, and a major reason why their salaries and support can, for example, be partly charged to the Merck and Co. budget.

7. *Insure that INBio staff in other programs know about his or her work* and make use of that knowledge for biodiversity prospecting, information dissemination, information processing, etc.

8. *Be willing to move on to other major taxonomic groups as needed.* As the inventory of one taxon or another nears completion, updating and facilitating others' work with the "finished" taxon may be only a part-time job. Some inventory managers may be asked to move into some other area of INBio information management (e.g., ecology, behavior, biodiversity prospecting, electronic data management, etc.). In any case, the inventory manager must place responsibility to INBio's broad spectrum of activities above a personal interest in a particular taxon. In turn, INBio must be willing to take the inventory manager's interests into account in decisions about how time is allocated.

9. *Insure that all of the above is done in a manner that helps Costa Rica develop "taxonomic self-sufficiency."* The goal should be confidence that taxonomic problems and identifications pose no insurmountable obstacles to the use of biodiversity and that the incoming biodiversity information is being placed in a stable taxonomic framework.

What do INBio Inventory Managers Need to do Their Work?

To carry out these nine activities, the inventory manager primarily needs the collection itself, access to a good library and electronic literature services, an occasional trip abroad (or loan of specimens) to examine types and other comparative material, and a willing taxonomist for taxonomic guidance and collaboration. But the INBio inventory manager also requires access to field vehicles so he or she can give feedback to the parataxonomists in the Biodiversity Offices and do some very focused collecting. Other needs include high-quality GIS and database-workstations, travel funds for self-directed learning and work with taxonomists at their home institutions, and operating funds to keep specimen processing fully up to date. Equally, the INBio inventory manager needs to be backed up by a fully funded publication process (electronic and hard copy) to insure distribution of the information gathered. Also needed are support funds so the inventory manager can host visiting taxonomists and help them get to specific field sites known to be of interest.

Where Does the Inventory Manager Come From?

Traditionally, taxonomists and museum curators have emerged from the ranks of those with a deep personal interest in taxonomic biology and, often, with great personal curiosity about a particular group of organisms. However, tropical countries cannot wait passively for such persons to appear spontaneously from their own populace, and relying on a surplus from developed countries severely retards efforts to develop self-sufficiency and a sense of responsibility for national biodiversity.

In Costa Rica, the universities turn out a steady flow of Bachelor's Degree graduates in biology, many of whom would find a career as an inventory manager to be attractive if it can be developed through on-the-job training without leaving Costa Rica for long periods. Also, many people working in other biology-related fields would be happy to switch to this biodiversity career. Several hundred major taxa of Costa Rican organisms are large enough to keep as many as 50 inventory managers busy for several decades. Since apprenticeships and on-the-job training make it possible for anyone with enthusiasm and university-level education in biology to become productive immediately, the number of INBio inventory managers is limited mainly by the availability of funds for meeting salary and operations costs.

Besides scarce funding, one of the barriers to becoming a happy inventory manager is the quite understandable tendency for taxonomists to want to "steal" them to become graduate students in taxonomy. It will be much more helpful if the taxonomist can invest in helping to make them very effective inventory managers, by a combination of apprenticeship and explicit guidance toward being very good at managing the taxonomic portion of a national biodiversity inventory.

Higher Degrees vs. On-the-job Training

The inventory manager at INBio has the mission of getting people to use, and in some cases pay for, information on Costa Rican wildland biodiversity. In the end, the user community should pay the direct costs of managing the wildlands containing biodiversity and the GNP should rise enough as a result of biodiversity use that society recognizes wildland biodiversity as a productive sector. The inventory manager thus translates raw biodiversity information into items that society is willing to pay for in votes, barter, and cash. However, in the developed world, so much social distance and so many bureaucratic tangles stand between the raw material (the bug in the woods) and the final product (a new medicine or a new strain of corn) that even taxonomists and museum curators may feel isolated from this process. As a result, getting a degree too often becomes an end in itself or a ticket to greater prestige, power, salary, or job security, rather than a moral contract with society and biodiversity.

These two visions of biodiversity information processes sometimes collide at INBio. Both Costa Rican peers and international mentors push the inventory manager to get a Ph.D. in taxonomy. Mentors in particular want to "bring a Latin American graduate student along" so that they feel that they are doing their part for tropical biodiversity and enlarge the group of specialists studying a certain group of species. But to the extent that the inventory managers are shunted off into Ph.D. programs in foreign countries, INBio's goals may be subverted.

A partial solution is to develop collaborative programs between INBio and Costa Rican universities, whereby the INBio inventory managers receive an M.S. for their on-the-job work. This would be quite possible in the educational climate commonly surrounding university-museum collaborations in developed countries. But considering how conservative developing-world universities tend to be and how threatening Costa Rican university faculty and students find INBio's national inventory staff, a better approach might be to present INBio's work as a source of direct and pragmatic solutions to widespread social problems. That way, Costa Rican universities will have a strong incentive to begin collaborating seriously with INBio staff, thus blurring the distinction between these new professions and more traditional academic-based ones.

National vs. Regional Inventory Managers

Although INBio is a national institution, it is under a logical pressure from some sectors to become regional—a sort of Central American INBio. *(See Chapter II.)* While parataxonomists tend to be wedded to a particular site, and taxonomists by definition follow species across national borders, such a shift would pit increased quality and depth in-country against broader scope regionally. Greater budgets and more inventory managers can solve some of the conflicts. So could better communication technology and more political will. Personal conflicts are trickier. A Costa Rican can manage the inventory for Costa Rican macromoths and still have a normal family life, but an inventory manager for Central American macromoths must be rather nomadic for several decades. An inventory manager may work very hard to put biodiversity to work within his or her own society, but be much less inclined to do the same for other countries. On the other hand, if INBio becomes regional, some inventory managers would have added incentive to specialize at managing information about all of Central America.

Expanding Costa Rica's national inventory to encompass Central America touches on quite thorny questions, as noted above. Who takes on the additional budgetary responsibility? Does Costa Rica have the right to place inventory information from other countries in the public domain? How should whatever commercial returns from biodiversity information be distributed? An expanded INBio and its inventory managers can, of course, become a custodian for Central American biodiversity information, but the enormous costs of doing so will require financial and political backing far beyond that available today. And if funds and support *were* available, each of the Central American countries might even want to develop its own INBio, though economies of scale would be a major consideration.

Remaining Barriers

If funding becomes available to cover salaries and operations for taxonomists and inventory managers, the major remaining deterrent to fully developing inventory managers and carrying out the inventory is an understandable reluctance by the developed world taxonomic community and its core institutions to fully share in the taxonomic industry. While this will mean the loss of absolute dominance by the developed world taxonomic community, it should result in much more scientific and personal opportunity for all concerned. We stand at the dawn of a new age of international collaboration in biodiversity management.

Taxonomists

The INBio process has been nurtured from its conception by a very small number of heroic taxonomists who have thrown their intellectual and moral support behind it. These pioneers have not only helped INBio develop parataxonomist courses, training for the inventory managers, guidebooks, collection management, computer capacity, and the ability to give government advice. They have also shed light on how to make participation in the INBio process more attractive to other taxonomists. Their collective wisdom follows:

1. *Develop good relations between INBio and the taxonomist's home administration.* The home administration may need coaching to grasp the value of the taxonomist's participation in a quite unorthodox process.
2. *Try to attract renown taxonomists who also enjoy their work and natural history.*
3. *Identify and meet the logistic, administrative, financial, and psychological needs of individual taxonomists.* Don't assume that all taxonomists have the same needs. One may need an airplane ticket. Another may need help with a difficult department chairman. Still another may need help writing a major proposal for funding both the INBio process and the taxonomist's home institution.

4. *Recognize that time is an extremely valuable resource to a taxonomist.* Nothing is more frustrating to a field scientist than to have to spend several days of his or her brief stay in a tropical country jumping through bureaucratic hoops.

5. *Don't try to force taxonomists to "do as the Romans when in Rome."* Often, taxonomists try to operate virtually outside society and politics: "you let me collect my butterflies and I will have no opinion about your dictatorship." To a certain degree, this isolationism can allow full attention to the task at hand and can be accommodated within the INBio process.

6. *Be a sincere, detailed, and appreciative user of a taxonomist's output.* Every identification is output, every effort made to show how to tell one bug from another is output, every minute spent helping an inventory manager to assemble a field guide is output. It is all "technology transfer" and should be rewarded as such.

7. *Recognize that taxonomists are not "big budget scientists."* They are accustomed to barter, and one of the most valuable kinds of barter is specimens and natural history that will help them solve the puzzles that they have been wrestling with throughout their professional lives. The challenge for INBio and others is thus allowing the taxonomist to keep on doing taxonomy without allowing economically disastrous "biodiversity leaks."

8. *Go to the taxonomists.* Most cannot leave their jobs easily, so money invested in sending INBio inventory managers abroad to visit the taxonomists for periods of intensive work will pay handsome dividends in technology transfer.

9. *Bring the taxonomists to INBio.* Eventually, INBio should have the resources to bring the taxonomists to the specimens where appropriate.

10. *Offer bright and enthusiastic collaborators as inventory managers, parataxonomists, and other INBio colleagues.*

Regional and National versus Monographic Work

For many taxonomists, the dream is to really "clean up" some major group of organisms—not only to make the species-level taxonomy unambiguous, but also to assign the species correctly to higher taxa and to understand the most likely evolutionary and biogeographic relationships among all of these taxa. Since most major taxa range across many countries and major habitat types, the taxonomist is not inclined to focus solely on a single region or country. Consequently, it will require a major effort for society to obtain a truly solid base of knowledge for all of tropical biodiversity. However, we cannot wait centuries for this information.

There are a variety of advantages for the taxonomist to also help with national or regional floras and faunas, especially if the "legwork" is carried out primarily by the parataxonomists and inventory managers. Very large series of specimens of both sexes and of various ages from many habitats offer major opportunities to sort out ecophenotypes and geographic variation.

Thorough collecting in one area often results in the discovery of sympatries that resolve questions related to sibling species. As the number of collections increase, natural history information accumulates. Equally important, as the organisms become better known locally, chances improve that the parataxonomists and inventory managers can collect additional specimens in a given taxon. Finally, the work done for a local flora and fauna is a valuable source of information for a definitive monograph for a taxon.

More administratively, work on local floras and faunas leads to finished intermediate products (electronic and hard-copy field guides, reference collections) that reveal actual results to funders and enhance users' interest (as opposed to an annual progress report for a monograph that will require 20 years to complete). In an upward spiral, this greater interest may then spur the collection of more natural history information and the growth of local political will to support the entire INBio process and biodiversity conservation, as well as systematics in general. It should be clear that taxonomic monographic work, and flora/fauna local identification guides and services, are fully complementary and both are vital.

Annex 2

BIODIVERSITY PROSPECTING CONTRACT

David Downes, Sarah A. Laird, Christopher Klein,
and Bonnie Kramer Carney

Part I introduces the draft agreement, explaining how it can be used when considering or negotiating specific transactions. Parts II and III contain the draft agreement itself and annexes to the agreement. Part IV discusses specific sections of the draft contract. Part V provides a general legal background to the draft contract.

I. Introduction—Using the Draft Contract

The Contract as a "Model." This contract is intended as an aid to the negotiation of contracts for the collection of biological samples. A wide variety of parties may negotiate these types of transactions in a wide variety of circumstances. Thus, the contract may serve as a starting point for discussions, but it must be modified to fit each case. In a field as new as biodiversity prospecting, it is impossible to design a "form contract" like those used in some established lines of business. (*See* Chapter IV for a discussion of the provisions included.)

The draft agreement is not a complete business agreement. Its purpose is to give negotiators useful information, not to provide an authoritative model, and it does not include all of the "boilerplate" provisions often found in business contracts (such as "force majeure" clauses) or all of the clauses frequently found in contracts for international transactions (such as provisions responding to currency regulations or investment rules).

255

For key terms that are most likely to differ from one contract to the next—such as the percentage of royalties—the contract includes blanks for negotiators to fill in. Terms that the parties are most likely to consider optional are enclosed in brackets. For clauses that parties are most likely to change or delete, examples of possible language are included in "Appendices" to the main body of the contract.

Similarly, the contract assigns certain duties to the Collector or the Pharmaceutical Company that under some circumstances the parties may decide to shift from the Pharmaceutical Company to the Collector, or vice versa. In addition, signatories may want to delete one or more obligations included in the draft contract.

Finally, the governing national or local law in the region from which the Samples are collected or in which either party is based may require certain changes or additions in the contract. When negotiating an agreement, a party should always consult with lawyers in the country where it is based or where activities will be conducted under the contract.

Parties to the Contract. The contract is drafted on the assumption that the parties are most likely to be, on the one side, a research institute or scientist based in the country where collection takes place (the "Collector"), and on the other side, a pharmaceutical company based in the United States (the "Pharmaceutical Company"). Most of the text is, however, consistent with the situation in which the Collector is an individual or organization based outside the country of collection. Modified, it might also be used by indigenous or local organizations within the country that may wish to contract with pharmaceutical companies to collect and supply Samples. The draft contract is not relevant to relationships involving basic taxonomic research with no direct commercial application, and it has limited relevance to transfers of crop genetic resources for use in agricultural genetic engineering or plant breeding.

The contract is drafted on the assumption that a Pharmaceutical Company based in the United States is contracting to buy Samples from a research scientist or institution. Nevertheless, if the Pharmaceutical Company is based in a different country, the contract could be modified accordingly. It could also be useful, with modifications, if the Pharmaceutical Company's place is taken by another type of enterprise, such as a biotechnology firm or a broker.

Additionally, a Collector and Pharmaceutical Company could sign the draft contract, and the Collector could sign a separate agreement with local or indigenous people to obtain their consent for collecting, arrange for the local or indigenous people to collect and supply Samples in exchange for payment of services, and to compensate them for knowledge supplied on traditional plant use, or a combination of these activities. Sections 1-5 of Appendix C to the draft contract include requirements of local participation and benefits, environmental assessment ("EA"), and public reporting that indigenous people and local communities may wish to include in any agreement whereby they agree to allow or participate in collecting.

II. Draft Contract

This Agreement is made the ____ day of _____, 199__ between _____, a corporation incorporated under the laws of the State of _____ of the United States of America with its principal place of business at _____ ("Pharmaceutical Company"); and _____, a _____ organized under the laws of _____ and located in the city of _____, in the country of _____ ("Collector").

WHEREAS the Pharmaceutical Company wishes to obtain Samples of biota (hereinafter "Samples") to screen for biological activity or other useful properties;

WHEREAS the Collector has access to the source of the Samples [as well as valuable trade secrets, know-how, and other intellectual property rights]; and

WHEREAS the parties have agreed, in consideration of the premises and obligations hereinafter set forth, to enter into and be legally bound by this Agreement:

Article 1 –   DEFINITIONS

"Net Sales" means the total gross revenues from sales of a Product, typically based on the financial exchange between buyer and seller at the point of distribution of the product.

"Collector" means the individual or organization that will collect Samples and provide them to the Pharmaceutical Company.

"Country of Collection" means the country in which the Sample Area is situated.

"Derived from," in defining "Product," shall refer to a product that is the actual isolated natural product or that is structurally based on the isolated natural product (i.e., where the natural product provides the lead for development of the invention), or that is in any other way created using in substantial part information, including ethnobotanical or traditional knowledge, contained or conveyed by or with a Sample.

"Ethnobiologist" means a person who studies how human cultures interrelate with their biological environment.

"Indigenous Person or People" means one or more persons belonging to an ethnic or cultural group living in and having long-standing traditional ties to the Sample Area.

"Local Person or People" means one or more persons living in or around the Sample Area and may include indigenous persons or people.

"Patent" means a United States patent and/or a patent from any other country that the Pharmaceutical Company acquires on a Product, including U.S. and other countries' plant patents and petty patents.

"Product" means any commercially valuable medicinal, pharmaceutical, or otherwise useful compound or useful combination of compounds derived from a Sample supplied under this Agreement.

"Sample" means a sample of a biological material that is distinct from all other samples, and that is one of the following:

a sample of part of the organism likely to contain significantly distinct active compounds (e.g. roots, leaves, flowers, wood, bark, fruit) from a taxonomically distinct species or subspecies of plant, fungus, or animal taken from the Sample Area;

a sample of soil, mud, or other medium for biota taken from the Sample Area that is likely to contain taxonomically distinct species or subspecies of microorganism, plant, animal, or fungus.

"Sample Area" means the territory from which the Collector will take the Samples, defined as _____[describe the territory].

"Trade Secret," as is defined under the Uniform Trade Secrets Act, means information that has competitive value because it is not generally known and is the subject of reasonable efforts to maintain its secrecy.

Article 2 –   COLLECTOR'S SAMPLE SUPPLY OBLIGATIONS

A.   The Collector shall supply Samples to the Pharmaceutical Company in regular batches of an agreed size, in a form and manner acceptable to the Pharmaceutical Company for screening, as specified in Appendix A.

B.   The Collector shall collect Samples according to the selection criteria in Appendix B. This may include selection provisions for Samples with

258

known ethnobiological uses, Samples collected at random, Samples collected taxonomically, soil Samples, or a combination of methods.

C. OPTION 1: The Collector shall label all Samples and provide the following information about each Sample: (1) name of species; (2) geographic location from which it came; (3) nature of habitat (e.g., rainforest stream bank, rainforest canopy); (4) time of day and season when collected; and (5) other information necessary to complete a minimal description under the standards of the relevant scientific discipline (i.e., botany, zoology or microbiology). The Collector shall ensure that each Sample is taxonomically authenticated according to generally accepted scientific standards and that an adequate record of any such authentication is delivered with the Sample to the Pharmaceutical Company. Voucher specimens will be kept by _____.

OPTION 2: The Collector need not provide Pharmaceutical Company with ecological or taxonomic information about a Sample, but shall code each Sample and shall maintain records so that it can, as far as is reasonably possible, gather additional quantities of the Sample where Pharmaceutical Company specifies in order to conduct additional testing of such Sample. Collector shall respond within a reasonable time [within ___ days] to any such requests for additional quantities of a Sample from Pharmaceutical Company.

Article 3 – COLLECTOR'S MISCELLANEOUS RESPONSIBILITIES

A. The Collector shall obtain and maintain all necessary permits, licenses, or other required approvals needed to collect and deliver Samples to _____ [location] under this Agreement, including, but not limited to, export controls and environmental laws, from the governmental authorities in the Country of Collection or from any private entities whose authorization is necessary under applicable law. In negotiating and signing this Agreement and carrying out its obligations, the Collector shall also comply with any national or international laws applicable in the Country of Collection and Sample Area that specifically concern the negotiation, signing, or performance of agreements for collection or delivery of biological Samples.

B. The Collector warrants that it has obtained the permits, licenses, or other approvals necessary to give it legal authority to negotiate and sign this Agreement.

C. The Collector shall use [at least ____ %] of the Pharmaceutical Company's advance payment, the annual payment for Samples collected, and any royalty payments for the purposes described in Appendix C.

D. The Collector warrants that it shall not obtain Samples or information about the ethnobotanical use of the Samples from Indigenous Peoples without obtaining their informed consent.

259

Article 4 –   PHARMACEUTICAL COMPANY'S OBLIGATIONS —
COMPENSATION

A.   The Pharmaceutical Company shall pay the Collector an advance payment of U.S. $_____ prior to the collection of any Samples, in order to initiate the agreed-upon workplan.

B.   Thereafter, the Pharmaceutical Company shall pay the Collector an annual fee of U.S. $_____ provided that the Collector fulfills the agreed schedule of supply of Samples.

C.   Should the Collector fail to supply the agreed upon numbers and quality of Samples (as specified in Appendix A), the Pharmaceutical Company may reduce its annual payment by an amount prorated to the shortfall in the supply of Samples.

Article 5 –   PHARMACEUTICAL COMPANY'S OBLIGATIONS —
SCREENING OF SAMPLES

A.   In cooperation with _____ , a medical research institution in the Country of Collection, the Pharmaceutical Company will screen all Samples for potential Products using its standard screening methods and criteria for evaluating commercial potential.

B.   In cooperation with _____ , a medical research institution in the Country of Collection, the Pharmaceutical Company shall screen Samples for uses relating to diseases common to the populations of the Country of Collection, such as _____. The Pharmaceutical Company shall notify the collector of positive results and, if it does not choose to pursue a patent on the substance producing the result, shall cooperate on arrangements for the Collector to pursue such a patent or for publication if the Collector so requests.

Article 6 –   PHARMACEUTICAL COMPANY'S OBLIGATIONS —
FUTURE COMPENSATION

A.   The Collector shall receive a quarterly royalty payment based on sales of any Product amounting to ___% of net sales for a patented Product and ___% of net sales for any other Product.

B.   In the event that a Sample or information provided by an Ethnobiologist or Local Person or People, or material collected from indigenous territories, leads to the identification of a Sample from which is ultimately derived a Product for a use similar to the one specified by the Ethnobiologist or the Local Person or People, such Local Person or People will receive a quarterly royalty of ___% of the net sales worldwide.

260

C. The Pharmaceutical Company shall continue to pay the royalties specified under this Article until the obligation terminates, as stated in Article 13.

D. The Pharmaceutical Company's obligations to pay royalties on Annual Net Sales shall not be diminished or otherwise affected if it issues any license relating to a Product to any entity.

E. The Collector shall have the right, for two years after any royalty payment under this Article, to verify that the royalty payment satisfies the requirements of this Agreement, as follows: At the request and expense of the Collector, the Pharmaceutical Company shall permit independent public accountants selected by the Collector, and reasonably acceptable to the Pharmaceutical Company, access to such books and records of the Pharmaceutical Company as are required to verify that the royalty payment(s) in question were calculated accurately and in conformance with the provisions of this Agreement. The Pharmaceutical Company's books and records subject to review pursuant to this provision shall not be revealed to the Collector, and the Collector shall cause said accountants to retain all such information in confidence during the term of this Agreement and for a period of five years thereafter.

Article 7 – PHARMACEUTICAL COMPANY'S MISCELLANEOUS OBLIGATIONS

A. During each annual period following the Effective Date of this Agreement, subject to the laws of the United States and the Collector's Country [or Country of Collection], the Pharmaceutical Company shall employ citizens of the Collector's country [or Country of Collection], with at least a ____ degree in a relevant discipline, designated by the Collector, to participate in research on supplied Samples. These persons will be employed as visiting researchers. Except for their status as visiting researchers, these citizens shall comply with and be subject to the ordinary terms under which the Pharmaceutical Company retains personnel, including relevant confidentiality agreements.

B. At each anniversary of the Effective Date of this Agreement, the Pharmaceutical Company shall report in writing to the Collector on the screening, research, and development ("R&D") relating to Samples provided under this Agreement, as well as on the performance of any other obligations of the Pharmaceutical Company in addition to such screening. The report shall include: a list adequately identifying all Samples screened; the highest stage of R&D to which each Sample was taken up to the time of writing and a summary of the R&D findings; applications for Patents for Products; grants of Patents for Products; an accounting of net sales, profits, and royalties paid under the Agreement on Products; and any commercial applications for any Product(s) being developed. The report shall be provided within ____ days following each anniversary of the Effective Date. This obligation shall extend

261

beyond the termination of other obligations under the Agreement, as specified in Article 12.D.

C. Only at the option of the Collector shall the Pharmaceutical Company, when publishing or authorizing publication of information regarding a Sample or Product, including research and development findings, describe (or take reasonable steps to ensure inclusion of a description of) the provenance of the Sample or Product as defined in this Article, unless otherwise directed by the Collector in writing. Any such description may be brief, but shall acknowledge the following facts: that the Collector provided the Sample; the taxonomic identity, geographic location, and (if known) ecological role of the species or variety represented by the Sample. If an Ethnobiologist or an Indigenous Person or People provided information that led to identification or better understanding of the Sample or Product, the Pharmaceutical Company shall also acknowledge that contribution in any publication if the Indigenous Person or People or the Ethnobiologist so desires. The Pharmaceutical Company shall take reasonable steps to ensure that its employees and agents comply with this obligation.

D. The Pharmaceutical Company (and its agents and employees) must execute the obligation described in Article 7.C only where appropriate and feasible. For instance, it shall make good faith efforts to comply with the obligation in publications in academic, scholarly, or scientific journals, and in patent applications where consistent with applicable law. It may be excused from compliance in, for instance, the creation of information inserts for pharmaceuticals, submissions to the *Physician's Desk Reference,* or advertising directed at physicians.

E. The Pharmaceutical Company warrants that it has obtained and promises that it shall maintain all necessary permits, licenses, or other required approvals for the negotiation and signing of this Agreement, and for the acceptance, payment for, and analysis of Samples under this Agreement, from the governmental authorities with jurisdiction over its activities under this Agreement, including, but not limited to laws regarding customs, tariffs, import restrictions, currency exchange, restraint of trade, or competition.

Article 8 –   PATENT RIGHTS

A. If, as a result of its screening any Sample supplied to it by the Collector, the Pharmaceutical Company identifies a Product that has commercial potential, the Pharmaceutical Company:

  i)   May, at its own expense, apply for patent protection for said Product in any country that the Pharmaceutical Company chooses. The Collector agrees to cooperate with the Pharmaceutical Company in obtaining any Patents under this Agreement.

ii)   Shall notify the Collector, identifying each Product and the Sample from which it was derived, of the filing of a patent application within 30 days after filing.

B.   The Collector shall have the right under this Agreement to assume the maintenance of the Patent if the Pharmaceutical Company decides to let such a patent lapse. The Pharmaceutical Company shall notify the Collector if it decides to cease to prosecute a patent application or to maintain an issued Patent on any Product, giving enough notice so that the Collector will be able to assume the prosecution or maintenance of the Patent.

C.   The Collector shall have the right to file for Patents on a Product in any country in which the Pharmaceutical Company chooses not to file for a Patent on that Product.

D.   The Pharmaceutical Company agrees to cooperate with the Collector in obtaining any Patents filed for under Section 8.C. above.

E.   The inventors named in any Patent may be, subject to the patent laws of the relevant jurisdiction, scientists affiliated with the Pharmaceutical Company and/or scientists affiliated with the Collector, and/or an Ethnobiologist or Local Person or People who have provided information about a Sample that led to the development of a patented Product.

F.   The Pharmaceutical Company shall use all reasonable measures, whether by maintaining action, suit, proceeding, or otherwise, against any person, firm, or corporation infringing any Patent(s) (except where it has ceased maintenance as provided for under Article 8.B), as well as any trade secrets belonging to the Collector, or trade secrets or trademarks relating to a Product, necessary to prevent such infringement or to recover damages. All costs and expenses of such action, suit, or proceeding shall be borne by the Pharmaceutical Company. Damages recovered in such action shall be applied to compensate the Collector up to the amount of its losses resulting from the infringement. For that purpose, the Collector shall assign any cause of action to the Pharmaceutical Company and otherwise cooperate in any way necessary, but without expense, in the prosecution of any action, suit, or proceeding.

Article 9 –   CONFIDENTIALITY

A.   Whenever it receives or takes possession of information from the Collector that the Collector has a duty to submit under this Agreement, and thereafter whenever such information is in its possession, the Pharmaceutical Company shall take all reasonable steps to keep confidential any trade secrets contained in that information, if the trade secrets are designated as confidential by marking of each page or part of a page (or other communication or record). The Pharmaceutical Company shall not, however, have any obligation to keep secret such information if it is not a trade secret or if it is made public by a source other than Pharmaceutical Company over which Pharmaceutical Company has no control and to whom Pharmaceutical Company did not supply the information.

B.   Whenever it receives or takes possession of information from the Pharmaceutical Company that the Pharmaceutical Company has a duty to submit under this Agreement, and thereafter whenever the information is in its possession, the Collector shall take all reasonable steps to keep confidential any trade secrets contained in that information, if the trade secrets are designated as confidential by marking of each page or part of a page (or other communication or record). The Collector shall not, however, have any obligation to keep secret such information if it is made public by a source other than Collector over which Collector had no control and to whom Collector did not supply the information, or by a government agency which obtained the information by virtue of its regulatory powers.

C.   No disclosure pursuant to the terms of this Agreement of a trade secret designated confidential as specified in Sections 9.A and 9.B above shall be deemed a relinquishment or publication of a trade secret.

Article 10 – EXCLUSIVITY

The Collector shall not release, deliver, or disclose to any other party any Sample (or material that is identical to a Sample) delivered to the Pharmaceutical Company for a period of _____ months after delivery to Pharmaceutical Company, except that: if the Pharmaceutical Company fails to conduct R&D aimed at developing a Product from a Sample or fails to report on such R&D as required under Article 7.B within ___ months after delivery of that Sample, then the Collector has the right to release, deliver, or disclose the Sample (or material identical to that Sample) to a third party.

Article 11 – RESOLUTION OF DISPUTES

A.   In the event of any dispute under this Agreement between the Pharmaceutical Company and the Collector, the parties shall negotiate or resort to mediation in good faith.

B.   OPTION 1: If efforts under Article 11.A fail, arbitration shall be the exclusive means of resolving disputes under this Agreement, except as otherwise provided here in Article 11. Arbitration shall be conducted under the arbitration rules of the United Nations Commission on International Trade Law, before one arbitrator to be selected by the parties from the list of knowledgeable persons attached to this Appendix. If the parties cannot agree on an arbitrator within ___ days after one party receives the other's notice of a claim, the arbitrator shall be appointed by _____. The language(s) of

264

the arbitration shall be _____. The place of arbitration shall be _____. The decision of the arbitration panel shall be final.

[In the case of a dispute regarding duties of confidentiality under Article 9, arbitration shall not be the exclusive means of dispute resolution and a party may resort to judicial action in the courts of _____.]

OPTION 2: If efforts under Article 11.A fail, arbitration shall be the exclusive means of resolving disputes under this Agreement, except as otherwise provided in this Article 11. Arbitration shall be conducted under the arbitration rules of the United Nations Commission on International Trade Law, before three arbitrators [to be selected from the list of knowledgeable persons attached to this Appendix], one selected by the Pharmaceutical Company, one selected by the Collector, and the third selected by the first two arbitrators. If the parties cannot agree on an arbitrator within __ days after one party receives the other's notice of a claim, the arbitrator shall be appointed by _____. The language(s) of the arbitration shall be _____. The place of arbitration shall be _____. The decision of the arbitration panel shall be final.

[In the case of a dispute regarding duties of confidentiality under Article 9, arbitration shall not be the exclusive means of dispute resolution and a party may resort to judicial action in the courts of _____.]

Article 12 – CHOICE OF LAW

This Agreement and the parties' rights and duties hereunder shall be interpreted under the laws of _____, without reference to conflicts-of-law provisions.

Article 13 – TERM OF AGREEMENT AND TERMINATION

A. The Collector's obligations regarding supply of Samples under Article 2 and the Pharmaceutical Company's obligations regarding compensation under Article 4 shall remain in force until the date specified in Appendix A to this Agreement. The duration of these obligations may be extended for further periods of _____ years by mutual written agreement. Any such agreement to extend the duration of these obligations shall be entered into at least six months before the obligations would otherwise terminate.

B. The Collector may terminate obligations under Article 2 and the Pharmaceutical Company may terminate obligations under Articles 5 and 7.A at any time upon six months' written notice to the other party.

C. The Pharmaceutical Company's obligations under Articles 6 and 7.B, C & D and the Collector's rights under Article 6 with respect to any Product under this Agreement shall extend until the latest date of expiration of the

Patent or Patents on that Product, or until 25 years after the effective termination of the Collector's obligations under Article 2, whichever date is earlier.

D. Obligations of confidentiality under Article 9 shall terminate only with the occurrence of the earliest of one of the following events: when the party asserting that designated information communicated to the other party is a trade secret publishes that information, or authorizes publication through a third party, or states in writing (in response to an inquiry from the other party or otherwise) that the information is no longer a trade secret; or when the information otherwise ceases to be a trade secret; or when ___ years have elapsed following the termination of collecting and compensation obligations under Articles 2, 3, 4, and 7.A.

Within one year from the termination of the obligations under Articles 2, 3, 4, and 7.A, either party has the right to demand the return, within a reasonable time, of materials submitted to the other party under the Agreement that were designated confidential as trade secrets.

E. Termination or expiration of the rights under this Agreement described in Sections 12.A and 12.B above shall be without prejudice to the rights and obligations of the parties described in Sections 12.C and 12.D above.

This Agreement, including the Appendices, contains the entire agreement of the parties with respect to the subject matter herein and may be amended only through a written document signed by both parties.

IN WITNESS WHEREOF, this Agreement is executed by the duly authorized officers effective as of the Effective Date first written above.

Signature	Signature
For _____	For _____
Pharmaceutical Company	Collector

III. Appendices to Draft Contract Between Pharmaceutical Company and Sample Collector

The provisions in Appendix A and Appendix B contain details about the performance of the contract that are likely to vary from one contract to the next. Appendix C is separated from the main contract because its provisions are different from typical commercial contracts in that they are particularly progressive and strive to meet high standards of conduct even where governmental or international regulation may not require it.

266

Although most of the provisions in Appendix C are unusual, they are not unique: many for-profit companies around the world are voluntarily setting high environmental standards for their businesses. The requirement that commercial collectors conduct initial and supplementary environmental assessments would appear to be a minimal obligation: if nothing else, collectors should make sure that their collecting activities do not harm the environment. Finally, given that much of the world's biodiversity-rich territory is within public lands, environmental and public accountability standards governing prospecting contracts are likely to become stronger over time. In this respect, much of Appendix C may merely prefigure future national regulatory standards.

Appendix A — Obligations for Supply of Samples

1. **Period of Delivery.** At the end of every period of ___ days, the Collector shall make a delivery of Samples to the Pharmaceutical Company at _____ , for acceptance by the Pharmaceutical Company.

2. **Number and Quality of Samples.** Each delivery shall contain no fewer than ____ and no more than ____ Samples. The Collector shall take reasonable steps necessary to ensure that Samples are collected, stored, shipped, and delivered in a condition good enough for purposes of full and reliable screening. The minimum size or amount of each sample is _____ .

3. **Dates of First and Last Delivery.** The Collector shall make the first delivery by _____ , 19___ . The Collector shall continue deliveries for a period of years, ending _____ , 19___ .

4. **Modification of Obligation.** If the Collector submits reasonable evidence that circumstances beyond its control have impaired its ability to meet its obligations under this Appendix A, then the Collector and Pharmaceutical Company shall negotiate in good faith a modification to such obligations. Such modification shall not affect any of the obligations of the Pharmaceutical Company.

Appendix B — Criteria for Selecting Samples

1. Samples will be collected by random or rational methods or a combination of the two. These include [select as many as appropriate]:

   a. Random collection of taxonomically diverse Samples, or randomly collected soil Samples, in the selected Sample Area.

   b. Taxonomic collection of Samples from species within a genus shown to have exhibited promising bioactive compounds.

c. Ethnobotanical collection of Samples that provides information on uses of Samples in traditional medical systems.

d. Ecological collection of Samples that provides information on potential chemical activity based on observed ecological relationships between plants, insects, and other animals.

2. ___ Samples will be collected using rational methods and ___ Samples using random methods.

Appendix C — Conservation And Local Benefits

To support and promote the goal of this Agreement and the parties' shared desire to encourage the conservation of biologically diverse ecosystems and local cultural resources, the parties agree to the following provisions:

1. Collector's Warranty of Local Consultations and Environmental Assessment ("EA"). In light of the widely recognized understanding that EA and local participation are essential to the preservation of biologically diverse ecosystems, the Collector warrants that it has:

a. Conducted an EA of this Agreement. The Collector also promises to report the results of the EA in its report referenced under Sections 2 and 5 of this Appendix. For purposes of this Appendix, EA means an investigation of the cumulative effects of collection activities conducted under this Agreement on the Sample Area; such investigation must be carried out by independent environmental auditing professionals experienced in environmental assessment of similar or analogous natural resources extraction activities, using the highest standards and most relevant techniques applied in similar or analogous activities. The goal of the EA shall be to determine (1) the cumulative environmental, economic, social, and cultural effects in the Sample Area and adjacent areas to the extent they may be affected, and (2) any violation of applicable laws, including laws concerning natural resources, environmental standards, relations with or rights of local communities, Indigenous Peoples or groups, or entry permits or approvals. The investigation shall include, but shall not be limited to, on-site visual inspection of the Sample Area and adjacent areas, review of relevant Collector and governmental records, and interviews with Collector's employees and local residents, including Indigenous People.

b. Obtained the informed consent needed to create this Agreement and carry out activities under it from appropriate representatives or governing bodies of Indigenous Peoples who traditionally reside in or use an area in which those activities are to be conducted. The Collector also warrants that it has obtained informed consent to conduct activities under this Agreement from any other Local People with legal authority to control access to an area in which those activities are to be conducted.

268

c. Published notice of the negotiation of this Agreement, including basic information about the contract, a request for comments or questions within a reasonable time, and information about how to submit comments or questions, among Local People in the Sample Area through appropriate means such as mail, telephone, or personal contact with traditional and official leaders of local communities; environmental, developmental or indigenous or human rights non-governmental organizations; government officials; or research scientists active in the Sample Area.

d. Asked for and received comments from those persons, through appropriate means, such as the methods for notice described in Section 1.c above, as well as through open meetings in local communities (held after reasonable notice), and has considered any written or oral comments received.

2. Publication of Conservation Purpose and Activities.

a. Except for the specific commercially sensitive terms in Articles _____, both parties shall make copies of this Agreement publicly available, by (among other reasonable means) sending a copy within a reasonable time in response to the request of any person.

b. Except for specific trade secrets as designated and identified under Articles 1 and 9.B, both Parties shall make public the annual reports required under Article 7.B of this Agreement and Section 5 of this Appendix by (among other reasonable means) sending a copy within a reasonable time in response to the request of any person.

c. The parties may charge reasonable fees for the material costs of copying and mailing information under this Section 2.

3. Collector's Use of Compensation.
The Collector shall apply at least ___ % of the compensation in the advance payment and ___ % of any royalties under this Agreement to expenditures incurred in performing the activities described in Section 4 of this Appendix C.

4. Collector's Conservation Obligations.
The Collector shall perform the following activities:

a. Consultation with local communities, government bodies, and conservation and development organizations regarding the planning and implementation of conservation measures that are compatible with and build upon local, including traditional and indigenous, cultures.

b. Public education and reporting (including workshops, town meetings, publications, and courses) on the Agreement between the Parties and its provisions for conservation and local benefits, and the implementation of those provisions.

c. Preparation of supplemental EAs of the Agreement and collection activities conducted under it, for each ___ year period in which collecting activities continue under this Agreement. These supplemental EAs need not duplicate investigations already conducted in the initial EA, but must include all investigation necessary and sufficient to update the initial EA, confirm or deny its predictions, and adequately describe the cumulative environmental, social, economic, and cultural effects of activities under this Agreement as of the date of the supplemental EA, including interviews with Collector's employees and local residents. The supplemental EAs shall be published in the Collector's annual report referenced in Sections 2 and 5 of this Appendix C.

d. Other measures devoted to preserving biological diversity in the Sample Area.

e. Obtain the informed consent to activities conducted under this Agreement of any Indigenous People. The Collector shall also obtain informed consent to conduct activities carried out under this Agreement from any other Local People with legal authority to control access to an area in which such activities are conducted.

5. **Collector's Report on Conservation Activities.** On the first anniversary of the Effective Date of this Agreement, and on each subsequent anniversary, the Collector shall report in writing to the public as specified in Section 2 above and to the Pharmaceutical Company on the expenditures of the advance payment and royalties, describing the progress of screening and research and development (R&D) relating to Samples provided under this Agreement, as well as the performance of any other obligations of the Pharmaceutical Company in addition to screening. The report shall include an EA or supplemental EA, whichever has most recently been conducted prior to publication, as described in Sections 1 and 4 of this Appendix C, and a report on consultations with Local People during the reporting period regarding the design, performance, and utility of the activities conducted under the Agreement.

6. **Right of Verification.** Parties described under Section 8 of this Appendix on enforcement shall have the right to verify that expenditures were made in accordance with Section 3 of this Appendix on the same terms under which the Collector has the right to verify royalties under Article 6.E of this Agreement.

7. **Termination of Obligations.** The obligations and rights under this Appendix shall terminate after one year from the termination of the collecting and compensation obligations under Articles 2 and 3.

8. Enforcement of Obligations. The obligations and rights under this Appendix may be enforced through specific performance, through the means provided for in Article 11 as modified in Section 8.a below, by the parties listed in Section 8.b. below.

    a. Enforcement shall proceed pursuant to Article 11 when the dispute is between the Collector and the Pharmaceutical Company. When a party listed under Section 8.b seeks to enforce the provisions of this Agreement, it may do so under either of the following procedures:

    (1) Through arbitration under the terms of Article 11, except that the Section 8.B. party names one arbitrator, and the party to the Agreement names the other, and the Section 8.B. party may dictate whether arbitration is binding or whether the arbitrated decision may be appealed as described in Section 8.a.(2) below.

    (2) By bringing an action for specific performance against the party whose obligation under this Agreement is at issue, in the Section 8.b. party's choice of either (a) a court with jurisdiction in the Country of Collection or (b) a court of the jurisdiction in which the defendant is organized or has its principal place of business. The parties to this Agreement promise not to raise and waive in advance any defense or objection to such an action under the doctrine of *forum non conveniens*.

    b. Parties empowered under this Agreement to enforce the obligations of this Appendix include: (1) either party to this Agreement; (2) any indigenous [or local] person or people [who has or have lived in or within __ kilometers of the Sample Area for at least __ months in the last __ years]; or (3) any of the following non-governmental, non-profit conservation organizations or their successors in interest, if they are also non-governmental, non-profit conservation organizations: [list organizations].

IV. Commentary on Contract Provisions

1. Types of Compensation. This contract covers several types of compensation. It provides for an advance payment, for annual payments for samples delivered, and for royalty payments contingent on the development of commercial products derived from the samples. The Pharmaceutical Company also agrees to sponsor visiting researchers from the Country of Collection. The requirement that the Pharmaceutical Company submit annual reports can also be viewed as compensation (information sharing), though it is better seen as a provision designed to monitor compliance and force performance of payment obligations. The non-monetary forms of compensation provided for in the draft contract are examples

271

chosen from a range of possibilities, more of which are discussed in Chapter IV of this book.

Negotiators should keep in mind that there are other mechanisms for compensation besides those included in the draft agreement. For instance, to facilitate technology transfer, some parties may consider forming a joint venture for some aspect of collection, extraction, or even product development or marketing. The viability of a joint venture should increase as technological capacities grow in countries where collection takes place.

2. **Definitions of "Sample" (Article 1).** This term is defined very broadly in this contract to include every variety of living organism. Collection contracts may be drafted to cover smaller categories of organisms, such as plants alone, according to the needs of the buyer and the expertise of the Collector.

3. **Warranty of Government Approval (Article 3A).** Warranties that a party to a contract has obtained necessary government approvals are standard in commercial agreements. Commonly, one party must obtain government approval as a precondition to the other party's performance of its contractual obligations.

4. **Contractual Agreement for Conservation Activities (Article 3C, Appendix C).** The provisions of Appendix C are included as options for parties wishing to memorialize and formalize conservation goals within the contract itself. They ensure that activities under the contract are public and that local people are involved in designing and conducting activities under the contract, including conservation measures. As mentioned, provisions 1–5 could also form part of a contract between the Collector and local or indigenous people in which local people exchange for monetary payments, services, and/or percentages of royalties, their labor, knowledge, and permission to enter a specified territory. Appendix C outlines a comprehensive environmental assessment process on which many variations are possible.

a. **Local Consultation and EA (Section 1).** These provisions formalize the Collector's commitment to ensuring local participation and avoiding environmental harm. The procedures that they establish will help both parties ensure that any legal requirements related to local or indigenous informed consent are satisfied. Because of the expense and scale of such an undertaking full EA provisions may be possible only for major collection programs.

Less expansive provisions requiring compliance with endangered species laws and certification of indigenous representatives' informed consent may be more suitable in many other cases.

b. Publication and Reporting (Sections 2, 5). These provisions formalize the parties' commitment to publicizing the benefits of the Agreement. They will help the parties garner the acceptance and approval of the general public, governmental officials, and the environmental community.

c. Use of Compensation (Section 3). This provision formalizes the parties' commitment to ensuring that the Agreement promotes conservation and equitable returns to local communities.

d. Enforcement (Section 8). Providing for benefits to go to third parties, and allowing third parties to take legal action to enforce the contract, are unusual but feasible in the contract law of some legal systems.[1]

5. Screening (Article 5). Parties will probably wish to describe in more detail the provisions for screening samples, and those provisions will probably vary, depending on the interests of the Pharmaceutical Company.

6. Verification of Performance (Article 7, Appendix C). The requirement in Article 7 that the Pharmaceutical Company submit annual reports is aimed not only at encouraging the sharing of information and know-how, but (like the provision for verification of royalty payments) also at checking compliance with the agreement. (The requirement in Appendix C that the Collector report on conservation measures—and permit verification of expenditures—has the same rationale.) By creating a record of the Pharmaceutical Company's research and development, the report will help the

---

[1]Most commercial contracts are enforceable only by the parties signing the contract, even if others stand to benefit from performance of the contract's promises. In certain circumstances, however, U.S. courts allow a "third-party beneficiary" to sue a contracting party for enforcement of a contract. For instance, if the contract explicitly provides for enforcement by a third party—such as the municipal government of a local community, or a person named to serve as a trustee for the natural ecosystem—then the courts will probably enforce it. However, the parties to the contract probably could later modify the contract to terminate either the duties or the right of third parties to enforce them, though at some point—courts disagree on exactly when—the third party's rights "vest" so that they cannot be terminated. (*See E. Allen Farnsworth, Contracts* §§ 10.1–10.4. 1982.)

Collector assess whether a commercial product of the Pharmaceutical Company was derived from a Sample submitted under the agreement. To reduce potential dispute over what the report should include, the parties may wish to draft a more detailed version that sets out more rigorous and detailed obligations for notification and verification of research developments, commercial possibilities, decisions about whether to patent, accounting, and research developments.

7. Patent Rights (Article 8) and Confidentiality (Article 9). Consistent with the few biodiversity prospecting agreements entered into so far, the draft contract accords the Pharmaceutical Company the right to patent any products that it derives from the Samples. The Collector has the right to subsequently own the patent to such a product only if the Pharmaceutical Company decides not to exercise its right to do so in a particular country. Subject to negotiation, the Collector could also be named in a patent (along with the Company).

The section on confidentiality, Article 9, provides that each side agrees to protect the trade secrets of the other. Note, however, that to the extent the Collector gives the Pharmaceutical Company any trade secrets related to a sample, the Pharmaceutical Company can appropriate them for its own use in developing derivative products, even though it cannot disclose them to third parties. This is probably not an important issue, however, unless the Collector conducts and reports on preliminary screening (which could lead to information constituting a trade secret) or relays "secret" ethnobotanical information (i.e., information regarding medical or other use of a sample traditionally kept secret or obtained from a traditional culture under promise of confidentiality).

Under this section, if one party discloses a trade secret to the other as required under the contract, the other agrees to take all reasonable steps to keep it secret, and the disclosure under the contract does not constitute a waiver of a trade secret.[2]

---

[2]The contract refers to a widely accepted definition of trade secrets under U.S. law found in the Uniform Trade Secrets Act. Harmonized international intellectual property standards proposed in the Uruguay Round of talks under the General Agreement on Tariffs and Trade would provide for the protection of such "undisclosed information" for the first time in international law.

8. Length and Termination of Agreement (Article 13). The different obligations under the Agreement must terminate at very different times if the goal of the agreement—to compensate sources of biodiversity for the commercial use of biodiversity—is to be accomplished.

9. Sample Supply Provisions (Appendix A). Section 4 on the modification of obligations is intended to cover ecological changes that make it difficult to meet the supply schedule; it permits arrangements for reductions in the number of samples supplied and corresponding reductions in payment.

V. General Legal Background

Part V.A. discusses the legal framework for contracts, noting basic legal issues peculiar to international transactions. Part V.B. discusses other international laws that could affect international biodiversity prospecting agreements.

A. Legal Framework for Contracts

1. Commercial Contracts in General

In Anglo-American law, the term contract defines a certain class of legally enforceable agreements.[3] To be enforceable, an agreement must consist of an exchange of bargained-for promises or actions, in which one party promises to perform one or more actions in exchange for the other party's promise to perform or performance of one or more actions.[4]

---

[3]*See* E. ALLEN FARNSWORTH, CONTRACTS § 1.1 (1982); *see also* REST. 2D CONTRACTS § 1 ("[a] contract is a promise or a set of promises for the breach of which the law gives a remedy").

[4]*See* FARNSWORTH, *supra* at § 1.1. Under this definition, a promise is legally enforceable only if it is made through bargaining, and made in exchange for past or future "consideration," i.e. something of value. See REST. 2D CONTRACTS §§ 17 (in general, "the formation of a contract requires a bargain in which there is...consideration"), 71(1) ("[t]o constitute consideration, a performance or return promise must be bargained for"). Not all contracts that satisfy this definition are legally enforceable. Where a court finds a contract to be contrary. to public policy—for instance, if it is a contract for performance of a crime—it will not enforce the contract. *See* FARNSWORTH at § 5.2.

To have a valid contract, there must be an offer, acceptance, and consideration. An offer is a manifestation of willingness to enter into a bargain. An acceptance is an indication that a party is willing to comply with the terms and conditions of the offer. Consideration is the motive, cause, or price that induces a party to enter into a contract.

The relationship between these elements is that the promisor makes an offer to the promisee in return for a certain consideration. If the promisee wishes to assent and thereby create a contract, he or she will accept the promise. At this point, both parties are bound to the agreement. It is important to note that a valid contract requires mutual "consideration"—i.e., each party must receive some benefit in return for being bound by the contract.

a. Contracts Compared to Letters of Intent

A letter of intent may or may not be a contract, depending on the circumstances under which it was prepared. A letter of intent is normally used to put into writing the preliminary understanding between parties who intend to enter into a contract. However, this may by itself constitute a contract, even if the parties intend to create a later and formal writing, but only if the parties have agreed on all issues relevant to the transaction, and if they intend to be legally bound by the letter. In other words, if there is evidence that a document that is entitled a letter of intent was meant by the parties to be a binding contract, then a court will treat it like one.

Letters of intent are often presented by one party to a transaction as a starting point for negotiations; they precede, rather than follow, negotiations, and may reflect a one-sided view of the transaction.

b. Differences in Bargaining Power

Frequently, the Pharmaceutical Company will be a much larger, wealthier enterprise than the collector. This makes for a tremendous difference in the parties' access to legal and technical services and, possibly, information relevant to the transaction (including information about legal rights, value of goods and rights being traded, etc.). Similar differences are apparent if buyers and developers of biodiversity seek to enter into contracts with indigenous peoples, even if the buyers are brokers or research firms much smaller than the major pharmaceuticals.

276

Governments in developed countries have rarely regulated the terms of contracts in which both parties are businesses, even when bargaining power is extremely disparate. In consumer transactions, in contrast, governments have enacted a host of regulations governing food, drugs, credit, and many other products, limiting the extent to which the two sides can vary so as to protect consumers (who have much less information and expertise at their disposal than many producers and sellers). In addition, governments in some countries give special scrutiny to transactions of certain groups—among them, indigenous peoples, purportedly (but not always practically) to protect them.

Currently, prospecting agreements are subject to no special regulations. Governments are, however, likely to enact regulations in coming years that could, among other things, at least partly offset differences in bargaining power.

c. Calculation of Royalties

The payment of royalties on the sale of products derived from compounds discovered in plants or animals is a new commercial practice, so few direct precedents exist to guide the calculation of royalty rates. In a new field of business like biodiversity prospecting, there is no pool of transactions, no clearly defined market, and thus no single market value or established royalty rate. Yet, analogous arrangements, such as payments for synthetic compounds (which are screened in the same manner as biological compounds) or royalties paid to states or landowners for the extraction of oil, minerals, or timber under natural resources exploitation leases or contracts provide some guidance. (For a discussion of royalties and biodiversity prospecting contracts, *see* Chapter IV.)

2. International Transactions

A number of issues set international and domestic transactions apart. They include: how and where disputes about the contracts are settled and contract requirements are enforced; "choice of law"; taxation; extraterritorial application of domestic laws, such as antitrust regulations; domestic laws particularly relevant to international transactions, such as customs rules; and national and international law on intellectual property.

a. Dispute Resolution and Enforcement of Contracts

Although contracts can be enforced in court under domestic laws, many domestic business agreements provide for methods of dispute-resolution that are less slow, complex, and expensive than judicial processes. In deciding how to resolve possible disputes in international transactions, negotiators must consider these issues, with some added twists.

Arbitration or Litigation? Going to court to enforce the contract is even more problematic at the international level than the domestic level. First, going to court with a claim regarding an international agreement tends to be even more expensive than domestic litigation, thanks mostly to travel expenses for litigants, counsel, and witnesses, the need for each party to hire two sets of lawyers, and in many cases the added cost of enforcing the judgment. Second, there are no universally accepted rules on how to decide which of various courts with overlapping jurisdiction has priority—especially troubling since parties may engage in "forum shopping" to gain various legal advantages. When this happens, parties may end up in multiple legal proceedings in a variety of courts, magnifying expenses, confusion, and delay. Third, courts in one country often refuse to enforce a foreign court's order for the production of evidence, and they frequently decline to honor a foreign court's judgment.[5]

For a number of reasons, "binding arbitration"—i.e., arbitration where the decision is final except under very special circumstances—as an exclusive remedy is a popular method for resolving commercial disputes at the international level. First, arbitration is generally cheaper than litigation. Second, the parties can specify in the agreement that all disputes will be taken to arbitration, thus avoiding the risk of "forum shopping" and multiple proceedings.[6] Third, courts in many countries, according to international treaties, will (a) recognize contract clauses providing for arbitration as the exclusive remedy and dismiss lawsuits brought to enforce such

---

[5]*See* Steven C. Nelson, *Alternatives to Litigation of International Disputes*, 23 INTERNATIONAL LAWYER 187, 188–92 (1989).

[6]*See* Nelson, *supra* at 193–99.

contracts, and (b) enforce arbitration judgments except in narrowly defined circumstances.[7]

There is, however, one circumstance in which businesses often prefer litigation to arbitration—if the violation of an obligation would lead to immediate, irreparable injury, especially when the amount of damages might be hard to peg in monetary terms. In cases in which the complaining party will want to enforce the obligation and end the injury as soon as possible, the contract may provide for direct recourse to specified courts.[8] Violations of confidentiality terms and the release of trade secrets is one such case, and the draft contract offers parties the option of judicial action rather than arbitration in such cases. Whether to take this approach also depends, however, on the nature and accessibility of the courts available to the parties, and such courts' power and willingness to enforce judgments. In addition, parties should decide whether they may have a better chance of ensuring confidentiality in arbitration than in more public judicial proceedings, thus better protecting trade secrets.[9]

---

[7]*See* New York Convention on the Recognition and Enforcement of Foreign Arbitral Awards, *done* Jun. 10, 1958, *entered into force,* 1959, entered into force for the United States, 1970, 21 U.S.T. 2517, T.I.A.S. 6997, 330 U.N.T.S. 3 (US implementation, United States Arbitration Act, 9 U.S.C. §§ 201–208). As of 1987, the Convention had 71 parties, including the United States. *See* REST. 3D, RESTATEMENT OF THE FOREIGN RELATIONS LAW OF THE UNITED STATES § 487, Rptrs. N.2 (Student ed., St. Paul, Minn., American Law Institute Publishers, 1990). Courts of ratifying nations must dismiss cases brought by parties to an agreement that provides for arbitration as the exclusive method for dispute resolution; the courts must also recognize and enforce judgments of arbitration panels if the case involves a commercial transaction and the parties to the transaction agreed in the contract to binding arbitration. *See* Nelson, *supra* at 194.

In the United States and other countries, exceptions to the judicial recognition of clauses for exclusive use of arbitration–such as public policy interests in regulating commerce through antitrust laws—are narrowly defined. *See* Nelson, *supra* at 196. Exceptions to the judicial recognition and enforcement of arbitral awards— for example, cases in which there is evidence that a member of the arbitration panel was corrupt—are also narrowly drawn. *See* REST. 3RD at § 487.

[8]If parties include a clause in the contract that specifies a certain court as the place in which a party may file an action on the contract, a court in the United States generally will enforce the clause. *See* REST. 3D at § 421(2)(e), (h), comment h.

[9]*See* Nelson, *supra* at 198.

What Kind of Arbitration? A number of international institutions provide arbitration services, and a number of well-developed sets of rules are often used by businesses.[10] Private institutions serving as arbitrators include the International Chamber of Commerce, the American Arbitration Association, and the Inter-American Commercial Arbitration Commission.[11] The services of most of these organizations are, however, expensive. In addition, proceedings are sometimes slow. For these reasons, many parties prefer to apply a standard set of rules under an *ad hoc* arbitration panel set up according to the terms of the contract. That is the approach reflected in the draft contract.

Of the available sets of standard arbitration rules, this contract refers to those of the United Nations Commission on International Trade Law (UNCITRAL),[12] which have been widely used and were the basis for the rules applied by the Iran-United States Claims Tribunal.[13] These rules detail the requirements for serving notice of an arbitration claim on the other party and for the arbitration procedure and decision; they also set time limits for various procedural steps, specify how arbitrators are to be appointed, and so on.

b. "Choice of Law"

This term simply refers to the laws that will be used to interpret the meaning of the language of a contract that involves different legal jurisdictions (because the parties are from different legal jurisdictions or because the contract was signed in a different jurisdiction from the parties, or the contract provides for activities that will be carried out in several jurisdictions or jurisdictions different from the parties' bases). To simplify questions of interpretation, parties to a contract frequently include a clause specifying a particular set of laws that will govern interpretation should any disagreement or uncertainty arise about the contract's meaning.

---

[10]*See* Nelson, *supra* at 193–99.

[11]*See* REST. 3RD, *supra* at § 487, Reporter's Note 4; Nelson, *supra* at 193.

[12]7 UNCITRAL Y.B. (pt.2) 22 (1976) (U.N. Doc. A/31/17) (as approved by the UN General Assembly)

[13]*See* Stewart Baker and Mark Davis, *Establishment of an Arbitral Tribunal Under the UNCITRAL Rules: The Experience of the Iran-United States Claims Tribunal,* 23 INTERNATIONAL LAWYER 81 (1989); Nelson, *supra* at 194.

Generally, a party will prefer that the law governing the contract is the law with which that party is most familiar. Another relevant factor may be the degree to which the law is developed and to which the judges are familiar with the subject of the agreement.

c. Extraterritorial Application of Domestic Laws

Parties should be aware that some domestic laws may apply internationally. For instance, U.S. antitrust laws apply in certain respects to international business. There have also been proposals in the United States Congress to specify that environmental or health laws apply to overseas activities. In the case of one such law, the National Environmental Policy Act (NEPA), extraterritorial application would mean that if the United States Government were involved in a transaction, it might have to examine the potential environmental effects.

d. Domestic Laws Governing International Transactions

A number of domestic laws are designed to regulate international transactions. Customs laws, for instance, may require importers (which would include the Pharmaceutical Company) to disclose information about goods (including their value calculated according to certain rules) at the border, may require government inspection of such goods, and may require payment of tariffs. In addition, customs laws may restrict certain imports, such as those that the United States Department of Agriculture imposes on certain agricultural goods.

The Country of Collection may have laws restricting exports, regulations restricting currency movement or exchange, and restrictions on foreign capital investment—all of which could be a factor if the parties decided to carry out a joint venture.

3. Other National Laws

In many countries, national laws establish procedures for exploiting natural resources. These procedures—including public auctions of exploitation rights, assessment of the environmental effects of exploitation, or compliance with environmental and other regulations—could apply to prospecting agreements. Collectors may need to obtain permits from various governmental authorities in order to enter public lands and remove specimens. The permission of private landowners or indigenous groups may also be required to enter and take samples from their lands. In addition, governments may establish special regulations to govern biodiversity prospecting agreements.[14]

Collectors should ensure that they are aware of all persons with plausible claims to any part of the Sample Area and that they consult with anyone with legitimate rights over the land or its resources. Failure to do so could expose the Collector (and possibly the Pharmaceutical Company) not only to public criticism, but also, conceivably, to litigation as well. Although the theories supporting claims to compensation would probably be novel extensions of existing law, there could be grounds for a claim for damages if, for example, samples of plants or animals are taken from recognized indigenous territory and later commercialized without informed consent or if scientists take blood samples from indigenous people that later served as the source of genetically engineered products.[15]

B. International Laws That Could Affect International Biodiversity Prospecting Agreements

Several additional areas of international law could bear on biodiversity prospecting agreements. *(See Chapter VI.)* Negotiators

---

[14]Costa Rica has established permitting procedures for biodiversity prospecting. The governments of several Central American countries announced plans to develop systems of regulation of biodiversity prospecting.

[15]Researchers are collecting blood samples of tribal peoples in order to preserve examples of gene pools nearing extinction. *See* Remarks of Jack Kloppenburg at the Rainforest Alliance *Tropical Forest Medical Resources and the Conservation of Biodiversity* Symposium, Jan. 24-25, 1992, New York. While declining to recognize that a plaintiff had a property interest in cell lines cultured from his own body parts, the California Supreme Court has permitted a plaintiff to seek a share in the profits from use of the cell lines on a theory of failure to obtain informed consent. *See Moore v. The Regents of the Univ. of California,* 51 Cal. 3d 120, 793 P.2d 479, 15 U.S.P.Q.2d 1753 (1990). Foreign plaintiffs have recovered cultural property from U.S. owners through common law claims in U.S. courts. *See Autocephalous Greek-Orthodox Church of Cyprus v. Goldberg & Feldman Fine Arts, Inc.,* 917 F.2d 278 (1990), *rehearing denied,* No. 89-2809, 1990 U.S. App. LEXIS 20,398 (7th Cir. Nov. 21, 1990) (en banc) (upholding replevin of Byzantine mosaics from Indiana art dealer to Cypriot Church).

should also keep in mind potential changes in international law that could affect such contracts. This section reviews international law in the following areas: (1) intellectual property; (2) human rights and indigenous rights; (3) cultural property; (4) aboriginal treaty law; and (5) the biodiversity convention.

1. Intellectual Property

The patent laws of many developing countries exclude certain substances, such as drugs or foods, from protection. If the country of collection does not permit patenting of a commercial product derived from a sample, the value of the right to market the product within that country is significantly diminished since any manufacturer of the product could compete freely with the licensee.

Such circumstances could change, however, as the patent laws of many developing countries grow stronger. Intellectual property issues are the subject of negotiation in the Uruguay Round of negotiations on the General Agreement on Tariffs and Trade (GATT), where developed countries, led by the United States, have pushed hard for increased protection of intellectual property rights.[16] The patenting of products under this contract, like all patenting of products with potential worldwide markets, is facilitated by the Paris Convention on Industrial Property, administered by the World Intellectual Property Organization (WIPO).

2. Human Rights and Indigenous Rights

Intellectual property rights—in the form of the rights of an "author" to "moral and material interests" in a scientific or artistic

---

[16]*See* Robert F. Housman & Durwood Zaelke, *Trade, Environment and Sustainable Development: A Primer*, 15 HASTINGS INT'L & COMP. L. REV. 535, 591–92 (1992); *GATT: Intellectual Property—Little Progress Expected in GATT Talks on Intellectual Property, Yerxa Says*, 8 INT'L TRADE REP. 471 (Mar. 27, 1991); *Uruguay Round: Trade-Related Aspects of Intellectual Property Rights (14–16 May)*, 72 GATT FOCUS NEWSL. 4–5 (July 1990). Similarly, the United States has pressured trading partners in bilateral relations as well, and as a result a number of U.S. trading partners have strengthened their intellectual property regimes. *See* Housman & Zaelke at 591; GATT FOCUS NEWSL. at 5.

"production"—are recognized in a number of international human rights instruments, such as the International Covenant on Economic, Social and Cultural Rights, which many countries have signed.[17] While international human rights laws require governments to protect the rights of persons within their jurisdiction, enforcement mechanisms for these laws are weak.

In any case, whether "author's rights" could cover traditional knowledge of the uses of flora and fauna, or knowledge passed down from one generation to another within a cultural or ethnic group, is open to debate. Under the proposed Draft Declaration of the Rights of Indigenous Peoples, however, indigenous peoples would clearly have the right to "special measures for protection, as intellectual property, of their traditional cultural manifestations, such as...cultigens, medicines and knowledge of the useful properties of fauna and flora."[18] In addition, they would have the right to own and control their lands.[19] If the United Nations General Assembly approves this language (which many countries may oppose), it would not be legally binding, but it could lend support for

---

[17]*See* Article 15, International Covenant on Economic, Social and Cultural Rights, G.A. Res. 2200A (XXI), Dec. 16, 1966, 21 U.N. GAOR Supp. (No. 16), UN Doc. A/6316 (1966), 993 U.N.T.S. 3, *entered into force* on Jan. 3, 1976; *accord* Article 27(2), Universal Declaration of Human Rights, G.A. Res. 217 A(III), Dec. 10, 1948, U.N. Doc. A/810 at 71 (1948); Article XIII, American Declaration of the Rights and Duties of Man, O.A.S. res. XXX, 6 Actas y Documentos 297-302 (1953) (adopted by the 9th Int'l Conf. of Am. States, Bogota, 1948); American Convention on Human Rights, Nov. 22, 1969, O.A.S. Treaty Ser. No. 36, OEA/Ser. L./V/II.23 doc. rev. 2, *entered into force* Jul. 18, 1978. These instruments also provide that no person shall be deprived arbitrarily of his or her property. *See, e.g.* Article [15], International Covenant on Economic, Social and Cultural Rights; Article [27] Universal Declaration of Human Rights, Article [XIII]; American Declaration of the Rights and Duties of Man; Article 21, American Convention on Human Rights.

[18]*See* UNITED NATIONS COMMISSION ON HUMAN RIGHTS, WORKING GROUP ON INDIGENOUS POPULATIONS, DISCRIMINATION AGAINST INDIGENOUS PEOPLES 34 (1991) (report of working group's ninth session) (UN Doc. No. E/CN.4/Sub.2/1991/40) (paragraph 18 of draft declaration). This language appears intended to protect indigenous peoples' traditional knowledge as inventions are protected under conventional patent law. It also appears intended to give traditional crop varieties ("cultigens") protection analogous to that provided to breeders of new plant varieties.

[19]*See id.* at ¶ 15.

indigenous intellectual property rights at the national level. National-level pressures could, in turn, obligate parties to biodiversity prospecting agreements to compensate indigenous peoples for the use of their traditional knowledge or for samples collected in indigenous territory.

Finally, the International Labour Organization's Convention No. 169 requires member governments to consult with indigenous peoples when considering exploitation of natural resources on indigenous lands, to respect indigenous peoples' "right...to participate in the use, management and conservation of these resources," and to ensure that indigenous peoples share in the benefits of exploitation "where possible."[20] If the Convention enters into effect, these provisions could affect future prospecting agreements by requiring governments to ensure that indigenous peoples are consulted when such agreements are drafted and that they benefit from them.[21]

3. Cultural Property

The Convention on the Means of Prohibiting and Preventing the Illicit Import, Export, and Transfer of Ownership of Cultural Property, administered by the United Nations Educational Scientific and Cultural Organization (UNESCO), establishes international obligations regarding "cultural property."[22] While it is unlikely that the Convention's drafters specifically contemplated that indigenous peoples' traditional knowledge of the medicinal value of biodiversity would, for purposes of protection, be considered

---

[20]*See* I.L.O. Convention No. 169 Concerning Indigenous and Tribal Peoples at art. 15.

[21]As of early 1993 only four countries had ratified the treaty, and it had therefore not yet entered into force. Telephone conversation with ILO Office, Washington, April 27, 1993.

[22]Nov. 14, 1970, 10 I.L.M. 289. Parties to the Cultural Property Convention include countries rich in biodiversity, such as Brazil, Colombia, Ecuador, India, Madagascar, Mexico, and Zaire, as well as the United States that is likely to be a major biotechnological and pharmaceutical user of imported biodiversity. *See* UNITED STATES DEPARTMENT OF STATE, TREATIES IN FORCE 302-303 (1992) (as of Jan. 1, 1992).

cultural property, the Convention's terms might reasonably be interpreted to include such property.[23]

States are obligated to control imports and exports of designated cultural property, to cooperate on measures to control cultural property trade, and to try to return cultural property "stolen from a museum or a religious or secular public monument or similar institution" to the party from which it was exported, at that party's request and at its own expense.[24] Currently, however, it is unlikely that the subject matter of a prospecting agreement will fall within a government's listed categories of cultural property, although this could change as awareness of the value of folk knowledge of biota grows.

4. Aboriginal Treaties

In certain countries, including Canada, the United States, and New Zealand, settler societies' governments negotiated one or more treaties with indigenous peoples. Many of these treaties establish rights relating to living creatures in certain territories, and in at least one country, native people have brought legal action under such a treaty, alleging that the patenting of varieties of plants derived from native flora are, along with the genetic manipulation of specimens of native flora, activities that can be conducted only with the approval of the native people.[25]

---

[23]Under the convention, each state party designates the categories of property within its jurisdiction to be considered "cultural property" within the Convention's terms and publishes lists of designated cultural property. *See* Articles 1, 5 and 6. Designated property can include "[r]are collections and specimens of fauna [and] flora,...property relating to history, including the history of science and technology...and social history," and "objects of ethnological interest." *See* Article 1. It can include "property "created by the individual *or collective* genius of nationals of the State." *See* Article 4 (emphasis added). These wide-ranging terms could be interpreted to include traditional knowledge of indigenous peoples or biodiversity found in a country's natural or domesticated ecosystems.

[24]*See id.* at Articles 9, 7(b)(ii), 13(2).

[25]*See Claim by Haana Murray, et al.*, Claim No. Wai. 262 (Waitangi Trib. filed Oct. 9, 1991). The claim arises under article 2 of the Treaty of Waitingi between the Maori and Great Britain, then the colonizing power in New Zealand, which provides that the Maori retain "full exclusive and undisturbed possession of their Lands and Estates Forests Fisheries and other properties...so long as it is their wish and desire." *See* NEW ZEALAND OFFICIAL YEARBOOK 55 (1990) (Wellington, Department of Statistics).

5. Convention on Biological Diversity

One of the hardest-fought issues in negotiations on the recently signed Convention on Biological Diversity was whether and how biodiversity source countries should benefit from the technological exploitation of biodiversity. The language in the convention that resulted from that battle could serve as the basis for future international regulation of prospecting agreements.[26] Under Article 15, countries must give other member countries access to their genetic resources (though they can impose terms on that access) and must give prior informed consent. Future meetings of parties to the convention could offer a useful forum for developing uniform rules on access to maintain minimum standards and ensure return of significant benefits.

Under Articles 15, 16, and 19, parties to the convention must help a biodiversity source country share in biotechnological research and development involving that country's genetic resources. The convention does not specify how this is to be done—conceivably, it could involve governmental or multilateral funding of technology transfer back to the source country, or regulations requiring source country participation in biotechnology research. Given the intense controversy over these provisions, there may be no binding rules under these provisions for some years. In the meantime, negotiated biodiversity prospecting agreements can be a useful method for promoting technology transfer.

---

[26]This and other possible steps under the Convention are discussed more fully in David R. Downes, *New Diplomacy for the Biodiversity Trade*. In press, *Journal of Transnational Law*, 1993.

Annex 3

THE CONVENTION ON BIOLOGICAL DIVERSITY AND INTELLECTUAL PROPERTY RIGHTS

Michael A. Gollin

The following textual analysis focuses on provisions that should be considered by policy-makers, legislators, and biodiversity prospectors as they determine the impact of the Convention on biodiversity prospecting, and in particular on intellectual property rights. This analysis, like Chapter VI, concludes that the Convention does not require technology transfer on anything but consensual terms, and overall will promote strengthened, not weakened, intellectual property protection around the world. Relevant passages from Agenda 21 support this conclusion.

The Convention on Biological Diversity is an unusual example of the conjuncture of environmental, trade, and intellectual property law (Housman and Zaelke, 1992). (Convention reprinted in Annex 4.) During preparations for the United Nations Conference on Environment and Development, developing-country negotiators decided to use their leverage as owners of genetic resources to promote biotechnology transfer (Porter, 1992). The United States opposed efforts to require companies to transfer technology. But even after extracting numerous concessions in the final round of negotiation of the Convention, it rejected the Convention, largely out of concern that it would undercut strong intellectual property protection, and weaken competitiveness. The U.S. ultimately became satisfied that the Convention need not have such negative effects. The Convention is likely to be ratified by most countries and will thus affect national conservation and intellectual property laws and international biodiversity prospecting practices.

Convention on Biological Diversity

Article 1:

The first article of the Convention explicitly includes the three objectives underlying this report—conservation of biodiversity, sustainable development of genetic resources, and "fair and equitable sharing" of the resulting benefits. The open question is the extent to which intellectual property, in conjunction with other laws, can help meet these goals. The Convention envisions harmonious links between conservation, intellectual property, environmental protection, research and development, and international financial aid—a complex, long-term undertaking by any standard.

Article 1 establishes the principle of reciprocity between access to genetic resources and transfer of relevant technologies. The Convention thus establishes a two-way street, respecting both biological resources and biotechnology.

Article 2:

This article defines basic terms of biodiversity prospecting in a largely uncontroversial manner. For example, "sustainable use" is defined as use "in a way and at a rate that does not lead to the long-term decline of biological diversity," so as to meet the needs of future generations, thus striking a balance between present and future needs.

A potential source of confusion arises in the definitions of "country of origin" and "country providing genetic resources." These terms implicitly assume that there is a single country with a particular species in its natural habitat and that one country provides those genetic resources. More commonly, however, there will be several countries and many sources in both categories, and the convention does not suggest how their rights should be allocated. It will therefore be necessary to focus on individual people or organizations with knowledge and access to resources, rather than on countries.

290

Article 3:

The Convention rejects the notion of genetic resources as a common good and recognizes the sovereign right to exploit domestic resources, subject to the responsibility to ensure that domestic activities do not damage the environment of other countries. The principal focus seems to be on destructive activities, such as international releases of noxious exotic species (say, gypsy moths or kudzu vines). More broadly, Article 3 can be read as a restriction on a nation's right to destroy the habitat of migratory species.

The responsibility to other countries' environments might arguably require a country to avoid supporting (e.g. by patenting) technologies that could cause destruction of biodiversity—for example, extraction of taxol from yew trees which could lead to destruction of the forests where they grow. Currently few, if any, patent systems contain mechanisms for assessing the environmental impact of a new technology. Moreover, patents rarely identify technology that derives from a habitat considered important for biodiversity. However, efforts to monitor or track genetic material—through required disclosure of the source of starting material in a patent application, laws protecting national genetic heritage, or contract provisions—are likely to increase as the demand for protecting biodiversity increases.

Article 4:

Under Article 4, the Convention establishes a two-tiered "jurisdictional scope." The provisions of the Convention apply to the actual components of biological diversity only within the limits of national jurisdiction. Countries are responsible for the effects of processes or activities carried out in one country, however, wherever those effects occur. This expansive extraterritorial application of the Convention may affect international technology transfer activities.

Article 7:

The identification, sampling, and monitoring of species and habitats called for in this section can be expected to produce valuable

291

work (including compilations of data, databases, and publications) that may be covered by copyright and trade secret rights. A key question is whether such information will be in the public domain.

The Convention does not preclude private efforts to inventory biodiversity and allows private ownership of resulting copyrights and trade secrets. Regardless of whether the information ultimately becomes public, it will be important to ensure that people who provide private information used in international monitoring authorize the further use of the information and that they receive fair compensation for their effort.

Article 8:

This Article promotes *in situ* conservation by calling on contracting countries to establish preserves, manage biological resources, remediate degraded systems, regulate releases of living genetically engineered organisms, help create conditions for conservation and sustainable use, protect endangered species, and mitigate adverse impacts.

Subsection (j) requires signatories to protect indigenous and local knowledge relevant to the conservation and sustainable use of biodiversity and "to encourage the equitable sharing of the benefits arising from utilization of such knowledge, innovations and practices." At first glance, this subsection might seem to obligate nations to reform their intellectual property laws so as to expressly recognize rights in local and indigenous knowledge. However, the force of the provision is limited by the phrase, "subject to its national legislation." For example, in the United States, the patent system may not easily extend to indigenous knowledge, but none of its provisions are clearly antithetical to the recognition of indigenous knowledge, and so there should be no need to reform the patent law.

Likewise, the protection of "customary use of biological resources," called for in Article 10(c), is qualified by the phrase "as far as possible and as appropriate." Countries should consider whether their trade secret and patent laws are adequate to protect customary usage. If not, reform may be necessary as described in Chapter VI.

Article 9:

This section encourages *ex situ* conservation in gene banks as an adjunct to *in situ* measures. As discussed in the extensive literature on the subject, intellectual property laws can directly protect and limit rights in gene banks, plantations, zoos, and other cultivated repositories of genetic resources. As discussed in Chapter VI, however, these measures can increase value in the wild sources of new genetic diversity only indirectly, and they may actually undercut support for wildland conservation.

Article 9(d) provides a basis for domestic regulation of access to biodiversity, through, for example, collectors' agreements and access restrictions. This article should be read in conjunction with Article 15(4), which is intended to facilitate access to genetic resources for environmentally sound uses "on mutually agreed terms." Access agreements are discussed in Chapter V of this report.

Article 10:

The goal of sustainable use is elaborated in Article 10. Subsection (c) requires contracting parties to protect "customary use of biological resources in accordance with traditional cultural practices." Intellectual property rights applicable to traditional practices might encourage communities to continue their practices by making it possible for them to receive revenues from licensing.

Article 11:

Article 11 requires countries to adopt, "as far as possible and as appropriate, economically and socially sound" incentives for the conservation and sustainable use of biodiversity. Such incentives can be provided by intellectual property rights, so this Article encourages developing countries to strengthen intellectual property laws that apply to the components of biological diversity. It also requires nations to establish national conservation and natural resources laws. Article 11 therefore provides a textual basis for the intellectual property rights framework described in Chapter VI of this report.

Article 15:

This article expands on the principle of national sovereignty over genetic resources, but commits countries to facilitate access for environmentally sound uses, thus limiting a country's freedom to "shut the greenhouse door." It further stipulates that access, "where granted, shall be on mutually agreed terms," (Article 15(4)) and that access will generally require a nation's prior informed consent (15(5)). The phrase "mutually agreed terms" appears again in the technology-transfer provisions, suggesting that the same standard of arms-length negotiation for a market price applies to both activities.

Article 15 relates only to genetic resources defined in Article 2 as "material containing functional units of heredity," as distinguished from extracts of organisms. Therefore, one could argue that the Convention requires access only to genetic resources, and that countries could shut the door on access to other biological resources such as chemical extracts. However, such an interpretation would be at odds with the Convention as a whole, which relates to sustainable use of all biological resources.

Article 15(3) emphasizes that the Convention applies primarily to genetic resources from countries of origin and from other countries that acquire genetic resources in accordance with the Convention. Apparently, countries that previously acquired genetic resources, or that acquire such resources from countries that are not party to the Convention, are not subject to the access restrictions of Article 15 and the technology-transfer provisions of Articles 16 and 19. This section thereby "grandfathers" prior uses, but the relevance to private entities is unclear (Duesing, 1992).

Article 15(6) suggests that one aspect of access agreements will be participation in scientific research on genetic resources. Article 15(7) goes farther, requiring appropriate legislative, administrative, or policy measures to promote the "fair and equitable" sharing of any proceeds from the commercial use of genetic resources, "upon mutually agreed terms." Such measures should include an intellectual property framework strong enough to protect the components of biological diversity and derivative products, including trade secrets, petty patents, and utility patents. Intellectual property rights facilitate technology transfer and cooperation through, for instance, cross-licensing arrangements.

One commentator has summarized the provisions of Articles 15, 16, and related provisions in terms of three mechanisms by which a country can benefit from use of its genetic resources: (1) participation in research using the resource; (2) receiving technology which embodies or utilizes the resource; and (3) sharing the financial benefits realized from commercial exploitation of the resource (Duesing, 1992). Intellectual property rights can be applied to facilitate all of these mechanisms.

Article 16:

Article 16 treats access to technology in a fashion parallel to the provisions for access to genetic resources in Article 15. Article 16 specifically links technology transfer to biodiversity conservation policy—a connection that some believe is peripheral to biodiversity and that the United States cited as a principal reason for not signing the Convention in 1992 (BNA, 1992). The section is so convoluted and ambiguous that the obligations of a signatory nation are not immediately clear. As a result, the United States initially made a worst-case interpretation of the language.

However, the language of Article 16, read in context, lends itself more easily to an interpretation that would promote productive international agreements without *requiring* them. In particular, any country that interprets Article 16 as requiring involuntary transfer of technology must be prepared for the counter-argument that the similar language in Article 15 requires involuntary transfer of genetic resources, a result no source country would happily accept.

Article 16 is addressed to governments, not private individuals. Critics of the Convention say that voluntary private agreements can be made without the intervention called for by the Convention. Nonetheless, given the social benefits of sustainable biodiversity prospecting, there is merit in requiring countries to promote voluntary biodiversity prospecting agreements, to "prime the pump" of the biodiversity prospecting trade (Duesing, 1992).

Critics add that this section raises the specter of compulsory licensing. While the Convention would tolerate foreign domestic laws providing for compulsory licensing, it would also tolerate U.S. laws excluding most types of compulsory licensing. The con-

295

cern underlying this criticism of the Convention appears to be that it is inconsistent with the U.S. position in the Trade Related Aspects of Intellectual Property negotiations under GATT, where the United States is seeking strong uniform intellectual property rights without compulsory licensing.

Article 16(1) calls for efforts to transfer or facilitate the transfer of biotechnology and other technologies relevant to the sustainable use of biological diversity. These technologies are not only the advanced biotechnology of developed nations, but also taxonomic expertise and traditional knowledge in source countries, too. This section further advances the principal of technological reciprocity: it would set up a two-way street, with biotechnology flowing from developed nations and both genetic resources and the local technology related to the sustainable use of biodiversity flowing from developing nations. Of course, developing countries stand to benefit if the flow is predominantly from high-technology to low-technology countries, but there is no certainty that agreements between parties in developed and developing countries would reach such a result.

Article 16(2) appears to reinforce the argument of critics in the U.S. that the technology flow is likely to be one-sided. It provides for "most favorable," concessional, or preferential terms for transfer to developing countries—a concept that would undercut principles of free international trade. However, the appearance of a technology giveaway is largely dispelled by the qualifications that the transfer need not be other than fair unless "as mutually agreed," and for the majority of technologies which are subject to patents and other intellectual property rights, transfer will be "on terms which recognize and are consistent with the adequate and effective protection of intellectual property rights." Thus, for example, the Convention cannot require preferential transfers for the United States because that would be inconsistent with U.S. law (e.g., exclusive rights under the Patent Act, and the Fifth Amendment prohibition on "taking" without just compensation). Thus, Article 16(2) need not have any disruptive effect on private property rights and transactions.

Subsections 16(3) and (4) promote legislative, administrative, and policy measures "as appropriate" to encourage access to and transfer of relevant technologies. Subsection (3) suggests that a country providing genetic resources should in return receive access to technology that makes use of the resources. Unlike the other subsections, subsection (3) relates only to genetic resources, not other related technologies. Critics of the Convention suggest that a developed country government would be required to take a compulsory license from a domestic biotechnology company and provide the technology to a developing nation. However, the language is qualified (once again) by the phrase "on mutually agreed terms," and, therefore, no such result is called for in the Convention.

Subsection (4) calls for legislative, administrative, or policy measures, "as appropriate," to encourage private firms to make such technology transfers. The qualification "on mutually agreed terms" in subsections (2) and (3) should eliminate fears that any license sought by a source country from, say, a U.S. firm negotiating access to genetic resources, would be compulsory.

Subsection (5) recognizes the influence of patents and intellectual property rights on implementing the Convention and calls on contracting parties to ensure that "such rights are supportive of and do not run counter to its objectives." One concern raised is that this provision, in conjunction with subsection (2), would permit countries to ignore intellectual property rights in order to expropriate technology (e.g., by compulsory licensing). However, the negotiating history shows that subsection (5) was adopted merely as a compromise between the two extreme views (a) that intellectual property rights are essential for technology transfer and (b) that they should be ignored (Porter, 1992:24–25). Subsection (5) therefore does not support either extreme position.

In effect, the subsection thus represents an agreement to disagree for now on whether particular intellectual property rights should be strengthened or weakened consistent with the Convention. As the other provisions of the Convention and the discussion in Chapter VI suggest, the advantages of an intellectual property approach as part of a legal framework for biodiversity prospecting will become plain as biodiversity prospecting actually increases. Rather than mandating unfavorable technology transfer, Article 16 can be read as promoting such non-compulsory measures as tax incentives, trade assistance, clearinghouses, and grants or awards for private companies agreeing to transfer biotechnology to countries providing genetic resources. In the long-run, Article 16 should strengthen intellectual property rights, not undercut them.

Article 17:

This section promotes the exchange of public domain information and technologies. Expanded information exchange entails a risk of inadvertent disclosure of trade secrets, a result that would be inconsistent with the goal of the incentives for biotechnology prospecting set forth in Article 11. The scope of intellectual property rights and their applicability to a given object (such as a microbial plasmid, a plant extract, or an animal gene) must be clearly defined so that the distinction between the public and protected domains is readily ascertainable and government agencies do not inadvertently disseminate protected information or technologies.

Article 18:

Article 18 requires contracting countries to promote technical and scientific cooperation with regard to the conservation and sustainable use of biological diversity through appropriate institutions (subsection 1), training (subsection 2) and clearinghouses (subsection 3). One measure that would be consistent with Article 18, discussed above in Chapters V and VI, is a licensing agency that would collect fees from recipients of samples and biological resources and distribute them to the suppliers. Such an agency could function as an alternative to the bilateral contracting arrangements discussed above in Chapter IV.

Subsection (4) specifically recognizes the importance of developing and using indigenous and traditional technologies. The best way to accomplish this goal is through intellectual property rights that may apply to such technology, including petty patents and trade secrets.

Subsection (5) calls upon countries to promote joint ventures. Examples of activities consistent with the subsection are the International Cooperative Biodiversity Groups that the U.S. National Institutes of Health is establishing and the Merck-INBio agreement.

Article 19:

Article 19, like Article 16, addresses preferential technology transfer, with a particular focus on biotechnology. Subsection (1), like Article 16(3), promotes participation in biotechnology research by source countries "as appropriate" and "where feasible." Subsection (2) requires parties to advance "priority access" to such biotechnology "on a fair and equitable basis" and "on mutually agreed terms." Like Article 16, these provisions are not clear. They may be interpreted as authorizing source countries to enact laws requiring technology transfer as a condition of access to habitats. Alternatively, Article 19 may be interpreted as allowing only consensual agreement for two-way technology transfer in a non-compulsory manner. In the context of the other sections, and consistent with the "mutually agreed" provision in Article 15, the latter interpretation is more supportable.

Articles 20 and 21:

These articles outline in general terms a commitment to establishing a financing mechanism and to providing necessary financial resources. The financing mechanism of the Convention has been criticized as being based on no particular standard. For perspective here, the revenues to be derived from intellectual property rights are not likely to exceed several hundred million dollars annually, while the cost of conserving biodiversity may be tens of billions of dollars. Trade in indigenous resources based on intellectual property rights will not be sufficient to finance biodiversity conservation.

Article 22:

This Article specifies that the Convention is subordinate to existing international agreements. Such agreements would include such international intellectual property treaties as the Paris Convention, the Berne Convention, the Patent Cooperation Treaty, and the International Convention for the Protection of New Varieties of Plants (UPOV). Article 22 therefore calls for recognition of intellectual property rights of parties to those agreements, except in the unlikely circumstance that such rights might pose a serious threat of damage to biological diversity.

Article 25:

Article 25(2)(c) establishes a body to "[i]dentify innovative, efficient, and state-of-the-art technologies and know-how relating to the conservation and sustainable use of biological diversity" and to promote their use. Such activities should, in conjunction with marketing efforts to increase the availability of know-how and technology, increase the importance of the intellectual property rights protecting them.

Article 27:

The enforcement provisions of the Convention under Article 27 include binding arbitration to resolve whether a signatory is in compliance. But the Convention will not have any binding effect on private citizens unless it is ratified and incorporated into domestic legislation (Sive, 1992). International agreements in areas subject to heavy domestic legislation and regulation (such as intellectual property and environmental protection) have no domestic effect without ratification.[1] Countries therefore have much discretion in maintaining their intellectual property systems as they see fit, without fear of violating the Convention. The Convention may influence the legislative process in signatory nations, but does not compel a particular outcome.

Agenda 21

Agenda 21 includes a number of provisions which bear on biodiversity prospecting and shed light on the approach of the Convention. Section 15 relates to biodiversity. Section 15.4(j), together with subsections (d) and (g), calls on governments to develop measures and arrangements to help source countries and their people share the benefits of "biotechnological development and the commercial utilization of products derived from [genetic] resources." Such measures include intellectual property rights. Section 15.5(e) calls for protection of indigenous and traditional knowledge, presumably through intellectual property rights.

Section 16 relates to biotechnology, predominately safety issues. Section 16.7, however, explicitly provides that governments should promote "rights associated with intellectual property and informal innovations, including farmers' and breeders' rights."

---

[1] *Restatement of Foreign Relations Law (3d)* § 113.

Likewise, Section 34 is directed to technology transfer, and Section 34.14 refers to "the need to protect intellectual property rights." Section 34.10 states that consideration should be given to patents and intellectual property rights in light of their impact on access to and transfer of environmentally sound technology. Section 34.18(e) calls upon governments to undertake "measures to prevent the abuse of intellectual property rights," including compulsory licensing. These last two provisions may be interpreted as supporting compulsory licensing and other restrictions on intellectual property. On the other hand, it is also open to evidence that intellectual property systems facilitate access and transfer of technology, in the long run, without compulsory licensing. In any event, acceptance of compulsory licensing may be part of the Grand Bargain for establishing an international consensus for strengthened, but locally tailored, intellectual property rights.

Conclusion

On balance, the Convention promotes free trade in genetic resources and the technologies relevant to them. The Convention underscores the importance of intellectual property rights—the currency of technology transfer—in countries with extensive genetic resources. It therefore creates a national self-interest in expanding the scope of intellectual property protection, a goal desired by many developed countries.

At the same time, the Convention provides a mechanism for financing biodiversity conservation and development and establishes an obligation for developed countries to finance those activities and to take actions to promote the transfer of technologies for the conservation and use of biodiversity—goals sought by developing countries.

The Convention was satisfactory to most countries. It was initially unsatisfactory to only a handful of countries, including the United States, largely because of Articles 16 and 19. During negotiations, however, those provisions were amended so that language restricting intellectual property rights was neutralized. The Convention has therefore been interpreted as consistent with U.S. policy goals. Experience with biodiversity prospecting will probably make it easier to build a consensus for action to which the United States will accede.

In the meantime, the Convention provides a road map to countries seeking to promote sound biodiversity-prospecting policies. The results should be a strengthened commitment to protecting wilderness, greater use of appropriate technologies for deriving benefits from genetic resources, and new mechanisms for providing a fair share of the benefits to those who care for wild habitats.

References

BNA's Patent, Trademark and Copyright Journal. 1992. PTO, biotech group explain objections to earth summit's biodiversity treaty. 44:120–121.

Duesing, J.H. 1992. The Convention on Biological Diversity: Its impact on biotechnology research. *AGRO food INDUSTRY HI-TECH* 3(4), p. 19.

Housman, R. and D. Zaelke. 1992. *Trade, Environment, and Sustainable Development: A Primer.* Hastings International and Comparative Law Review. 15:535–612.

Porter, G. 1992. *The False Dilemma: The Biodiversity Convention and Intellectual Property Rights.* Environmental and Energy Study Institute, Washington, D.C.

Sive, D. 1992. Sustainable development was Rio theme. *National Law Journal* 9/21/92, p. 16.

Annex 4

UNITED NATIONS CONVENTION ON BIOLOGICAL DIVERSITY

Preamble

The Contracting Parties,

Conscious of the intrinsic value of biological diversity and of the ecological, genetic, social, economic, scientific, educational, cultural, recreational and aesthetic values of biological diversity and its components,

Conscious also of the importance of biological diversity for evolution and for maintaining life sustaining systems of the biosphere,

Affirming that the conservation of biological diversity is a common concern of humankind,

Reaffirming that States have sovereign rights over their own biological resources,

Reaffirming also that States are responsible for conserving their biological diversity and for using their biological resources in a sustainable manner,

Concerned that biological diversity is being significantly reduced by certain human activities,

Aware of the general lack of information and knowledge regarding biological diversity and of the urgent need to develop scientific, technical and institutional capacities to provide the basic understanding upon which to plan and implement appropriate measures,

Noting that it is vital to anticipate, prevent and attack the causes of significant reduction or loss of biological diversity at source,

Noting also that where there is a threat of significant reduction or loss of biological diversity, lack of full scientific certainty should not be used as a reason for postponing measures to avoid or minimize such a threat,

Noting further that the fundamental requirement for the conservation of biological diversity is the *in-situ* conservation of ecosystems and natural habitats and the maintenance and recovery of viable populations of species in their natural surroundings,

Noting further that *ex-situ* measures, preferably in the country of origin, also have an important role to play,

Recognizing the close and traditional dependence of many indigenous and local communities embodying traditional lifestyles on biological resources, and the desirability of sharing equitably benefits arising from the use of traditional knowledge, innovations and practices relevant to the conservation of biological diversity and the sustainable use of its components,

Recognizing also the vital role that women play in the conservation and sustainable use of biological diversity and affirming the need for the full participation of women at all levels of policy-making and implementation for biological diversity conservation,

Stressing the importance of, and the need to promote, international, regional and global cooperation among States and intergovernmental organizations and the non-governmental sector for the conservation of biological diversity and the sustainable use of its components,

Acknowledging that the provision of new and additional financial resources and appropriate access to relevant technologies can be expected to make a substantial difference in the world's ability to address the loss of biological diversity,

Acknowledging further that special provision is required to meet the needs of developing countries, including the provision of new and additional financial resources and appropriate access to relevant technologies,

Noting in this regard the special conditions of the least developed countries and small island States,

Acknowledging that substantial investments are required to conserve biological diversity and that there is the expectation of a broad range of environmental, economic and social benefits from those investments,

Recognizing that economic and social development and poverty eradication

are the first and overriding priorities of developing countries,

Aware that conservation and sustainable use of biological diversity is of critical importance for meeting the food, health and other needs of the growing world population, for which purpose access to and sharing of both genetic resources and technologies are essential,

Noting that, ultimately, the conservation and sustainable use of biological diversity will strengthen friendly relations among States and contribute to peace for humankind,

Desiring to enhance and complement existing international arrangements for the conservation of biological diversity and sustainable use of its components, and

Determined to conserve and sustainably use biological diversity for the benefit of present and future generations,

Have agreed as follows:

Article 1. Objectives

The objectives of this Convention, to be pursued in accordance with its relevant provisions, are the conservation of biological diversity, the sustainable use of its components and the fair and equitable sharing of the benefits arising out of the utilization of genetic resources, including by appropriate access to genetic resources and by appropriate transfer of relevant technologies, taking into account all rights over those resources and to technologies, and by appropriate funding.

Article 2. Use of Terms

For the purposes of this Convention:
"Biological diversity" means the variability among living organisms from

all sources including, *inter alia*, terrestrial, marine and other aquatic ecosystems and the ecological complexes of which they are part; this includes diversity within species, between species and of ecosystems.

"Biological resources" includes genetic resources, organisms or parts thereof, populations, or any other biotic component of ecosystems with actual or potential use or value for humanity.

"Biotechnology" means any technological application that uses biological systems, living organisms, or derivatives thereof, to make or modify products or processes for specific use.

"Country of origin of genetic resources" means the country which possesses those genetic resources in *in-situ* conditions.

"Country providing genetic resources" means the country supplying genetic resources collected from *in-situ* sources, including populations of both wild and domesticated species, or taken from *ex-situ* sources, which may or may not have originated in that country.

"Domesticated or cultivated species" means species in which the evolutionary process has been influenced by humans to meet their needs.

"Ecosystem" means a dynamic complex of plant, animal and micro-organism communities and their non-living environment interacting as a functional unit.

"Ex-situ conservation" means the conservation of components of biological diversity outside their natural habitats.

"Genetic material" means any material of plant, animal, microbial or other origin containing functional units of heredity.

"Genetic resources" means genetic material of actual or potential value.

"Habitat" means the place or type of site where an organism or population naturally occurs.

"In-situ conditions" means conditions where genetic resources exist within ecosystems and natural habitats, and, in the case of domesticated or cultivated species, in the surroundings where they have developed their distinctive properties.

"In-situ conservation" means the conservation of ecosystems and natural habitats and the maintenance and recovery of viable populations of species in their natural surroundings and, in the case of domesticated or cultivated species, in the surroundings where they have developed their distinctive properties.

"Protected area" means a geographically defined area which is designated or regulated and managed to achieve specific conservation objectives.

"Regional economic integration organization" means an organization constituted by sovereign States of a given region, to which its member States have transferred competence in respect of matters governed by this Convention and which has been duly authorized, in accordance with its internal procedures, to sign, ratify, accept, approve or accede to it.

"Sustainable use" means the use of components of biological diversity in a way and at a rate that does not lead to the long-term decline of biological diversity, thereby maintaining its potential to meet the needs and aspirations of present and future generations.

"Technology" includes biotechnology.

Article 3. Principle

States have, in accordance with the Charter of the United Nations and the

305

principles of international law, the sovereign right to exploit their own resources pursuant to their own environmental policies, and the responsibility to ensure that activities within their jurisdiction or control do not cause damage to the environment of other States or of areas beyond the limits of national jurisdiction.

Article 4. Jurisdictional Scope

Subject to the rights of other States, and except as otherwise expressly provided in this Convention, the provisions of this Convention apply, in relation to each Contracting Party:

(a) In the case of components of biological diversity, in areas within the limits of its national jurisdiction; and

(b) In the case of processes and activities, regardless of where their effects occur, carried out under its jurisdiction or control, within the area of its national jurisdiction or beyond the limits of national jurisdiction.

Article 5. Cooperation

Each Contracting Party shall, as far as possible and as appropriate, cooperate with other Contracting Parties, directly or, where appropriate, through competent international organizations, in respect of areas beyond national jurisdiction and on other matters of mutual interest, for the conservation and sustainable use of biological diversity.

Article 6. General Measures for Conservation and Sustainable Use

Each Contracting Party shall, in accordance with its particular conditions and capabilities:

(a) Develop national strategies, plans or programmes for the conservation and sustainable use of biological diversity or adapt for this purpose existing strategies, plans or programmes which shall reflect, *inter alia*, the measures set out in this Convention relevant to the Contracting Party concerned; and

(b) Integrate, as far as possible and as appropriate, the conservation and sustainable use of biological diversity into relevant sectoral or cross-sectoral plans, programmes and policies.

Article 7. Identification and Monitoring

Each Contracting Party shall, as far as possible and as appropriate, in particular for the purposes of Articles 8 to 10:

(a) Identify components of biological diversity important for its conservation and sustainable use having regard to the indicative list of categories set down in Annex I;

(b) Monitor, through sampling and other techniques, the components of biological diversity identified pursuant to subparagraph (a) above, paying particular attention to those requiring urgent conservation measures and those which offer the greatest potential for sustainable use;

(c) Identify processes and categories of activities which have or are likely to have significant adverse impacts on the conservation and sustainable use of biological diversity, and monitor their effects through sampling and other techniques; and

(d) Maintain and organize, by any mechanism data, derived from identification and monitoring activities pursuant to subparagraphs (a), (b) and (c) above.

Article 8. *In-situ* Conservation

Each Contracting Party shall, as far as possible and as appropriate:
(a) Establish a system of protected areas or areas where special measures need to be taken to conserve biological diversity;
(b) Develop, where necessary, guidelines for the selection, establishment and management of protected areas or areas where special measures need to be taken to conserve biological diversity;
(c) Regulate or manage biological resources important for the conservation of biological diversity whether within or outside protected areas, with a view to ensuring their conservation and sustainable use;
(d) Promote the protection of ecosystems, natural habitats and the maintenance of viable populations of species in natural surroundings;
(e) Promote environmentally sound and sustainable development in areas adjacent to protected areas with a view to furthering protection of these areas;
(f) Rehabilitate and restore degraded ecosystems and promote the recovery of threatened species, *inter alia*, through the development and implementation of plans or other management strategies;
(g) Establish or maintain means to regulate, manage or control the risks associated with the use and release of living modified organisms resulting from biotechnology which are likely to have adverse environmental impacts that could affect the conservation and sustainable use of biological diversity, taking also into account the risks to human health;
(h) Prevent the introduction of, control or eradicate those alien species which threaten ecosystems, habitats or species;
(i) Endeavour to provide the conditions needed for compatibility between present uses and the conservation of biological diversity and the sustainable use of its components;
(j) Subject to its national legislation, respect, preserve and maintain knowledge, innovations and practices of indigenous and local communities embodying traditional lifestyles relevant for the conservation and sustainable use of biological diversity and promote their wider application with the approval and involvement of the holders of such knowledge, innovations and practices and encourage the equitable sharing of the benefits arising from the utilization of such knowledge, innovations and practices;
(k) Develop or maintain necessary legislation and/or other regulatory provisions for the protection of threatened species and populations;
(l) Where a significant adverse effect on biological diversity has been determined pursuant to Article 7, regulate or manage the relevant processes and categories of activities; and
(m) Cooperate in providing financial and other support for *in-situ* conservation outlined in subparagraphs (a) to (l) above, particularly to developing countries.

Article 9. *Ex-situ* Conservation

Each Contracting Party shall, as far as possible and as appropriate, and predominantly for the purpose of complementing *in-situ* measures:
(a) Adopt measures for the *ex-situ* conservation of components of biological diversity, preferably in the country of origin of such components;

(b) Establish and maintain facilities for *ex-situ* conservation of and research on plants, animals and micro-organisms, preferably in the country of origin of genetic resources;

(c) Adopt measures for the recovery and rehabilitation of threatened species and for their reintroduction into their natural habitats under appropriate conditions;

(d) Regulate and manage collection of biological resources from natural habitats for *ex-situ* conservation purposes so as not to threaten ecosystems and *in-situ* populations of species, except where special temporary *ex-situ* measures are required under subparagraph (c) above; and

(e) Cooperate in providing financial and other support for *ex-situ* conservation outlined in subparagraphs (a) to (d) above and in the establishment and maintenance of *ex-situ* conservation facilities in developing countries.

Article 10. Sustainable Use of Components of Biological Diversity

Each Contracting Party shall, as far as possible and as appropriate:

(a) Integrate consideration of the conservation and sustainable use of biological resources into national decision-making;

(b) Adopt measures relating to the use of biological resources to avoid or minimize adverse impacts on biological diversity;

(c) Protect and encourage customary use of biological resources in accordance with traditional cultural practices that are compatible with conservation or sustainable use requirements;

(d) Support local populations to develop and implement remedial action

in degraded areas where biological diversity has been reduced; and

(e) Encourage cooperation between its governmental authorities and its private sector in developing methods for sustainable use of biological resources.

Article 11. Incentive Measures

Each Contracting Party shall, as far as possible and as appropriate, adopt economically and socially sound measures that act as incentives for the conservation and sustainable use of components of biological diversity.

Article 12. Research and Training

The Contracting Parties, taking into account the special needs of developing countries, shall:

(a) Establish and maintain programmes for scientific and technical education and training in measures for the identification, conservation and sustainable use of biological diversity and its components and provide support for such education and training for the specific needs of developing countries;

(b) Promote and encourage research which contributes to the conservation and sustainable use of biological diversity, particularly in developing countries, *inter alia*, in accordance with decisions of the Conference of the Parties taken in consequence of recommendations of the Subsidiary Body on Scientific, Technical and Technological Advice; and

(c) In keeping with the provisions of Articles 16, 18 and 20, promote and cooperate in the use of scientific advances in biological diversity research in developing methods for conservation and sustainable use of biological resources.

Article 13. Public Education and Awareness

The Contracting Parties shall:

(a) Promote and encourage understanding of the importance of, and the measures required for, the conservation of biological diversity, as well as its propagation through media, and the inclusion of these topics in educational programmes; and

(b) Cooperate, as appropriate, with other States and international organizations in developing educational and public awareness programmes, with respect to conservation and sustainable use of biological diversity.

Article 14. Impact Assessment and Minimizing Adverse Impacts

1. Each Contracting Party, as far as possible and as appropriate, shall:

(a) Introduce appropriate procedures requiring environmental impact assessment of its proposed projects that are likely to have significant adverse effects on biological diversity with a view to avoiding or minimizing such effects and, where appropriate, allow for public participation in such procedures;

(b) Introduce appropriate arrangements to ensure that the environmental consequences of its programmes and policies that are likely to have significant adverse impacts on biological diversity are duly taken into account;

(c) Promote, on the basis of reciprocity, notification, exchange of information and consultation on activities under their jurisdiction or control which are likely to significantly affect adversely the biological diversity of other States or areas beyond the limits of national jurisdiction, by encouraging the conclusion of bilateral, regional or multilateral arrangements, as appropriate;

(d) In the case of imminent or grave danger or damage, originating under its jurisdiction or control, to biological diversity within the area under jurisdiction of other States or in areas beyond the limits of national jurisdiction, notify immediately the potentially affected States of such danger or damage, as well as initiate action to prevent or minimize such danger or damage; and

(e) Promote national arrangements for emergency responses to activities or events, whether caused naturally or otherwise, which present a grave and imminent danger to biological diversity and encourage international cooperation to supplement such national efforts and, where appropriate and agreed by the States or regional economic integration organizations concerned, to establish joint contingency plans.

2. The Conference of the Parties shall examine, on the basis of studies to be carried out, the issue of liability and redress, including restoration and compensation, for damage to biological diversity, except where such liability is a purely internal matter.

Article 15. Access to Genetic Resources

1. Recognizing the sovereign rights of States over their natural resources, the authority to determine access to genetic resources rests with the national governments and is subject to national legislation.

2. Each Contracting Party shall endeavour to create conditions to facilitate access to genetic resources for environmentally sound uses by other Contracting Parties and not to impose restrictions that run counter to the objectives of this Convention.

3. For the purpose of this Convention, the genetic resources being provided by a Contracting Party, as referred to in this Article and Articles 16 and 19, are only those that are provided by Contracting Parties that are countries of origin of such resources or by the Parties that have acquired the genetic resources in accordance with this Convention.

4. Access, where granted, shall be on mutually agreed terms and subject to the provisions of this Article.

5. Access to genetic resources shall be subject to prior informed consent of the Contracting Party providing such resources, unless otherwise determined by that Party.

6. Each Contracting Party shall endeavour to develop and carry out scientific research based on genetic resources provided by other Contracting Parties with the full participation of, and where possible in, such Contracting Parties.

7. Each Contracting Party shall take legislative, administrative or policy measures, as appropriate, and in accordance with Articles 16 and 19 and, where necessary, through the financial mechanism established by Articles 20 and 21 with the aim of sharing in a fair and equitable way the results of research and development and the benefits arising from the commercial and other utilization of genetic resources with the Contracting Party providing such resources. Such sharing shall be upon mutually agreed terms.

Article 16. Access to and Transfer of Technology

1. Each Contracting Party, recognizing that technology includes biotechnology, and that both access to and transfer of technology among Contracting Parties are essential elements for the attainment of the objectives of this Convention, undertakes subject to the provisions of this Article to provide and/or facilitate access for and transfer to other Contracting Parties of technologies that are relevant to the conservation and sustainable use of biological diversity or make use of genetic resources and do not cause significant damage to the environment.

2. Access to and transfer of technology referred to in paragraph 1 above to developing countries shall be provided and/or facilitated under fair and most favourable terms, including on concessional and preferential terms where mutually agreed, and, where necessary, in accordance with the financial mechanism established by Articles 20 and 21. In the case of technology subject to patents and other intellectual property rights, such access and transfer shall be provided on terms which recognize and are consistent with the adequate and effective protection of intellectual property rights. The application of this paragraph shall be consistent with paragraphs 3, 4 and 5 below.

3. Each Contracting Party shall take legislative, administrative or policy measures, as appropriate, with the aim that Contracting Parties, in particular those that are developing countries, which provide genetic resources are provided access to and transfer of technology which makes use of those resources, on mutually agreed terms, in-

310

cluding technology protected by patents and other intellectual property rights, where necessary, through the provisions of Articles 20 and 21 and in accordance with international law and consistent with paragraphs 4 and 5 below.

4. Each Contracting Party shall take legislative, administrative or policy measures, as appropriate, with the aim that the private sector facilitates access to, joint development and transfer of technology referred to in paragraph 1 above for the benefit of both governmental institutions and the private sector of developing countries and in this regard shall abide by the obligations included in paragraphs 1, 2 and 3 above.

5. The Contracting Parties, recognizing that patents and other intellectual property rights may have an influence on the implementation of this Convention, shall cooperate in this regard subject to national legislation and international law in order to ensure that such rights are supportive of and do not run counter to its objectives.

Article 17. Exchange of Information

1. The Contracting Parties shall facilitate the exchange of information, from all publicly available sources, relevant to the conservation and sustainable use of biological diversity, taking into account the special needs of developing countries.

2. Such exchange of information shall include exchange of results of technical, scientific and socio-economic research, as well as information on training and surveying programmes, specialized knowledge, indigenous and traditional knowledge as such and in combination with the technologies referred to in Article 16, paragraph 1. It shall also, where feasible, include repatriation of information.

Article 18. Technical and Scientific Cooperation

1. The Contracting Parties shall promote international technical and scientific cooperation in the field of conservation and sustainable use of biological diversity, where necessary, through the appropriate international and national institutions.

2. Each Contracting Party shall promote technical and scientific cooperation with other Contracting Parties, in particular developing countries, in implementing this Convention, *inter alia*, through the development and implementation of national policies. In promoting such cooperation, special attention should be given to the development and strengthening of national capabilities, by means of human resources development and institution building.

3. The Conference of the Parties, at its first meeting, shall determine how to establish a clearing-house mechanism to promote and facilitate technical and scientific cooperation.

4. The Contracting Parties shall, in accordance with national legislation and policies, encourage and develop methods of cooperation for the development and use of technologies, including indigenous and traditional technologies, in pursuance of the objectives of this Convention. For this purpose, the Contracting Parties shall also promote cooperation in the training of personnel and exchange of experts.

5. The Contracting Parties shall, subject to mutual agreement, promote the establishment of joint research pro-

311

grammes and joint ventures for the development of technologies relevant to the objectives of this Convention.

Article 19. Handling of Biotechnology and Distribution of Its Benefits

1. Each Contracting Party shall take legislative, administrative or policy measures, as appropriate, to provide for the effective participation in biotechnological research activities by those Contracting Parties, especially developing countries, which provide the genetic resources for such research, and where feasible in such Contracting Parties.

2. Each Contracting Party shall take all practicable measures to promote and advance priority access on a fair and equitable basis by Contracting Parties, especially developing countries, to the results and benefits arising from biotechnologies based upon genetic resources provided by those Contracting Parties. Such access shall be on mutually agreed terms.

3. The Parties shall consider the need for and modalities of a protocol setting out appropriate procedures, including, in particular, advance informed agreement, in the field of the safe transfer, handling and use of any living modified organism resulting from biotechnology that may have adverse effect on the conservation and sustainable use of biological diversity.

4. Each Contracting Party shall, directly or by requiring any natural or legal person under its jurisdiction providing the organisms referred to in paragraph 3 above, provide any available information about the use and safety regulations required by that Contracting Party in handling such organisms, as well as any available information on the potential adverse impact of the specific organisms concerned to the Contracting Party into which those organisms are to be introduced.

Article 20. Financial Resources

1. Each Contracting Party undertakes to provide, in accordance with its capabilities, financial support and incentives in respect of those national activities which are intended to achieve the objectives of this Convention, in accordance with its national plans, priorities and programmes.

2. The developed country Parties shall provide new and additional financial resources to enable developing country Parties to meet the agreed full incremental costs to them of implementing measures which fulfil the obligations of this Convention and to benefit from its provisions and which costs are agreed between a developing country Party and the institutional structure referred to in Article 21, in accordance with policy, strategy, programme priorities and eligibility criteria and an indicative list of incremental costs established by the Conference of the Parties. Other Parties, including countries undergoing the process of transition to a market economy, may voluntarily assume the obligations of the developed country Parties. For the purpose of this Article, the Conference of the Parties, shall at its first meeting establish a list of developed country Parties and other Parties which voluntarily assume the obligations of the developed country Parties. The Conference of the Parties shall periodically review and if necessary amend the list. Contributions from other countries

and sources on a voluntary basis would also be encouraged. The implementation of these commitments shall take into account the need for adequacy, predictability and timely flow of funds and the importance of burden-sharing among the contributing Parties included in the list.

3. The developed country Parties may also provide, and developing country Parties avail themselves of, financial resources related to the implementation of this Convention through bilateral, regional and other multilateral channels.

4. The extent to which developing country Parties will effectively implement their commitments under this Convention will depend on the effective implementation by developed country Parties of their commitments under this Convention related to financial resources and transfer of technology and will take fully into account the fact that economic and social development and eradication of poverty are the first and overriding priorities of the developing country Parties.

5. The Parties shall take full account of the specific needs and special situation of least developed countries in their actions with regard to funding and transfer of technology.

6. The Contracting Parties shall also take into consideration the special conditions resulting from the dependence on, distribution and location of, biological diversity within developing country Parties, in particular small island States.

7. Consideration shall also be given to the special situation of developing countries, including those that are most environmentally vulnerable, such as those with arid and semi-arid zones, coastal and mountainous areas.

Article 21. Financial Mechanism

1. There shall be a mechanism for the provision of financial resources to developing country Parties for purposes of this Convention on a grant or concessional basis the essential elements of which are described in this Article. The mechanism shall function under the authority and guidance of, and be accountable to, the Conference of the Parties for purposes of this Convention. The operations of the mechanism shall be carried out by such institutional structure as may be decided upon by the Conference of the Parties at its first meeting. For purposes of this Convention, the Conference of the Parties shall determine the policy, strategy, programme priorities and eligibility criteria relating to the access to and utilization of such resources. The contributions shall be such as to take into account the need for predictability, adequacy and timely flow of funds referred to in Article 20 in accordance with the amount of resources needed to be decided periodically by the Conference of the Parties and the importance of burden-sharing among the contributing Parties included in the list referred to in Article 20, paragraph 2. Voluntary contributions may also be made by the developed country Parties and by other countries and sources. The mechanism shall operate within a democratic and transparent system of governance.

2. Pursuant to the objectives of this Convention, the Conference of the Parties shall at its first meeting determine the policy, strategy and programme priorities, as well as detailed criteria and guidelines for eligibility for access to and utilization of the financial resources including monitoring and

evaluation on a regular basis of such utilization. The Conference of the Parties shall decide on the arrangements to give effect to paragraph 1 above after consultation with the institutional structure entrusted with the operation of the financial mechanism.

3. The Conference of the Parties shall review the effectiveness of the mechanism established under this Article, including the criteria and guidelines referred to in paragraph 2 above, not less than two years after the entry into force of this Convention and thereafter on a regular basis. Based on such review, it shall take appropriate action to improve the effectiveness of the mechanism if necessary.

4. The Contracting Parties shall consider strengthening existing financial institutions to provide financial resources for the conservation and sustainable use of biological diversity.

Article 22. Relationship with Other International Conventions

1. The provisions of this Convention shall not affect the rights and obligations of any Contracting Party deriving from any existing international agreement, except where the exercise of those rights and obligations would cause a serious damage or threat to biological diversity.

2. Contracting Parties shall implement this Convention with respect to the marine environment consistently with the rights and obligations of States under the law of the sea.

Article 23. Conference of the Parties

1. A Conference of the Parties is hereby established. The first meeting of the Conference of the Parties shall

be convened by the Executive Director of the United Nations Environment Programme not later than one year after the entry into force of this Convention. Thereafter, ordinary meetings of the Conference of the Parties shall be held at regular intervals to be determined by the Conference at its first meeting.

2. Extraordinary meetings of the Conference of the Parties shall be held at such other times as may be deemed necessary by the Conference, or at the written request of any Party, provided that, within six months of the request being communicated to them by the Secretariat, it is supported by at least one third of the Parties.

3. The Conference of the Parties shall by consensus agree upon and adopt rules of procedure for itself and for any subsidiary body it may establish, as well as financial rules governing the funding of the Secretariat. At each ordinary meeting, it shall adopt a budget for the financial period until the next ordinary meeting.

4. The Conference of the Parties shall keep under review the implementation of this Convention, and, for this purpose, shall:

(a) Establish the form and the intervals for transmitting the information to be submitted in accordance with Article 26 and consider such information as well as reports submitted by any subsidiary body;

(b) Review scientific, technical and technological advice on biological diversity provided in accordance with Article 25;

(c) Consider and adopt, as required, protocols in accordance with Article 28;

(d) Consider and adopt, as required, in accordance with Articles 29 and 30, amendments to this Convention and its annexes;

(e) Consider amendments to any protocol, as well as to any annexes thereto, and, if so decided, recommend their adoption to the parties to the protocol concerned;

(f) Consider and adopt, as required, in accordance with Article 30, additional annexes to this Convention;

(g) Establish such subsidiary bodies, particularly to provide scientific and technical advice, as are deemed necessary for the implementation of this Convention;

(h) Contact, through the Secretariat, the executive bodies of conventions dealing with matters covered by this Convention with a view to establishing appropriate forms of cooperation with them; and

(i) Consider and undertake any additional action that may be required for the achievement of the purposes of this Convention in the light of experience gained in its operation.

5. The United Nations, its specialized agencies and the International Atomic Energy Agency, as well as any State not Party to this Convention, may be represented as observers at meetings of the Conference of the Parties. Any other body or agency, whether governmental or non-governmental, qualified in fields relating to conservation and sustainable use of biological diversity, which has informed the Secretariat of its wish to be represented as an observer at a meeting of the Conference of the Parties, may be admitted unless at least one third of the Parties present object. The admission and participation of observers shall be subject to the rules of procedure adopted by the Conference of the Parties.

Article 24. Secretariat

1. A secretariat is hereby established. Its functions shall be:

(a) To arrange for and service meetings of the Conference of the Parties provided for in Article 23;

(b) To perform the functions assigned to it by any protocol;

(c) To prepare reports on the execution of its functions under this Convention and present them to the Conference of the Parties;

(d) To coordinate with other relevant international bodies and, in particular to enter into such administrative and contractual arrangements as may be required for the effective discharge of its functions; and

(e) To perform such other functions as may be determined by the Conference of the Parties.

2. At its first ordinary meeting, the Conference of the Parties shall designate the secretariat from amongst those existing competent international organizations which have signified their willingness to carry out the secretariat functions under this Convention.

Article 25. Subsidiary Body on Scientific, Technical and Technological Advice

1. A subsidiary body for the provision of scientific, technical and technological advice is hereby established to provide the Conference of the Parties and, as appropriate, its other subsidiary bodies with timely advice relating to the implementation of this Convention. This body shall be open to participation by all Parties and shall be multidisciplinary. It shall comprise government representatives competent in the relevant field of expertise. It

shall report regularly to the Conference of the Parties on all aspects of its work.

2. Under the authority of and in accordance with guidelines laid down by the Conference of the Parties, and upon its request, this body shall:

(a) Provide scientific and technical assessments of the status of biological diversity;

(b) Prepare scientific and technical assessments of the effects of types of measures taken in accordance with the provisions of this Convention;

(c) Identify innovative, efficient and state-of-the-art technologies and know-how relating to the conservation and sustainable use of biological diversity and advise on the ways and means of promoting development and/or transferring such technologies;

(d) Provide advice on scientific programmes and international cooperation in research and development related to conservation and sustainable use of biological diversity; and

(e) Respond to scientific, technical, technological and methodological questions that the Conference of the Parties and its subsidiary bodies may put to the body.

3. The functions, terms of reference, organization and operation of this body may be further elaborated by the Conference of the Parties.

Article 26. Reports

Each Contracting Party shall, at intervals to be determined by the Conference of the Parties, present to the Conference of the Parties, reports on measures which it has taken for the implementation of the provisions of this Convention and their effectiveness in meeting the objectives of this Convention.

Article 27. Settlement of Disputes

1. In the event of a dispute between Contracting Parties concerning the interpretation or application of this Convention, the parties concerned shall seek solution by negotiation.

2. If the parties concerned cannot reach agreement by negotiation, they may jointly seek the good offices of, or request mediation by, a third party.

3. When ratifying, accepting, approving or acceding to this Convention, or at any time thereafter, a State or regional economic integration organization may declare in writing to the Depositary that for a dispute not resolved in accordance with paragraph 1 or paragraph 2 above, it accepts one or both of the following means of dispute settlement as compulsory:

(a) Arbitration in accordance with the procedure laid down in Part 1 of Annex II;

(b) Submission of the dispute to the International Court of Justice.

4. If the parties to the dispute have not, in accordance with paragraph 3 above, accepted the same or any procedure, the dispute shall be submitted to conciliation in accordance with Part 2 of Annex II unless the parties otherwise agree.

5. The provisions of this Article shall apply with respect to any protocol except as otherwise provided in the protocol concerned.

Article 28. Adoption of Protocols

1. The Contracting Parties shall cooperate in the formulation and adoption of protocols to this Convention.

2. Protocols shall be adopted at a meeting of the Conference of the Parties.

3. The text of any proposed protocol shall be communicated to the Contracting Parties by the Secretariat at least six months before such a meeting.

Article 29. Amendment of the Convention or Protocols

1. Amendments to this Convention may be proposed by any Contracting Party. Amendments to any protocol may be proposed by any Party to that protocol.

2. Amendments to this Convention shall be adopted at a meeting of the Conference of the Parties. Amendments to any protocol shall be adopted at a meeting of the Parties to the Protocol in question. The text of any proposed amendment to this Convention or to any protocol, except as may otherwise be provided in such protocol, shall be communicated to the Parties to the instrument in question by the secretariat at least six months before the meeting at which it is proposed for adoption. The secretariat shall also communicate proposed amendments to the signatories to this Convention for information.

3. The Parties shall make every effort to reach agreement on any proposed amendment to this Convention or to any protocol by consensus. If all efforts at consensus have been exhausted, and no agreement reached, the amendment shall as a last resort be adopted by a two-third majority vote of the Parties to the instrument in question present and voting at the meeting, and shall be submitted by the Depositary to all Parties for ratification, acceptance or approval.

4. Ratification, acceptance or approval of amendments shall be notified to the Depositary in writing. Amendments adopted in accordance with paragraph 3 above shall enter into force among Parties having accepted them on the ninetieth day after the deposit of instruments of ratification, acceptance or approval by at least two thirds of the Contracting Parties to this Convention or of the Parties to the protocol concerned, except as may otherwise be provided in such protocol. Thereafter the amendments shall enter into force for any other Party on the ninetieth day after that Party deposits its instrument of ratification, acceptance or approval of the amendments.

5. For the purposes of this Article, "Parties present and voting" means Parties present and casting an affirmative or negative vote.

Article 30. Adoption and Amendment of Annexes

1. The annexes to this Convention or to any protocol shall form an integral part of the Convention or of such protocol, as the case may be, and, unless expressly provided otherwise, a reference to this Convention or its protocols constitutes at the same time a reference to any annexes thereto. Such annexes shall be restricted to procedural, scientific, technical and administrative matters.

2. Except as may be otherwise provided in any protocol with respect to its annexes, the following procedure shall apply to the proposal, adoption and entry into force of additional annexes to this Convention or of annexes to any protocol:

(a) Annexes to this Convention or to any protocol shall be proposed and adopted according to the procedure laid down in Article 29;

(b) Any Party that is unable to approve an additional annex to this Convention or an annex to any protocol to which it is Party shall so notify the Depositary, in writing, within one year from the date of the communication of the adoption by the Depositary. The Depositary shall without delay notify all Parties of any such notification received. A Party may at any time withdraw a previous declaration of objection and the annexes shall thereupon enter into force for that Party subject to subparagraph (c) below;

(c) On the expiry of one year from the date of the communication of the adoption by the Depositary, the annex shall enter into force for all Parties to this Convention or to any protocol concerned which have not submitted a notification in accordance with the provisions of subparagraph (b) above.

3. The proposal, adoption and entry into force of amendments to annexes to this Convention or to any protocol shall be subject to the same procedure as for the proposal, adoption and entry into force of annexes to the Convention or annexes to any protocol.

4. If an additional annex or an amendment to an annex is related to an amendment to this Convention or to any protocol, the additional annex or amendment shall not enter into force until such time as the amendment to the Convention or to the protocol concerned enters into force.

Article 31. Right to Vote

1. Except as provided for in paragraph 2 below, each Contracting Party to this Convention or to any protocol shall have one vote.

2. Regional economic integration organizations, in matters within their competence, shall exercise their right to vote with a number of votes equal to the number of their member States which are Contracting Parties to this

Convention or the relevant protocol. Such organizations shall not exercise their right to vote if their member States exercise theirs, and vice versa.

Article 32. Relationship between This Convention and Its Protocols

1. A State or a regional economic integration organization may not become a Party to a protocol unless it is, or becomes at the same time, a Contracting Party to this Convention.

2. Decisions under any protocol shall be taken only by the Parties to the protocol concerned. Any Contracting Party that has not ratified, accepted or approved a protocol may participate as an observer in any meeting of the parties to that protocol.

Article 33. Signature

This Convention shall be open for signature at Rio de Janeiro by all States and any regional economic integration organization from 5 June 1992 until 14 June 1992, and at the United Nations Headquarters in New York from 15 June 1992 to 4 June 1993.

Article 34. Ratification, Acceptance or Approval

1. This Convention and any protocol shall be subject to ratification, acceptance or approval by States and by regional economic integration organizations. Instruments of ratification, acceptance or approval shall be deposited with the Depositary.

2. Any organization referred to in paragraph 1 above which becomes a Contracting Party to this Convention or any protocol without any of its member States being a Contracting

Party shall be bound by all the obligations under the Convention or the protocol, as the case may be. In the case of such organizations, one or more of whose member States is a Contracting Party to this Convention or relevant protocol, the organization and its member States shall decide on their respective responsibilities for the performance of their obligations under the Convention or protocol, as the case may be. In such cases, the organization and the member States shall not be entitled to exercise rights under the Convention or relevant protocol concurrently.

3. In their instruments of ratification, acceptance or approval, the organizations referred to in paragraph 1 above shall declare the extent of their competence with respect to the matters governed by the Convention or the relevant protocol. These organizations shall also inform the Depositary of any relevant modification in the extent of their competence.

Article 35. Accession

1. This Convention and any protocol shall be open for accession by States and by regional economic integration organizations from the date on which the Convention or the protocol concerned is closed for signature. The instruments of accession shall be deposited with the Depositary.

2. In their instruments of accession, the organizations referred to in paragraph 1 above shall declare the extent of their competence with respect to the matters governed by the Convention or the relevant protocol. These organizations shall also inform the Depositary of any relevant modification in the extent of their competence.

3. The provisions of Article 34, paragraph 2, shall apply to regional economic integration organizations which accede to this Convention or any protocol.

Article 36. Entry Into Force

1. This Convention shall enter into force on the ninetieth day after the date of deposit of the thirtieth instrument of ratification, acceptance, approval or accession.

2. Any protocol shall enter into force on the ninetieth day after the date of deposit of the number of instruments of ratification, acceptance, approval or accession, specified in that protocol, has been deposited.

3. For each Contracting Party which ratifies, accepts or approves this Convention or accedes thereto after the deposit of the thirtieth instrument of ratification, acceptance, approval or accession, it shall enter into force on the ninetieth day after the date of deposit by such Contracting Party of its instrument of ratification, acceptance, approval or accession.

4. Any protocol, except as otherwise provided in such protocol, shall enter into force for a Contracting Party that ratifies, accepts or approves that protocol or accedes thereto after its entry into force pursuant to paragraph 2 above, on the ninetieth day after the date on which that Contracting Party deposits its instrument of ratification, acceptance, approval or accession, or on the date on which this Convention enters into force for that Contracting Party, whichever shall be the later.

5. For the purposes of paragraphs 1 and 2 above, any instrument deposited by a regional economic integration organization shall not be counted as ad-

ditional to those deposited by member States of such organization.

Article 37. Reservations

No reservations may be made to this Convention.

Article 38. Withdrawals

1. At any time after two years from the date on which this Convention has entered into force for a Contracting Party, that Contracting Party may withdraw from the Convention by giving written notification to the Depositary.

2. Any such withdrawal shall take place upon expiry of one year after the date of its receipt by the Depositary, or on such later date as may be specified in the notification of the withdrawal.

3. Any Contracting Party which withdraws from this Convention shall be considered as also having withdrawn from any protocol to which it is party.

Article 39. Financial Interim Arrangements

Provided that it has been fully restructured in accordance with the requirements of Article 21, the Global Environment Facility of the United Nations Development Programme, the United Nations Environment Programme and the International Bank for Reconstruction and Development shall be the institutional structure referred to in Article 21 on an interim basis, for the period between the entry into force of this Convention and the first meeting of the Conference of the Parties or until the Conference of the Parties decides which institutional structure will be designated in accordance with Article 21.

Article 40. Secretariat Interim Arrangements

The secretariat to be provided by the Executive Director of the United Nations Environment Programme shall be the secretariat referred to in Article 24, paragraph 2, on an interim basis for the period between the entry into force of this Convention and the first meeting of the Conference of the Parties.

Article 41. Depositary

The Secretary-General of the United Nations shall assume the functions of Depositary of this Convention and any protocols.

Article 42. Authentic Texts

The original of this Convention, of which the Arabic, Chinese, English, French, Russian and Spanish texts are equally authentic, shall be deposited with the Secretary-General of the United Nations.

IN WITNESS WHEREOF the undersigned, being duly authorized to that effect, have signed this Convention.

Done at Rio de Janeiro on this fifth day of June, one thousand nine hundred and ninety-two.

Annex I
IDENTIFICATION AND MONITORING

1. Ecosystems and habitats: containing high diversity, large numbers of endemic or threatened species, or wilderness; required by migratory species; of social, economic, cultural or scientific importance; or, which are representative, unique or associated with key evolutionary or other biological processes;

2. Species and communities which are: threatened; wild relatives of domesticated or cultivated species; of medicinal, agricultural or other economic value; or social, scientific or cultural importance; or importance for research into the conservation and sustainable use of biological diversity, such as indicator species; and

3. Described genomes and genes of social, scientific or economic importance.

Annex II
Part 1
ARBITRATION

Article 1

The claimant party shall notify the secretariat that the parties are referring a dispute to arbitration pursuant to Article 27. The notification shall state the subject-matter of arbitration and include, in particular, the articles of the Convention or the protocol, the interpretation or application of which are at issue. If the parties do not agree on the subject matter of the dispute before the President of the tribunal is designated, the arbitral tribunal shall determine the subject matter. The secretariat shall forward the information thus received to all Contracting Parties to this Convention or to the protocol concerned.

Article 2

1. In disputes between two parties, the arbitral tribunal shall consist of three members. Each of the parties to the dispute shall appoint an arbitrator and the two arbitrators so appointed shall designate by common agreement the third arbitrator who shall be the President of the tribunal. The latter shall not be a national of one of the parties to the dispute, nor have his or her usual place of residence in the territory of one of these parties, nor be employed by any of them, nor have dealt with the case in any other capacity.

2. In disputes between more than two parties, parties in the same interest shall appoint one arbitrator jointly by agreement.

3. Any vacancy shall be filled in the manner prescribed for the initial appointment.

Article 3

1. If the President of the arbitral tribunal has not been designated within

two months of the appointment of the second arbitrator, the Secretary-General of the United Nations shall, at the request of a party, designate the President within a further two-month period.

2. If one of the parties to the dispute does not appoint an arbitrator within two months of receipt of the request, the other party may inform the Secretary-General who shall make the designation within a further two-month period.

Article 4

The arbitral tribunal shall render its decisions in accordance with the provisions of this Convention, any protocols concerned, and international law.

Article 5

Unless the parties to the dispute otherwise agree, the arbitral tribunal shall determine its own rules of procedure.

Article 6

The arbitral tribunal may, at the request of one of the parties, recommend essential interim measures of protection.

Article 7

The parties to the dispute shall facilitate the work of the arbitral tribunal and, in particular, using all means at their disposal, shall:

(a) Provide it with all relevant documents, information and facilities; and

(b) Enable it, when necessary, to call witnesses or experts and receive their evidence.

Article 8

The parties and the arbitrators are under an obligation to protect the confidentiality of any information they receive in confidence during the proceedings of the arbitral tribunal.

Article 9

Unless the arbitral tribunal determines otherwise because of the particular circumstances of the case, the costs of the tribunal shall be borne by the parties to the dispute in equal shares. The tribunal shall keep a record of all its costs, and shall furnish a final statement thereof to the parties.

Article 10

Any Contracting Party that has an interest of a legal nature in the subject-matter of the dispute which may be affected by the decision in the case, may intervene in the proceedings with the consent of the tribunal.

Article 11

The tribunal may hear and determine counterclaims arising directly out of the subject-matter of the dispute.

Article 12

Decisions both on procedure and substance of the arbitral tribunal shall be taken by a majority vote of its members.

Article 13

If one of the parties to the dispute does not appear before the arbitral tribunal or fails to defend its case, the other party may request the tribunal to continue the proceedings and to make its award. Absence of a party or a failure of a party to defend its case shall not constitute a bar to the proceedings. Before rendering its final decision, the arbitral tribunal must satisfy itself that the claim is well founded in fact and law.

Article 14

The tribunal shall render its final decision within five months of the date on which it is fully constituted unless it finds it necessary to extend the time-limit for a period which should not exceed five more months.

Article 15

The final decision of the arbitral tribunal shall be confined to the subject-matter of the dispute and shall state the reasons on which it is based. It shall contain the names of the members who have participated and the date of the final decision. Any member of the tribunal may attach a separate or dissenting opinion to the final decision.

Article 16

The award shall be binding on the parties to the dispute. It shall be without appeal unless the parties to the dispute have agreed in advance to an appellate procedure.

Article 17

Any controversy which may arise between the parties to the dispute as regards the interpretation or manner of implementation of the final decision may be submitted by either party for decision to the arbitral tribunal which rendered it.

Part 2
CONCILIATION

Article 1

A conciliation commission shall be created upon the request of one of the parties to the dispute. The commission shall, unless the parties otherwise agree, be composed of five members, two appointed by each Party concerned and a President chosen jointly by those members.

Article 2

In disputes between more than two parties, parties in the same interest shall appoint their members of the commission jointly by agreement. Where two or more parties have separate interests or there is a disagreement as to whether they are of the same interest, they shall appoint their members separately.

Article 3

If any appointments by the parties are not made within two months of the date of the request to create a conciliation commission, the Secretary-General of the United Nations shall, if asked to do so by the party that made the request, make those appointments within a further two-month period.

Article 4

If a President of the conciliation commission has not been chosen within two months of the last of the members of the commission being appointed, the Secretary-General of the United Nations shall, if asked to do so by a party, designate a President within a further two-month period.

Article 5

The conciliation commission shall take its decisions by majority vote of its members. It shall, unless the parties to the dispute otherwise agree, determine its own procedure. It shall render a proposal for resolution of the dispute, which the parties shall consider in good faith.

Article 6

A disagreement as to whether the conciliation commission has competence shall be decided by the commission.

ABOUT THE AUTHORS

Bonnie Kramer Carney is an attorney with Morgan and Finnegan, Attorneys at Law, New York.

David Downes is an attorney with the Center for International Environmental Law, in Washington D.C.

Dr. Rodrigo Gámez is the Director of the National Biodiversity Institute (INBio) of Costa Rica. Formerly he was Director of University of Costa Rica's Institute of Cellular and Molecular Biology.

Michael A. Gollin practices intellectual property and environmental law in Washington, D.C., concentrating on biotechnology and environmental technology matters. He is organizing an indigenous resources trade project.

Dr. Winnie Hallwachs is a biologist and technical advisor to INBio and the Guanacaste Conservation Area in Costa Rica.

Dr. Daniel H. Janzen is a Professor of Biology at the University of Pennsylvania, and Technical Advisor to INBio and the Guanacaste Conservation Area in Costa Rica.

Dr. Jorge Jimenez is Director of the Division of Biodiversity Inventory, INBio, Costa Rica.

Dr. Calestous Juma is Executive Director of the African Centre for Technology Studies, Nairobi, Kenya.

Christopher Klein is an attorney with Morgan and Finnegan, Attorneys at Law, New York.

Sarah A. Laird is a Research Fellow with the Rainforest Alliance. Formerly she was director of the Periwinkle Project at Rainforest Alliance in New York.

Eugenia Leon is Director of Administration, INBio, Costa Rica.

Dr. Carrie A. Meyer is an Associate in WRI's Program in Economics and Population. Before that she was a Professor of Microeconomics and Economic Development at George Mason University in Virginia.

Gerardo Mirabelli is Director of the Division of Biodiversity Information Management, INBio, Costa Rica.

Dr. Alfio Piva is Director of the Division of Biodiversity Information Distribution, INBio, Costa Rica.

Dr. Walter V. Reid is an ecologist and Vice President for Program at WRI. Before that he was a Senior Associate in WRI's Program in Forests and Biodiversity.

Bernard Sihanya is an Assistant Policy Analyst with the African Centre for Technology Studies, Nairobi, Kenya.

Dr. Ana Sittenfeld is the Director of the Division of Biodiversity Prospecting at INBio.

ABOUT THE INSTITUTIONS

World Resources Institute

World Resources Institute is a research and policy organization helping governments, the private sector, environmental and development organizations, and others address a fundamental question: How can societies meet human needs and nurture economic growth while preserving the natural resources and environmental integrity on which life and economic vitality ultimately depend?

WRI's books and reports present accurate information about global resources and environmental conditions, analyses of emerging issues, and creative yet workable policy responses. To deepen public understanding, the institute also undertakes briefings, seminars, and conferences and offers material for use in print and broadcast media.

In developing countries, WRI provides field services and technical support for governments and nongovernmental organizations working to ensure the sustainable use of natural resources. For further information contact WRI, 1709 New York Ave. NW, Washington, D.C. 20006. Tel: 202/638-6300, Fax: 202/638-0036.

The National Biodiversity Institute (INBio)

The National Biodiversity Institute (Instituto Nacional de Biodiversidad, or INBio) is a private non-profit Costa Rican institution dedicated to the conservation of the country's wildland biodiversity through facilitating its use as a resource for society's intellectual and sustainable economic development. INBio operates under the assumption that a developing tropical society will succeed in conserving a major portion of its wildland biodiversity only if this area can generate enough intellectual and economic income to pay for its upkeep and also contribute to the national economy in rough proportion to its area.

Costa Rica's history of several decades of classical conservation has provided the raw materials for biodiversity conservation through non-destructive use. The next steps, for which INBio was created in 1989, are to determine what these raw materials are—through a direct and detailed inventory—and to facilitate their non-damaging use by all sectors of society. Requests for further information should be addressed to Dr. Rodrigo Gámez, Executive Director, INBio, Apdo. 22-3100, Santo Domingo, Heredia, Costa Rica. Tel: 506/36-7690, Fax: 506/36-2816.

Rainforest Alliance

The Rainforest Alliance is a non-profit organization dedicated to the conservation of the world's endangered tropical forests. Our unique mission is to develop and promote sound economic alternatives to tropical deforestation. These alternatives are designed in concert with local people, to develop forest products and businesses that offer long-term, stable income for people living in or near forests. An important part of this work involves educating the public, in the U.S. and the tropics, about what they can do to help save the remaining tropical forests before it's too late.

Contact Rainforest Alliance, 65 Bleecker Street, New York, NY 10012-2420, Tel: 212/677-1900, Fax: 212/677-2187.

African Centre for Technology Studies

The African Centre for Technology Studies (ACTS) is an international non partisan, not-for-profit institution established to conduct policy research, provide training, offer advice and disseminate information on the application of science and technology to sustainable development. The Centre operates through its head-

328

quarters in Nairobi and the ACTS Biopolicy Institute at Maastricht, The Netherlands. Requests for further information should be addressed to African Centre for Technology Studies, P.O. Box 45917, Nairobi, Kenya, Tel: 254-2/744047, Fax 743995.

INDEX

Aboriginal treaties, 286
Advance payments
    INBio-Merck agreement, 31,
      109–110
    plant sample description, 108
    size, 108–111
Agenda 21, 209
Agricultural research, 12–15
    patents, 22
AIDS
    low-dose human alpha interferon
      for, 206
Asian Development Bank, 26
Asian Symposium on Medicinal
    Plants and Other Natural Products
    "Code of Ethics for Foreign Col-
      lectors of Biological Samples,"
      108
Author's rights, 283–284

Bacillus thuringiensis, 14
Belize Ethnobotany Project, 122
Benefit sharing
    Convention on Biological Diver-
      sity and, 4, 292, 300
    developing countries, 4
    INBio attitude, 78, 82, 84
    intellectual property rights and,
      33–34, 185

local communities, 30–32
traditional knowledge and, 36–38,
    104, 122–123
See also specific companies by
    name
Berne Convention, 299
Biodegradable plastic, 15
Biodiversity definition, 69
Biodiversity Marketing and Commer-
    cialization Board (Indonesia), 26
Biodiversity prospecting. *See also*
    National Biodiversity Institute
    agricultural research, 12–15
    companies active in plant screen-
      ing, 8–13
    company-collector contracts,
      30–32, 255–287
    databases, 67, 77–78, 82
    demand for resources, 6–7, 12–15
    evolution of institutions, 18–19
    financial issues, 15–18
    guidelines, 26–46
    intellectual property rights, 19–22,
      32–38
    intermediaries, 24–26, 27–30
    international agreements, 23–24,
      44–46
    legal guarantees, 38–42
    legislative issues, 94–96

QH
75
B535
1993

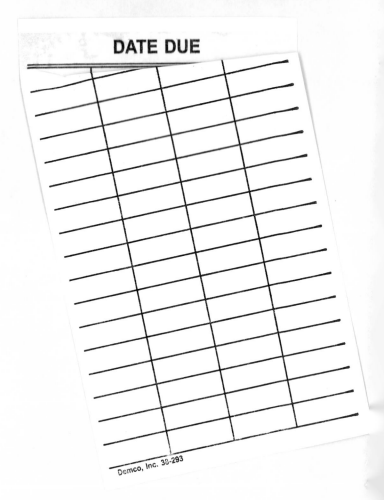